The Workman's Manual of Engineering Drawing

THE

WORKMAN'S MANUAL

OF

ENGINEERING DRAWING.

THE

WORKMAN'S MANUAL

OF

ENGINEERING DRAWING

BY

JOHN MAXTON, Engineer

INSTRUCTOR IN ENGINEERING DRAWING, ROYAL NAVAL COLLEGE, GREENWICH;
FORMERLY OF R.S.N.A. SOUTH KENSINGTON, UNIVERSITY COLLEGE, ETC.

With nearly Three Hundred and Fifty Woodcuts and Seven Plates

THIRD EDITION, CAREFULLY REVISED

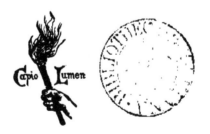

LONDON

LOCKWOOD & CO., 7, STATIONERS' HALL COURT

LUDGATE HILL

1875

PREFACE.

THE object of the present book is to enable the working engineer to instruct himself in an important branch of his business. Although especially designed for this purpose, the latter part will be found useful to the general student; while it is hoped that to the master, who is already familiar with the subject, it may be found convenient as a book of reference.

ENFIELD ROAD NORTH,
LONDON, *June*, 1871.

CONTENTS.

Gas Fittings.—The vertical distance of the light from the drawing table should be about 2 feet, and the tube—in one or more joints—so arranged as to admit of the light being moved horizontally, or raised or lowered to any suitable position. The socket for the burner should be inclined outwards at an angle of 45° from the vertical, so that, when the burner is in its place, and the gas lit, it would throw the light down upon the paper.*

Sundries.—A drawing-office, or a room adjoining it, should also contain the following :—A duster, a wash-hand basin, soap,† towel, and a supply of water.

CHAPTER II.

MATERIALS.

DRAWING BOARDS.

THE first requisite for the mechanical draughtsman is a drawing board of suitable dimensions. The two most useful sizes are those for whole and half-sheets of double elephant drawing paper. The board should be fully half an inch each way larger than the paper, as the latter would not adhere properly where the gum or glue is applied unless the edge is within the board.

Drawing boards are generally made either of mahogany or of fir. The latter is commonly used, on account of its being the cheapest; but the best drawing boards are made from old mahogany tables or shop counters, such wood having become well seasoned, and therefore less liable to warp. The French polish is planed off, so as to prevent staining the paper.

---

* Under the most favourable circumstances it is more difficult to draw or colour by artificial than by daylight.

† It being quite essential to have the hands clean. The basin is also more convenient than an ordinary tumbler for the use of the sponge as well as for washing out palettes.

A section of a form of board more in favour in former times than now is shown in Fig. 1. This form is good in so

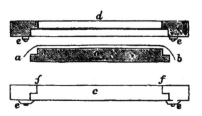

Fig. 1.

far as it saves the trouble of gumming down the paper at the edge, but is expensive.

In the above sections *a b* represents the paper, which, when damped, is placed on the lower board *c*; the frame *d*, which fits closely all round the edge of the lower board, is then squeezed down over the paper as shown at *f*, and secured by the fastenings *e e*.

The price of a board of this description for a whole sheet of double elephant would be—

Of mahogany . . 3 ft. 6 in. × 2 ft. 6 in. × ¾ in. 25*s.*
  ,, half-sheet 2 6 × 1 9 × ⅔ 15*s.*
  ,, smaller size 1 10 × 1 6 × ½ 7*s.*
Of fir, whole sheet size . . . . 12*s.*
  ,, half-sheet size . . . . 8*s. 6d.*

The price of an ordinary well-seasoned plain board for a whole sheet of double elephant would be—

Of mahogany . . . . 18*s.*
  ,, half-sheet size . . . . . 13*s.*
Of fir, whole sheet size . . . . . . 7*s.*
  ,, half ,, ... 4*s. 6d.*

Ordinary drawing boards are made in a variety of ways to prevent warping, of which the following are specimens :—

Fig. 2 represents a common method of finishing the ends of mahogany boards, the corners being mitred and tongued.

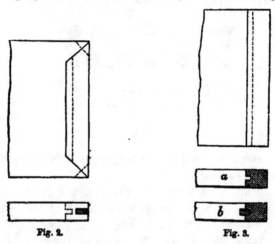

Fig. 2.   Fig. 3.

In Fig. 3 the end piece is put on with a tongue, as at *a*, worked out of the solid wood, or with a feather or tongue let in as at *b*.

In Fig. 4 the end piece is mortised on.

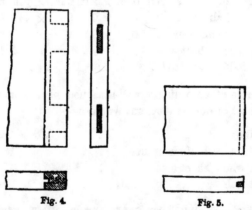

Fig. 4.   Fig. 5.

In Fig. 5 a strip of oak is fitted into a groove. This plan is very good for small fir boards.

When those of Figs. 3 and 4 are of fir, however well seasoned, they are apt to contract a little with heat, and the extremities of the end pieces are certain to project, and, if not planed off, cause the lines by a T-square to be untrue, as shown at Fig. 6. Fir boards are more easily acted on by the weather than those of mahogany.

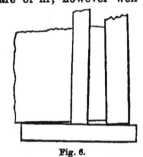

Fig. 6.

If no cross ends are put on, two bars across the back, as at Fig. 7, would prevent the board bending. In this case

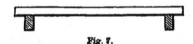

Fig. 7.

only one side of the board can be used; a disadvantage, as it is sometimes convenient to have a sheet of paper on each side at the same time (the one not in immediate use being covered over to prevent its being soiled). These bars are more applicable to small-sized boards. A large-sized fir board is better without cross ends, but having cross bars to prevent its warping, in which case some provision is necessary to allow it to expand and contract by the weather without damaging the board. The best of these are made with a series of grooves in the back about 2 inches apart, ⅛th of an inch

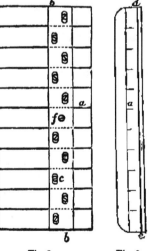

Fig. 8.   Fig. 9.

wide, and cut half-way through the thickness, as shown at

a, Figs. 8 and 9. The bars *b* at each end of the board on the back, Fig. 8, being secured by a screw nail *f*, passing through

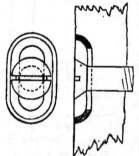

the bar and nearly through the board, in the centre of it; the wood being allowed to expand or contract on each side by other screws sliding in little brass slots as at *c*, Fig. 8, of which Fig. 10 is a full-sized view, and Fig. 11 the corresponding section. A narrow strip of hard wood, generally ebony, is inserted along one side

Fig. 10.   Fig. 11.   and one end of the board, a little

from the edge, as at *d e*, Fig. 9, to allow the square to slide more easily. This is the most approved modern fir board,* and when of a size for a whole sheet of double elephant paper costs about 12*s.* 6*d.*, and for half-sheet size about 8*s.* It is almost needless to add that all drawing boards should have

the sides and ends perfectly square to each other. A good test of this is obtained by measuring across the board by the *cape and corner* method, in the direction of the

Fig. 12.   dotted lines, (Fig. 12). When correct, the

length *a b* is equal to the length *c d*.

CHAPTER III.

SQUARES.

DRAWING, or T-squares, so called from their resemblance in shape to that letter, are of various sorts. They are gene-

---

* Its only disadvantage is that it is impossible, as in the previous example given, to have a sheet of paper on both sides.

rally made of mahogany, pear tree, or ebony. The common sort is that represented in Fig. 13. It has an immovable stock *a*, and a blade *b*, mortised into it. The blade should be as long as the longest side of the drawing board. If for a whole sheet of double elephant, the length should be 3 feet 6 inches, the breadth 2¼ inches, and the thickness ₃/₁₆ of an inch. The stock should be 1 foot long, 2½ inches broad, and ⅞ inch thick.

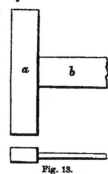

Fig. 13.

The price of such square of mahogany would be 8*s.* 6*d.*
„   „   pear tree   „   4*s.* 6*d.*

A smaller size for half-sheet double elephant will, for most purposes, be found more convenient. The size should be: blade 2 feet 6 inches long, breadth 2 inches, thickness ₃/₁₆ inch; and the stock 10 inches long, breadth 2 inches, and the thickness ½ inch.

The price of such square of mahogany would be 2*s.*
„   „   pear tree   „   3*s.* 6*d.*

Squares having the stock projecting only on one side, Fig. 14, are suitable for working on a fixed straight-edge, as,

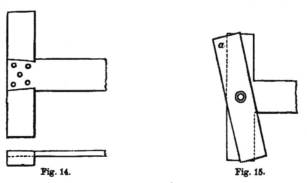

Fig. 14.   Fig. 15.

in making large illustrative drawings for lectures on paper

fixed on a wall, the blade of the square lies close to the paper, a necessity for drawing a straight line correctly.

A square having a movable stock, shown at *a*, Fig. 15, is useful for drawing a series of lines at an angle to the side of the board and parallel to each other.

The price, fitted with screw pin and nut, of the
    larger size, in mahogany, would be about .   5*s*. 6*d*.
Ditto, pear tree . . . . 7*s*.
Ditto, ebony . . . . 11*s*. 6*d*.
Smaller size, in mahogany. . . . . 4*s*.
      ,,   pear tree . . . . 5*s*.

They are frequently made with a tongue projecting from the stock, as at *b*, Fig. 16, which keeps the blade more flat to the board. It is generally of ebony, let into the stock. This kind is a little more expensive than those already described.

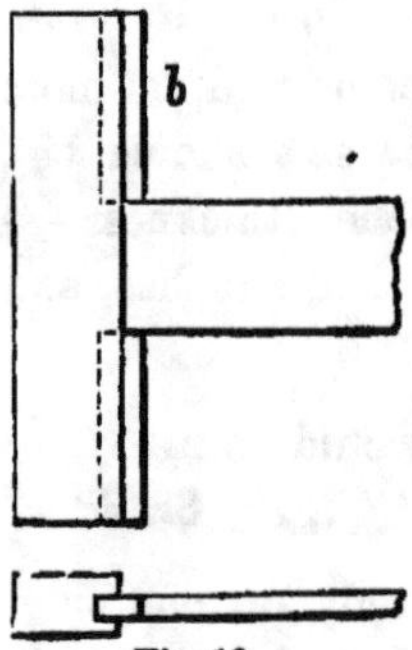

Others have the blade broader towards the stock, as in Fig. 17. This shape admits of the blade being kept steadier to the board, but only one side of it can be used for drawing lines square to the board, whereas, if an accident should occur to one edge of a parallel blade, the other edge can be made use of.

Fig. 16.

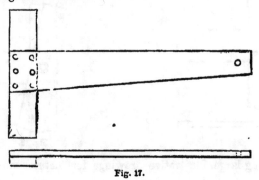

Fig. 17.

Blades, such as in Fig. 17, are simply put on above the stock, without either dovetails or mortises, the additional breadth affording ample room for a sufficient number of screw nails to render it secure. This square also allows the little set squares to be used beyond the edge of the drawing board if necessary.

The price of such square, if of pear tree (ebony

edged), with 3 feet 6 inches blade, is about .   7s. 6d.

And of a 2 feet 6 inches blade   .   .   .   .   .   5s. 6d.

It is much better to have the edge of the blade as shown at a, Fig. 18, than to have it bevelled, as they frequently are, as shown at b, as, in the latter case, in making dotted lines the pen is apt to get overlifted.

Fig. 18.

Every square should have a ⅜ inch hole near the outer end of the blade to hang it up by, being the best way to preserve a T-square in its integrity.

A square is usually tested by first drawing a line with it on any plane surface having a straight side against which to bear the stock of square during the operation, and then turning it upside down and observing if the same edge of blade still coincides with the line, the stock bearing as before. If it has a shifting stock, care must be taken that the shifting edge is screwed up firmly, flush with the fixed part.

Pear-tree squares are preferable to those of mahogany, being less liable to warp, the material being thin, though mahogany has always a cleaner appearance than those of the lighter woods when frequently used.

CHAPTER IV.

DRAWING INSTRUMENTS, MOULDS, ETC.

It is a common error to suppose that any sort of instruments will suit a beginner. On the contrary he ought, in fairness to himself, to have the very best he can procure. Instruments of the proper quality can be purchased separately; or very good second-hand sets, containing most of the necessary instruments, can be had for 30s. A new set in a box containing everything for ordinary use costs from £3 10s. to £4. First-class boxes of instruments frequently have duplicates of many of those contained in an ordinary set, with scales, moulds for curves, sets of colours, palettes, beam compasses, having pencil and ink feet for sliding on a straight edge for drawing large circles, or round telescopic metal bar for the same purpose (the price of a single instrument of the latter description, plain, with 3 feet metal tube, ranges from £1 5s. to £2 10s.), such sets run up in price to £15, or even more. When such boxes cannot be afforded, a set for ordinary engineering drawing must at least contain the following instruments. Compasses, pencil and ink legs with lengthening bar, pencil and ink bows, drawing pen, file and knife, little screw keys, parallel rulers, drawing pins, and scales.

Compasses, &c.—The most useful being those having jointed legs, one being removable, and with pencil and ink legs to fit in for drawing ordinary sized circles, and with a lengthening bar for large circles. The price of which set, if of brass, including file with knife end, is about 13s. 6d., of electrum 18s. to 21s.

Pencil and Ink Compasses (or bows) for the smaller circles, having a joint in each leg, so that in drawing a circle the lower parts may be as vertical as possible (for reasons explained in Chapter X.). Price of each instrument, plain, of brass, 2s. 6d. to 3s., if of electrum, 4s. and 5s. Some bows are fitted with a needle point projecting from a small shoulder or flat point, these when used on a mahogany board never make a hole in the paper larger than a needle would, even when inserted up to the shoulder: but with a fir board, in drawing many circles from the same centre, shoulder and all are apt to work in and do that which the needle point was intended to avoid.

Drawing Pen, which if purchased separately (and it is the instrument of all others that requires replacing), cannot give satisfactory results under a price of 2s. 6d., those having the lower part of the holder of a square form, to show the direction of the points, being preferable.   As this instrument is more used than any of the others, it frequently requires touching up at the points.   The ink foot of compasses, and the ink bows, also require touching up occasionally,* and consequently the half of ink legs should have a joint, so that when entirely unscrewed it can be lifted up and permit attention to the points, as well as allow of cleaning out any dry ink.   The best thing for cleaning out such instruments is a common steel writing pen, with the one half broken off at the split.   When a drawing pen or other ink points get blunt they ought to be sharpened up on a piece of common school slate with water, oil preventing the ink flowing freely.

Most drawing pens unscrew in the centre, having a pricker fitted in the upper part or handle; this is necessary occasionally for copying irregular figures to be made of the same size as the copy, by pricking the lines of the copy through to the new sheet below it.   If not so fitted in drawing pen they are to be had separately, price 2s.   It is a common practice for the same purpose to put a fine needle into the uncut end of a pencil.

File with *Knife* fitted at one end; the former part is useful for touching up an instrument, and for putting a fine point on the pencil, and the latter for pointing pencils, or for cutting off a finished drawing.

Screw Keys.—There ought always to be a little screw key or keys furnished along with compasses and bows to tighten or slacken them when found necessary.   They should neither shut nor open too easily.

Parallel Rulers.—The common sort formed of two parallel parts is better than the single bar with a roller at each end,

* Instrument makers charge about 3d. for setting-up a pen or ink points.

which indeed for practical engineering drawings is seldom used. In choosing the former it should be specially noticed that they have no loose play, or they would be quite useless. The ordinary length is 6 inches, and price in ebony, 2d. per linear inch.

Drawing Pins.—A dozen or two of brass-headed drawing pins are always necessary for fastening down a sheet of either drawing or tracing paper when not to be coloured upon; good ones are to be had at 4d. per dozen.

Scales of feet with twelfths (or inches) are seldom to be had of useful lengths in boxes containing the other instruments. It is better to purchase them separately. See next chapter.

When a great many circles are required to be drawn from the same centre, such centre in the paper is apt to get enlarged into a hole under the best conditions; to obviate which, little round discs of horn about ⅜ths of an inch diameter, with three fine projecting points, are to be had, one of which when placed above where the centre is to be, completely preserves the paper; cost about 4d. each.

A half circular piece of horn or metal about 4 inches diameter, called a protractor, having degrees marked on the circumference, is useful for measuring angles, and can be either had in a set or separately (further reference to this instrument is made in Chapter XL), price, 4½ inches diameter, of horn 6d., ivory 2s. 6d., brass 4s., electrum 7s.

Proportional compasses are seldom sold with an ordinary set of instruments; they are so constructed with double ends as to save much time and labour in reducing or enlarging a drawing from a copy, as in taking a measurement with one pair of legs the proper alteration in size is given by the other pair, whereas with ordinary compasses the method of trial and error is required. Those made with a shifting centre for various proportions, cost, if of 6 inch, brass, from 6s. to 13s., plain, if of electrum, 9 inch, £2 15s. Wholes and halves, or bisecting compasses having a fixed centre, are exceedingly useful for making a drawing from a copy either half or double the size.   Price in electrum, 20s.

Besides the above-mentioned there are many other instruments for engineering drawing which may be referred to here.   They are generally to be had of the same maker.

A bordering pen, having a tongue fitted between the ordinary points, is useful for drawing thick lines at one operation. Price 5s. to 6s.

Some instrument boxes contain a double drawing pen, each ink end complete in itself, and so jointed that two lines can be drawn of any moderate width apart at one operation.   This instrument is more used, however, by civil than by practical engineers, being employed for detailed railway plans, curves in railway lines, &c.   Its price varies between 4s. 6d. and 7s.

Spring dividers are useful for dividing the teeth of wheels, or for dividing into any number of equal parts, as scales of feet, inches, &c.   Ink bows are sometimes made in the same way, opening of themselves when the nut of the leg is unscrewed, but as they are never made with a joint in the legs they are not so good, for the reasons given in Chapter X. Price of dividers, pencil, and ink, 6s. 6d. to 7s. 6d. per set of three, electrum 10s.; each set in a case.   The same of electrum, with needle points, 24s., extra quality, 27s.

Some boxes contain a little instrument called a wheel pen for dotting-in lines or circles, being made to fit into the compasses for the latter process.   It is similar to a spur fitted between ink ends and revolving as it is drawn along, the ink being supplied at the back of the wheel.   It is seldom used for practical engineering drawings, as it makes much coarser dots than draughtsmen generally like.   Price, single, with sets of wheels, having dots of different patterns, 6s. 6d. to 8s. 6d.

NOTE.—Before laying aside the drawing pen and ink leg of compasses, &c., after using, they should be cleaned out and unscrewed a little, so as to preserve the elasticity of the spring as much as possible.*

For long regular or irregular curves, strips of wood called batons will be found essential; these are accompanied with lead weights fitted on soles of wood. These batons are of various lengths, some are thicker at one end than at the other, as shown in the subjoined sections (Fig. 19), of natural

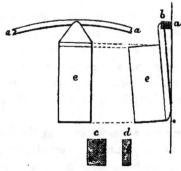

Fig. 19.

size, c d, some are thick in the middle and tapered off towards each end. The lead weight e may be 4 or 5 inches long, 2 inches deep, and from 1 to 2 inches broad, though the sizes vary. They are generally covered in with mahogany, the sole is notched in front lower edge as at b, so as to keep the baton a, when set, in position. As the curve line has to pass through points already laid off, a weight like that described is generally placed on the baton at each point. These weights are also useful for holding down a sheet flat. The price of six lead weights, covered in with mahogany, Admiralty size, and six lancewood batons, is about 60s. Small

* Should the little screw of pen or ink legs get lost, or overhauled in the thread from wear and tear, they may still be put to use by tying a piece of fine wire or fine string round the leg between the middle and points, which can be shifted up or down to produce the thickness of line required; or if the spring that opens the ink points loses its elasticity, or gets broken, a little piece of india-rubber or cork fitted in between will act very well until refitted in a proper manner.

lead weights for the purpose of keeping a sheet of paper flat cost 1s. 6d. plain, incased in mahogany, 8s. 6d. each.

Much drawing cannot be done without a good straight-edge, 7 or 8 feet long, 2½ inches broad, and ¼ of an inch thick, having one edge bevelled within ₃⅟₂ of an inch from the lower edge.* The price of a 7 feet mahogany straight-edge is about 8s. 6d., hardwood, 6s., steel, 81s.

Three little triangular set squares of pear tree, or vulcanite, of 55°, 45°, and 80°, each of them having one right angle, are essential, the two former angles for projecting shadows, &c., and the last for drawing in six-sided figures, such as nuts. It is better not to have the rectangular sides of the former less than 4 inches long. The price of pear-tree set squares, if 4 inches, 4d., 6 inches, 5d., 8 inches, 6d.; vulcanite of the same sizes, 1s., 1s. 6d., and 2s. respectively.

As engineering is so much concerned with shipbuilding, a few parabolic moulds are desirable for any ship sections that occur in marine engineering drawings, as well as for drawing curved shadows in machinery drawings generally; also arcs of circles of large diameter will be found useful for drawing-in barrelled rods, and for various other curved details. The following representations of moulds present a series of curves, each set containing what it would require two or three of the others previously indicated to produce. These are given of full size, so that a similar set in thin wood can easily be made by pricking any of the three examples given through to the wood, or by first tracing them and pricking through the tracing on to the wood. After having delineated it carefully with a fine pointed pencil, the required mould can be cut out with a sharp penknife, then filed and sand-papered. Pear or lime tree is the best material for such purposes. They are to be had of various patterns and sizes, and in sets.

---

* To prove a straight-edge, draw a line along the edge, turn it over, or place it end for end with the edge towards the line; if they still coincide it is correct.

In the annexed diagram each of the three moulds is differently lined and dotted so as to distinguish them, while occupying little space. Price of any pattern of the same sizes as in example, pear tree, 6d. each, or 5s. per dozen ; if of vulcanite, 1s. to 3s. each; a set of 9 pear-tree long curves costs 7s. 6d., or 15 for 12s. 6d. ; 40, Admiralty pattern, pear tree, in a case, 86s. ; ditto, vulcanite, 60s.

It is hardly needful to say that the draughtsman must always possess a good 2 ft. rule for taking the dimensions of machinery to be drawn to a scale. The rule should have a brass slide, for the more conveniently measuring small orifices. Price of a boxwood slide rule variously graduated, from 4s. 6d. Also, external and internal calibers should be procured, and several little strips of wood for taking distances from models.

A good steel writing pen for printing, or for making wood or iron fractures, should be kept. For circles too small for ink bows a good steel *crowquill* is wanted. This should have as thick a holder as a writing pen, otherwise it is difficult to command. A pen intended for such a purpose should never be applied to any other.

An ordinary magnifying glass will be found useful for examining the points of drawing pen, ink bows, &c., showing better what is required to them in touching them up, if not drawing satisfactorily.

For ordinary mechanical drawings pencils marked H H are the best ; * and for rougher purposes a common pencil.

A good 6 inch sponge, fine grained, is necessary.

India-rubber of the common dark description, is the best

---

* In handling a new pencil, there is more command over it when it is long, than when it gets cut down to about 3 or 4 inches. It is impossible to draw well with a short pencil. When a pencil gets inconveniently short it can be attached to the end of a longer piece by simply gumming a strip of writing paper about an inch broad round the joint two or three turns, or a crayon holder may be used. When pencils are cut away, until about an inch or so long, they should be thinned to fit compasses or bows, as pencils for such purposes of the proper size and of HH quality are seldom to be had.

Plate I.

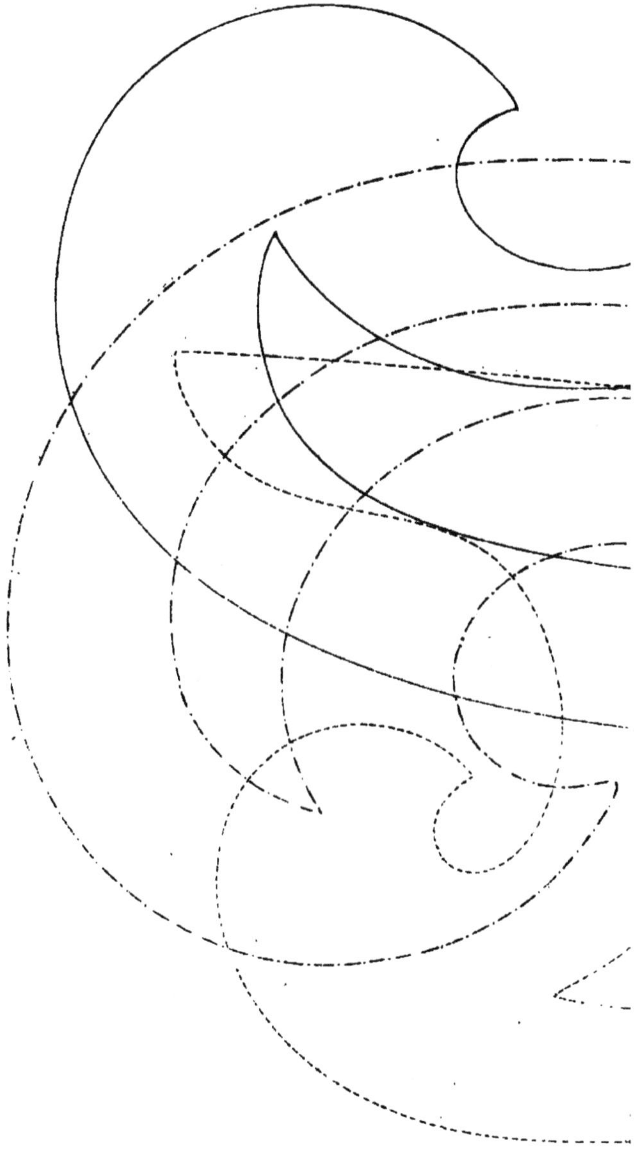

for ordinary drawing paper, especially if the paper is to be coloured on.

For the machine-made paper, where the pencil lines are more difficult to rub out, vulcanised india-rubber is the best.

An ink eraser may be useful for removing a blot from the paper, but should never be used on any surface to be coloured.

Further remarks upon these subjects will be found in the succeeding chapters.

CHAPTER V.

SCALES.

THE best and most durable scales are of ivory; and though boxwood is often used, it will not stand so much tear and wear as the former.

A good useful engineer's scale ought to have from $\frac{1}{8}$th (and progressing by an eighth) up to 3 inches to a foot.

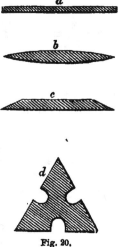

Fig. 20.

Scales are usually made in four different forms in their cross sections, as shown at *a*, *b*, *c*, and *d*, Fig. 20. They are generally a little over 1 foot long, and about $1\frac{1}{8}$ inch broad.

The form of edge shown at *c*, when the rule has the required scale, is useful for applying direct to the drawing, especially for minute parts, without measuring off the distance by the compasses. The scale *d* is of a convenient form, having two more additional scales at a third edge for the same purpose; *a* is the best form, if required at any time as a little straight-edge.

Price of ivory scales, best quality }
   (as at *a, b, c*), each . . . } 8*s.* 6*d.*, second quality 7*s.*

Boxwood, ditto . . . . . 2*s.* 9*d.*

Ivory, triangular (*d*), 12 inches }
   long . . . . } 21*s.* to 25*s.*

Ditto, 6 inches long . . . . 9*s.* to 10*s.* 6*d.*

Boxwood, ditto, 12 inches long 7*s.*

Ditto, 6 inches long . . . . 4*s.*

There are very good sets of single scales on pasteboard, and sold in cases large enough to contain all the ordinary useful scales. These are cheap compared with the sorts already referred to, and each has the scale at the edge, which is convenient, yet by frequently using them they get soiled and dirty looking, and the compasses soon begin to *tell* on the divisional lines.

Price, 18 inches long, 1*s.* each, or per dozen, in a case, 10*s.*

There is a form of scale, not so much in use now among engineers as formerly, divided differently from those just described, and of which the subjoined diagram (Fig. 21) is a

Fig. 21.

representation. It is still the form of scale put on the drawings of ship designs. In the present example there are six horizontal spaces formed by parallel lines. The last foot at each end is divided into inches by the diagonal lines, so that from the vertical line *o* at either end of scale on the second line to the first diagonal is 1 inch, and to the second diagonal 11 inches; from *o*, on the third line, to the first diagonal is 2 inches, and to the second diagonal 10 inches; and so on up to 6 inches. This scale is generally made "double ended;" so that it is immaterial, therefore, which end is used. There are other modifications of this scale, but the example here given will be found sufficiently explanatory for the rest. They are to be had of the same materials as those first described.*

In civil architecture it will generally be found that the scale on the different *orders* is not feet and inches, but minutes and seconds (or tenths), the minute being divided into 10 seconds.

A new and useful scale † for the measurement of lines has come into use in the offices of engineers, architects, surveyors, &c. It is called a "Dionome," and gives by mere inspection every measure of a line from the $\frac{1}{16}$th of an inch to 6 inches, and the price of which is only 1s.

CHAPTER VI.

COLOURS, INKS, PALETTES, AND BRUSHES.

Colours.—The colours usually required for engineering drawings comprise Prussian blue, crimson lake, gamboge, burnt umber, yellow ochre, light (or Indian) red, indigo, flake white, and carmine.

An engineering draughtsman, under ordinary circumstances, may get on very well with these, but in colouring sections, &c., of steam-ships (referred to further on), requiring some little decorative art, other colours will be found necessary.

Complete sets of colours include all the foregoing, and others—as sienna, sepia, &c.—which are used in civil architecture. Excepting the carmine, which costs 10s. per whole cake and 5s. per half cake, they can be had of good quality at 1s. per whole cake. At a less price they are apt to be gritty, and unfit for the purpose required.

Neutral tint for shading, when sold in cake, is frequently

---

* Scales should never be used, as they too frequently are, as paper-cutters, which process soon serrates the edges.

† By Spanton.

too chalky for engineering drawings; it is, therefore, better to mix it up of the different transparent colours which compose such tint (for the component parts see Chapter XVI.).

Fluid colours of carmine, blue, green, &c., are to be had in bottles at 1s. each, and are more used in drawings of ship designs than for engineering drawings.

Inks.—Indian ink varies a great deal as to quality; indeed, it is difficult to get the genuine article. There are two sorts, one having a rough and the other a smooth exterior. The smooth is found generally to be the best, it shades better than the other, and the lines made by the smooth are not so apt to *run* in colouring over them. If the cake is of the best sort, the end, after rubbing when moist, should present a brownish hue. The cakes are sold of various sizes, and their quality being supposed to be equal, their price varies accordingly, though the shilling size is generally of better quality than the larger sort. A shilling cake, in constant ordinary use by one person, will last twelve months, frequently longer.

Fluid Indian ink can be had in bottles at 2s. 6d. each, used for lining only, that in cake being best for the shading tint.

Palettes.—Two sorts are necessary, one having a sloping recess for rubbing down Indian ink, and having three or more little round recesses or cups adjoining for mixing up tints; and a second palette is required having three or more sloping recesses only, for rubbing down each colour required separately, either for using each by itself, or before for mixing up a tint. The average price is 6d. each. Little saucers fitting into each other, called cabinet-nests, to keep colour moist when not using, are to be had; those having five in the set, small size, cost 1s., middle 1s. 8d., large 1s. 6d. There are also little glass tumblers made for draughtsmen for containing the water for shading, and having little indentations in the rim for holding the brush when not in use for the moment. Price about 8d. each.

Brushes.—In choosing colour brushes they should be gently drawn through the lips, and if on being bent against anything they still keep their elasticity, they may be considered fit for use, but if they keep the *bend* they should be rejected. They should always terminate in a point when moistened.

The prices of ordinary brushes vary very much at different shops. For all ordinary drawings there should be three sizes, and in pairs, those on each end of holder being similar.

Prices :—

2—$\frac{1}{4}$ inch long, sable, per pair, and holder				7d.
2—$\frac{1}{2}$ ditto	ditto	ditto	1s. 4d.
2—$\frac{3}{4}$ ditto	ditto	ditto	2s. 6d.

Sable is preferable to camel hair, as it retains its elasticity for a longer period. The cost of the latter is about two-thirds less.

The holder should be about 5 inches long—the brush at one end being used for the tint, and that on the opposite end for water.

Brushes of a larger size may be sometimes found necessary for large washes of tint. When selecting such, the ones fitted in sheet iron, instead of quill, are preferable, and will stand rough work longer.

Prices :—

Camel hair, 1$\frac{1}{4}$ inch long and $\frac{3}{8}$ inch diameter, with holder, about . . . . 1s.   each.
Camel hair, 1 inch long and $\frac{1}{4}$ inch diameter, with holder, about . . . . 6d. „
Sable, 1$\frac{1}{4}$ inch long and $\frac{1}{4}$ inch diameter, with holder, about . . . . 7s. 6d. „

CHAPTER VII.

DRAWING AND TRACING PAPERS, ETC.

Drawing Paper.—The paper most commonly used for practical engineering drawings is double elephant. Of this there are two sorts—rough and smooth. The latter will be found the best for shading. Antiquarian is a larger sized sheet, and generally has a good surface to draw upon; and so has atlas paper; but neither are half so much used as the elephant. Machine-made or what is called cartridge drawing paper, has not so good a surface as any of the above, neither is it so white, its principal recommendation being found in its dimensions, it being procurable in rolls any reasonable length. It has a rough and a smooth side, the latter being the proper side to draw upon. It is frequently used for shipbuilding drawings, the other papers being too short in most cases; it is also used for large illustrations for lectures.

The following table gives the names, with their sizes, and prices per single sheet, of the several kinds of drawing paper in general use. In purchasing a quantity, the price would, of course, be proportionally less :—

Name of Paper.	Length in inches.	Breadth in inches.	Price.
Cartridge (thin cartoon)	Continuous	57	6d. per yard, or 25 yards 7s. 4d.
Do. (thick)	Do.	52	11d. per yard, best 1s. 4d.
Drawing Cartridge	54	27	8d. per sheet.
Antiquarian	53	30	3s. „
Double Elephant	40	27	8d. to 9d. „
Columbier	35	23½	7d. „
Atlas	34	26	7d „
Imperial	30	21	4½d. „
Elephant	28	23	4d. „

The prices in different shops vary a little, and the sizes of those bearing the same name will sometimes be found to differ a little from the above.

Drawing paper, ready mounted on cloth :—

Price per yard, 54 inches wide, 5s

,,   40   ,,   8s.

Tracing Paper.—Tracing paper is sold of many sizes, and of as many prices, seldom two shops being alike in this respect; but the following will be found about the average prices for the sizes given :—

40 inches by 80 inches, 6d. per sheet.

80   ,,   20   ,,   8d.   ,,

24 yards, continuous, 42 inches wide, ordinary, from 7s. to 9s.

Extra stout, 16s.

Home-made tracing paper is much less expensive than that purchased at the shops. Common silk (or *tissue*) paper can be had at something less than a halfpenny per sheet, of the ordinary size, when purchased in quantities. To prepare it, mix a proportion of 1 of boiled linseed oil to 5 of turpentine in a cup. Put a single sheet of the paper at a time on an inverted tea tray, large enough to allow, at least, the half of sheet to lie flat. The mixture should then be put on with a small sponge, one coating only, and that not too thickly; each sheet after such process should be hung over a string stretched across the room, and when all the clear oily marks entirely disappear it will be ready for use.

Tracing Cloth.—Tracing cloth, 88 inches wide, costs about 1s. 6d. per yard.

Best continuous, 28 inches wide, 80s. per 21 yards.

CHAPTER VIII.

PREPARATION FOR DRAWING ON BOARDS.

To draw easily, and accurately, the paper must be stretched tight on the board; in other words, it must be quite flat. If the paper is not stretched quite tight, the process of

colouring would cause the paper to buckle up where moistened, and it would not lie flat again when dry. To get
the sheet satisfactorily tight, it must be first expanded by
damping it all over with a sponge and clean water, putting
weights on each corner of the paper to keep it in as flat a
position as possible during the process. It is better not to
place the paper on the board to which it is to be gummed,
as the very place which is required to be kept dry for the
joint would be apt to get wetted ; any other flat horizontal
surface will suit for the purpose. It was formerly the
custom, far more than now, to take the right side of the
paper for drawing on, supposed to be that in which the
name of the maker of the paper in the watermark can be
read off. In the case of the paper most in use, both sides
will be found so nearly alike as to render the difference, if
any, of no practical importance. If any sheet has really a
better looking or smoother side than another, the smoothest
side is generally the best for drawing on.

As the less the surface of paper is sponged the better, the
side not to be drawn on should be equally sponged all over
with a sponge nearly dry, and all tiny *pools* of water lying
in the hollows of the surface carefully removed. When the
clear watery surface begins to look dry, or rough, repeat the
process a second time, allowing the water to sink in, as
before. As long as clear water lies on the surface, the
paper may go on expanding during the process of fixing
down the sheet, and much trouble may follow from the
edges not lying flat, under which circumstances the only
remedy is to take up the sheet where fixed, and let it rest a
little. After the water from the second sponging has sunk
in sufficiently, it is time to turn over the paper, having the
drier or proper surface for drawing on uppermost, and while
thus damp the edge must be fixed down firmly all round,
either with hot or cold glue, or thick office gum.* If an

---

* Fluid gum is the quickest adhesive with which to put down a
sheet, though cold glue is perhaps the cleanest. Hot glue, though it

ordinary sheet, and having a *long* way, the long sides should be fixed down before the ends; a square, or straight-edge, should be placed ⅜ths of an inch inwards from edge of paper, and weights upon it to keep it firm, and the edge of the paper turned up against it. If cold glue is to be used, it should be a piece about 3 inches long and straight on the rubbing edge, and moistened with cold or hot water (the latter being preferable), then rubbed against the turned-up edge of the paper and the board, when it will become adhesive. The edge of the paper should next be turned down and rubbed hard with the rounded end of a penknife or a piece of hard wood for the purpose, always through a strip of drawing paper about 6 inches long. In putting on a sheet with fluid gum, both the board and edge of paper should be gummed; a joint either of gum or hot glue seldom requires rubbing down, as in the cold glue process, unless the edge should rise here and there.

After the four sides have been put down, it is a safe precaution to put a brass-headed pin in each corner, and a few along the sides and ends. These assist in preventing the joint from giving way. If the sheet contracts quicker than the joint dries, a slight sponging over the surface of the sheet, keeping an inch clear of the sides, is also a safeguard.

In putting on a large sheet, which is apt to get too dry before the sides are all fixed down, a damp piece of calico, or similar fabric, is the best thing to lay on it, always keeping it clear of the edge of the sheet, the paper is thus kept expanded until the joint is dry all round. The paper, on removing the cloth, then contracts, and becomes perfectly tight for drawing on.

generally performs its work well, is *messy*, and as such, not to be recommended. The fluid gum sold in bottles is generally too thin for such purposes; the proper proportion should be equal gum with equal water, and it should be kept ready for use in a phial having a wide neck, closed by a cork with a little hole in the top of it in which to place the brush when not in use. The brush should be a hard one, about half inch long, and kept entirely for the purpose.

In putting down a very long sheet, such as for ship drawings, instead of fixing down the long sides first, as in ordinary sized sheets, it is easier to fasten down the ends first,
as otherwise when such a length of sheet begins to contract,
the sides would give a good deal of trouble. When the
ends are put down they should be well pinned; then in
each of the long sides, 8 or 9 inches of the edge in the
middle of length, should be turned up, having made a little
incision at each end of the little length previously, such
length should be gummed, or glued, and pinned down; intermediate spaces should be opened up and treated similarly.
The process should be repeated until both sides are fully
fixed down. When the paper has become quite dry, the
pins must be removed, so as to allow the square to do its
work.

Sometimes in putting on a sheet with assistance, when it
is damped and ready for turning over on the board, the
edges might have the gum or fluid glue first put on, and,
with a person at each end, it can be turned over easily on to
its board and rubbed down, granting the gum or glue has
not dried too quickly on a very large sheet. Or the paper
may be fixed to the board without assistance, by placing the
board as nearly vertical as it will stand against the wall or
other firm object, and taking the sheet so prepared and
hanging it on the board in the same way as in papering the
wall of a room, immediately after which it should be placed
horizontally. A board with a newly-stretched sheet should
never be placed against the wall, or in any upright position
to dry, as the moisture in the paper is apt to sink gradually
down, and by the upper joint drying, and the paper con-
tracting and pulling it upwards at the same time, the lower
joint gets loosened. Neither should a board with, or without, a sheet on it be placed at any time against a wall whose
dryness is doubtful, for where there is the least damp the
board runs the risk of being warped, and if any sheet
stretched upon it, would be destroyed by getting cloudy;

and if it has anything drawn on it so much the worse. A newly-stretched sheet should never be held to the fire to dry, as the edge joint is likely to be pulled up before it is sufficiently dry. It should be allowed always to dry naturally in a horizontal position.

A frame fitting over a board, as described in Chapter II., Fig. 1, without any adhesive, is seldom or never resorted to now for practical engineering drawings.

Long cartridge paper has a surface that does not suit well for some large drawings, when it is better to join the smaller sized sheets of superior surface. This can be done very neatly by thinning the edges to be joined by fine sand or glass paper, held tightly by the hand (or glued) around a flat piece of wood about 6 inches long, 2 inches broad, and ¼ inch thick. The edges of the paper, which are to be joined, should be cut quite straight, after which each sheet should be placed separately, with the cut edge close to the edge of the table or a drawing board, and a straight-edged piece of wood, against which to bear in using the sand paper, placed above the paper about ⅜ths of an inch, or the breadth of what is to be the joint, inwards from the edge of paper, and held firmly by weights. The projecting ⅜ths of the paper, beyond the straight-edge, should then be rubbed with the sand-paper till it is quite thin at the outer edge; the same process should be repeated to the end of the other sheet, taking care previously that the corresponding surfaces to be drawn upon will be together when joined. Each edge of paper, so rubbed, should have a thin coating of gum. Having placed the sheets so that the joint will be somewhere on the middle of any flat surface, such as a table or a drawing board, a slip of drawing paper, at least 1½ inches broad, should then be placed over the joint, and well rubbed on the top with the rounded end of a penknife; never in any case should the intervening slip of paper be omitted. If the paper thus joined is not afterwards to be damped for stretching, a strip of smooth wood, or a straight-edge, with a few weights, should be laid on the joint, causing it to dry flat. If, however, the paper has to be stretched on a board, it should be done while the joint is still damp. The joint should be carefully avoided in sponging the paper. When the paper is gummed round the edge, and put down in the ordinary way, a brass pin should be placed in each end of the joining of paper, and three or four on each side of it, about 1 inch apart in the common margin. A sheet formed thus, in two parts, should never have any drawing on it sponged, in the way referred to in Chapter XVI., or the joining ends would run the risk of being separated during contraction.

On any unstretched sheet of drawing paper finer ink lines are more easily drawn, the fibre of the paper not being separated by expansion. When a small unstretched sheet, kept in roll, is to be drawn upon, it will always be found to lie better to the board by keeping the hollow, or concave side, uppermost. The corners should be stuck down with a little gum, rather than pins, as the latter are apt to interfere with the free action of the T-square ; but when for colouring, however small the sheet, it must be stretched and gummed down all round, for the reason already stated.

A damp sheet should never be covered up with brown paper, or the like, as such coverings are apt to leave a cloudy mark.

When the sheet is quite dry, white paper is the best covering, particulars regarding which are noticed at the end of next chapter.

Should there be at any time two drawings, one on each side of a board, one of them not being required for a time, and the other worked at, a sheet of paper should be put above the former, and gummed down all round at the edge, and a brass pin put in each corner, so as to keep the under surface from being chafed by the table, which it certainly otherwise would be after being handled about.

CHAPTER IX.

STRETCHING FRAME.

I_F_ a drawing has to be made in a highly-finished style for framing, it is better to first attach the paper to the cloth already fastened to the plain stretcher, which has to be placed in the proper frame, otherwise colours and shade lines are apt to run and blot, besides running the risk of the drawing not drying on the cloth quite fair and square. Especially is this advice necessary to the draughtsman who has not been accustomed to mount his own drawings. A stretching-frame should be strong enough to resist the tension of the paper when dry, and for any length above 18 inches should have a bar or bars across. The inner top sides of stretchers should be slightly rounded over, as shown in the subjoined cross section (Fig. 22); if these corners were left square they would be apt to show a soiled mark on the paper by the time a drawing was finished. A large frame, 6 or 8 feet

Fig. 22.

long, should have two cross bars, dividing the length of frame into three equal parts, and of such thickness as when let in flush at the back the top sides only come up to the rounding of the sides, as shown; and they should be let into the sides only about one-third across, so as not to weaken them. The sides and ends of a stretcher 8 or 9 feet long, and 2 feet across, should be 4 inches by ⅞ths of an inch. The frame being ready, linen or calico—the former being preferable—should be procured as white as it can be had, and it should be spread out on a table or other flat surface, and, the face side of stretcher being laid next to it, the edges of the cloth should be pulled over and nailed to the back; the ends first, then the middles of the sides, and in every intermediate space until the tacks are only about 4 inches apart, taking care always to pull it tight in putting

any tack when opposite to another. If the edge is folded
for the tacking, the two thicknesses will tend to hold the
tacking better than if single. The paper to be stretched
should be laid flat on a surface covered by a clean table-
cloth, the side of paper to be drawn on of course being
·under. Sponge the paper with clean water, and let it dry
in a little ; and then with cold flour paste, free from knots
and gritty matter, applied with a flat brush (whitewash one
if the sheet is large), give the paper one or two good coats ;
place the frame with the cloth on the paper, and rub the
back of the cloth well ; turn it over and rub down the edges,
which should be in a little from outer edge of frame. If
any little blisters should arise from the paste not having
been sufficiently cold, they should be pricked with a fine
needle, and the paper rubbed down. When paper thus
stretched on cloth is quite dry, it will be found nearly as
stiff to draw on as a drawing-board. As the cloth at the
edge of the frame will not present a good edge for the
accurate working of the T-square, a strip of parallel wood,
rectangular in section, and equal to the thickness of the
frame, should be nailed on temporarily.

In making a drawing, mounted as described on a frame,
the horizontal lines have to be worked as in long drawings
on boards, by measuring up in two places in the length from
the bottom, and applying a straight-edge. A long T-square,
however accurate in itself, and however square the ends of
boards or frames may be to the sides, would be rendered
inaccurate by the least particle of grit, the end of the blade
seriously so. It may be as well to mention here, that in
shading and colouring a stretched drawing on a frame it is
better to lean the hand on a thin broad straight-edge, or
clean strip of plank long enough to reach over the ends of
frame, and which will prevent the hand indenting the
paper.

In covering up a drawing in progress, either on boards or
stretchers, when not actually working at it, brown paper or

newspapers should never be used for the purpose—the former being greasy or tarry, and the latter apt to soil from the printed matter. Clean white paper is the best, and can be had of large size for such purposes, or several sheets can be pasted together. The best way for preserving a drawing when likely to be indefinitely prolonged, is to gum all round the edge of the cover, after the principal centre lines have been drawn in, and cut a door in it suitable to the size of the piece of drawing that is being worked at, and, when put aside, another whole sheet should be pinned all round the edge on the top of the other. A drawing cannot be kept too clean.

Drawing paper, when purchased ready mounted on cloth, is useful for various kinds of drawings, but more frequently for those of civil than mechanical engineers. It is never damped and stretched for drawing on, and rarely buckles up in being coloured. For any drawing to be afterwards framed, those whose business it is can put it on a stretching frame quite tightly, without at all injuring it.

CHAPTER X.

COMMENCING A DRAWING.

DRAWING is the art of representing objects on a plane surface in such a manner that the delineation shall perfectly accord with the natural appearance of those objects. It is also the laying down the outlines of any object tastefully and correctly; and the process depends chiefly on the dexterous use of the various instruments employed, and upon preserving a strict proportion of details, so that the whole and all the parts may agree with the scale on which the drawing is constructed.

It is usual to stand when drawing, especially in making large drawings. In making small drawings, however, sitting may do well enough, as they can be conveniently worked at.

Having seen that the drawing-paper is properly stretched on the board, quite dry, and free from blemish, and, the board and square having been proved correct, a good flat point must be put on the H H pencil by a sharp penknife. Though a round point is preferable for filling in any little circular work, a flat point will do more straight work without repairing. The wood should be cut away as far back as ⅜ths of an inch from the end. In using the penknife for this purpose, it will be found less liable to break the lead if the blade of the knife is held at an angle than if square across; the point can be trimmed up either on a small smooth file, or on fine sand (or glass) paper. The point of the pencil must not be so fine as to break off, and should be kept sharp by a little application of the sand-paper.

A pencil should never be wetted, as afterwards it would be impossible to rub out; besides, it is quite unnecessary.

Before using the T-square for the day, it should be wiped free from dust with the cloth kept for such purposes.

In using a square which has a shifting stock for lines to be parallel to the board, care must always be taken that it is not the shifting part of the stock that bears against the board, instead of the fixed side; the screw nut of such stock should always be uppermost.

For drawing horizontal lines the square must be kept firm with the left hand against the left edge of the drawing-board, and never, by any means, on the right side; and for drawing vertical lines the square must be kept firm, with the left hand, against the bottom edge of the board, and never against the top edge.

The lines should always be drawn along the front edge of the square, and never along the edge at the back, and always on the same side of the blade, even though the stock is not a shifting one. For the same drawing the same square should always be used.

The little triangles of thin wood (referred to in Chapter IV.), having one angle rectangular, when placed against the

T-square, are useful for drawing any series of lines at right angles to the T-square, or parallel to each other; but, unless for a series of lines, it is more trouble adjusting the square in its position across the board than shifting the T-square itself.

Having previously laid off, just visibly, the point through which the line is to be drawn, and placed the T-square in position, the top of the pencil should incline a little outwards, so as to permit the point to move close to the lower edge of the square; the top of the pencil should also incline a little towards the right. The line should invariably be drawn from the left to the right.

In making circles with pencil compasses (supposing them of the description recommended in Chapter IV., with a joint in each leg), the lower portions of each leg should be kept nearly vertical, otherwise the central point will make a large hole in the paper, which ought always to be avoided. If the circle is to be a small one, the central leg should be kept a little longer than the pencil one: for in most cases it will go a little way into the paper. A good small circle can never be drawn if the centre leg is the shortest. In drawing a circle, the bows (or compasses) should be held by the top, and kept in as upright a position as circumstances will admit of.

Before entering into the subject of copying by the pencil from an original drawing, &c., it is requisite to give, in a concise way, a few hints in geometry, the uses of which are continually recurring in mechanical drawing.

CHAPTER XI.

HINTS ON GEOMETRY.

GEOMETRY is the science which treats of the properties and relations of magnitudes.

These magnitudes are either solids, surfaces, or lines.

c 3

Solids have length, breadth, and thickness.

A surface is the face of a solid, and has only length and breadth.

A line has only length, without either breadth or thickness, and may be called the boundary of a surface.

A point has neither length, breadth, nor thickness—it has simply position; and in the crossing of two lines there is the point of intersection—it has only position.*

Lines.—Lines are either straight or curved.

A mixed line is composed of curves and straight lines (Fig. 23).

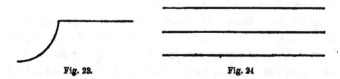

Fig. 23.   Fig. 24

Parallel straight lines are those which are equally distant from each other at every part, and however far they may be produced at either end can never meet (Fig. 24).

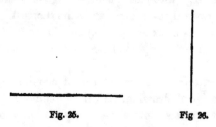

Fig. 25.   Fig 26.

A horizontal line is a line parallel to the horizon (Fig. 25).

A vertical line is a line upright from the horizon (Fig. 26).

* In attempting to represent lines and points on the surface of paper by means of drawing instruments, the representations can never more than approximate to the things intended to be shown. For the finest line that can be drawn will have *some* breadth; and, indeed, if it had no breadth it could not be visible. In the same way, a point may be represented by a very minute dot on the surface; still, as it *some* surface, it is not a geometrical point.

Angles.—An angle is the amount of opening between two lines which meet. It will be understood that the lengths of

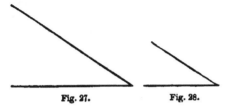

Fig. 27.   Fig. 28.

the lines have nothing to do with the size of the angle : thus, these two angles (Figs. 27 and 28) are said to be equal.

If the lines are both straight, it is called a rectilineal angle; if both curved, a cúrvilineal angle. The lines are the sides of the angle; the point of meeting is the vertex of the angle.

Right Angle.—When one straight line stands upon another, so as to make the two angles equal, each of these angles is called a right angle (Fig. 29); and one line is said to be perpendicular to the other. A line which is not perpendicular to another is oblique to it.

Acute Angle, less than a right angle (Fig. 30).

Obtuse Angle, greater than a right angle (Fig. 31).

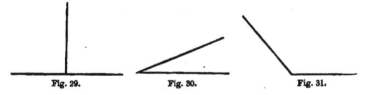

Fig. 29.   Fig. 30.   Fig. 31.

Surfaces.—Surfaces are either curved or flat. Flat surfaces are called *planes.* Curved surfaces máy be called *deflected.* The hollow side is called *concave;* the other *convex.*

Triangles.—The three angles of any triangle added together are equal to two right angles.

Any side may be called the base.

Triangles are denominated according to the magnitude of their angles.

A right-angled triangle, having one right angle (Fig. 32). The side opposite which is called the hypothenuse; the other sides are, indiscriminately, one of them the base, and the other the perpendicular.

An acute-angled triangle, having its three angles acute (Fig. 33).

An obtuse-angled triangle, having an obtuse angle (Fig. 34).

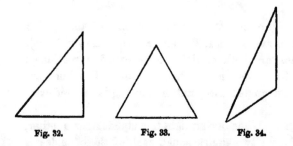

Fig. 32.   Fig. 33.   Fig. 34.

Triangles are also divided according to their sides.

An equilateral triangle, having three sides which are equal (Fig. 35).

An isosceles triangle, having two sides which are equal (Fig. 36).

A scalene triangle, having all three sides unequal (Fig. 37).

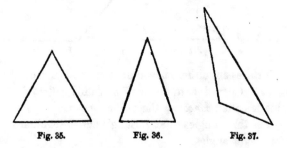

Fig. 35.   Fig. 36.   Fig. 37.

Quadrilaterals.—A quadrilateral figure is that which is bounded by four lines.

When the opposite sides are parallel, it is called a parallelogram (Fig. 38).

When a parallelogram has right angles, it is called a rectangle (Fig. 39).

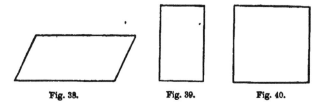

Fig. 38.   Fig. 39.   Fig. 40.

Square, having four right angles and four equal sides (Fig. 40).

Rhombus, or lozenge, having its sides equal, and only its opposite angles equal (Fig. 41).

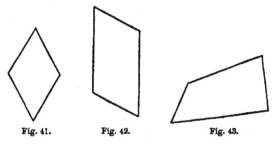

Fig. 41.   Fig. 42.   Fig. 43.

Rhomboid, having its sides parallel, and only its opposite sides equal (Fig. 42).

Trapezium, having neither pair of its sides parallel (Fig. 43).

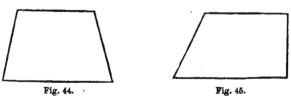

Fig. 44.   Fig. 45.

Trapezoid, having two sides parallel (Fig. 44).

Right-angled trapezoid, having two right angles (Fig. 45).

Isosceles trapezoid, having two opposite sides equal (Fig. 46).

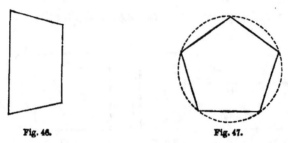

Fig. 46.   Fig. 47.

Figures on planes and of more than four sides are called polygons.

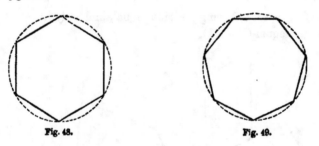

Fig. 48.   Fig. 49.

When the sides and angles of a polygon are equal, it is a regular polygon; when they are otherwise, it is an irregular polygon.

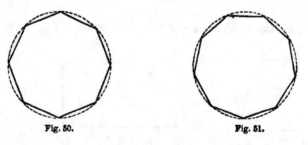

Fig. 50.   Fig. 51.

Pentagon, five sides and five angles equal (Fig. 47).
Hexagon, six sides (Fig. 48).

Heptagon, seven sides (Fig. 49).
Octagon, eight sides (Fig. 50).
Nonagon, or Enneagon, nine sides (Fig. 51).

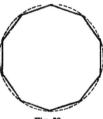

Fig. 52.

Fig. 53.

Decagon, ten sides (Fig. 52).
Undecagon, eleven sides (Fig. 53).
Duodecagon, twelve sides (Fig. 54).
Diagonal.—A line joining the vertices of two angles of a figure not adjacent (Fig. 55).

Fig. 54.

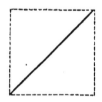

Fig. 55.

Circles.—*Circumference,* a curve line of which the points are equally distant from a point or common centre. The circle is the area bounded by the circumference (Fig. 56).

Diameter, a line passing through the centre and terminated both ways by the circumference (Fig. 57) (the proportion of diameter to circumference is as 1 to 3·14).

The portion of the circle cut off by the diameter is a semi-circle.

Radius, a line drawn from the centre to the circumference ; equal to half a diameter. All the radii are obviously equal (Fig. 58).

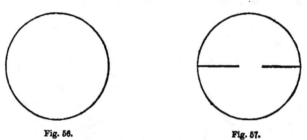

Fig. 56.   Fig. 57.

Arc, a part of the circumference (Fig. 59).

Chord, a line joining two points of a circumference, or the extremities of an arc (Fig. 60).

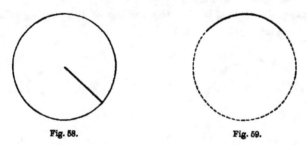

Fig. 58.   Fig. 59.

Segment, part of a circle cut off by a chord (Fig. 61).

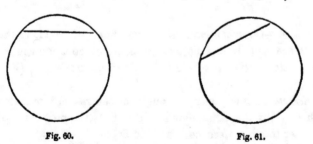

Fig. 60.   Fig. 61.

Sector, space cut off by two radii (Fig. 62).

Inscribed line, a line terminated both ways by the circumference (Fig. 63).

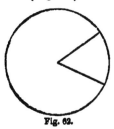

Fig. 62.

Fig. 63.

Inscribed angle, the summit at the circumference, and the sides consisting of two chords (Fig. 64).

Inscribed triangle, the summits of the three angles at the circumference (Fig. 65).

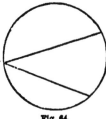

Fig. 64.

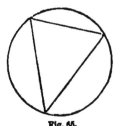

Fig. 65.

Tangent, touching the circle without cutting it, meeting only at one point, called the point of contact (Fig. 66).

Fig. 66.

Fig. 67

Secant, a line drawn from the centre through the extremity of an arc to meet the tangent drawn from the other extremity, as the dotted line (Fig. 67).

Concentric lines, having the same centre, and therefore parallel (Fig. 68).

Eccentric lines, having different centres (Fig. 69).

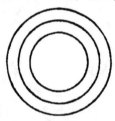

Fig. 68.   Fig. 69.

Ordinate, a straight line drawn from any point of a curve perpendicular to the diameter, as the dotted lines (Fig. 70).

Abciss, the part of the diameter cut off by the ordinate (Fig. 71).

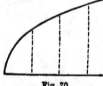
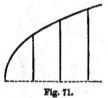

Fig. 70.   Fig. 71.

Spiral, starting from a centre and removing from it gradually (Fig. 72).

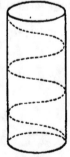

Fig. 72.   Fig. 73.

Helix, turning on a cylinder, and uniformly advancing lengthwise (Fig. 73).

Tangent circles (Fig. 74).

Circumscribed polygon (Fig. 75).

Ellipse (Fig. 76). The longest diameter is called the *major axis*, and the shortest diameter the *minor axis*.

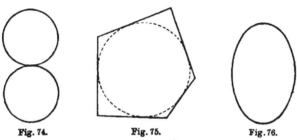

Fig. 74.   Fig. 75.   Fig. 76.

Solids (*regular*).—Of solids there are a great variety. As planes are bounded by lines, and derive their names from the character and disposition of these lines, so solids are bounded by surfaces either plane or curve, and derive their titles therefrom. Regular solids, bounded exclusively by planes, cannot have fewer than four sides.

Tetrahedron, having the faces composed of four equilateral triangles (Fig. 77).

Hexahedron, having six faces equal squares (Fig. 78).

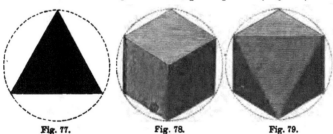

Fig. 77.   Fig. 78.   Fig. 79.

Octahedron, having eight faces equilateral triangles (Fig. 79).

Dodecahedron, having twelve faces equal pentagons (Fig. 80).

Icosahedron, having twenty faces equilateral triangles (Fig. 81).

Triangular prism, having three sides in the base (Fig. 82).

Quadrangular prism, having four sides in the base (Fig. 88).

Truncated prism, the remainder of a prism which has been cut obliquely (Fig. 84).

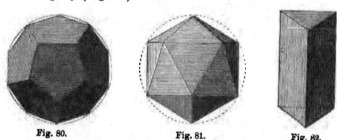

Fig. 80.   Fig. 81.   Fig. 82.

Hexagonal prism, having six sides in the base (Fig. 85).

Triangular pyramid, having three sides in the base and terminating in a point (Fig. 86).

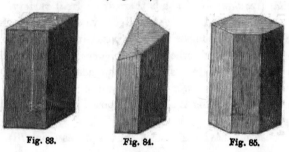

Fig. 83.   Fig. 84.   Fig. 85.

Quadragular pyramid, having a quadrilateral for the base (Fig. 87).

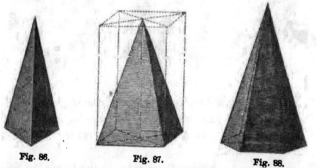

Fig. 86.   Fig. 87.   Fig. 88.

Hexagonal pyramid, having a hexagon for the base (Fig. 88).

Cylinder, generated by the motion of a circle parallel to itself, and at right angles to its own plane (Fig. 89).

Cone, having a circle for its base, and terminated by a point (Fig. 90).

Inclined pyramid (Fig. 91).

Fig. 89.   Fig. 90.   Fig. 91.

Inclined cylinder (Fig. 92).

Sphere, the curve surface of which is at all points equally distant from the centre (Fig. 93).

Spheroid, or elongated sphere, something like an ellipse in its side elevation (Fig. 94).

Fig. 92.   Fig. 93.   Fig. 94.

Degrees.—Angles are described as of so many degrees. It is usual to divide the circumference of a circle into 360 equal parts, called degrees; these again are divided into

minutes, and the latter into seconds ; and known by the following signs :—Degrees, ° ; minutes, ′ ; seconds, ″.

. The fourth of a circle, as shown in diagram (Fig. 95), is
an angle of 90°. The lines A B and C D are at right angles,
A B being perpendicular to C D. When the radii are thus at
right angles, the sector is called a quadrant.

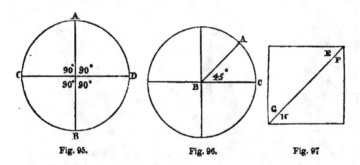

Fig. 95.   Fig. 96.   Fig. 97

The eighth of a circle (Fig. 96) is an angle of 45°, as A B C,
and it is also shown (Fig. 97) as the angles formed by a line
drawn through to the opposite (but not adjacent) angles of a
square, and is called its diagonal. E, F, G, H, have each an
angle of 45°.

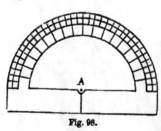

Fig. 98.

A little half-circular instrument, called a protractor (Fig.
98) (referred to in Chapter IV.),
is useful for setting off any required angle, having the degrees marked all round the edge,
the centre, A, of the instrument,
being placed on the point on
base line to which the other line forming the angle is to
be drawn. It is also useful for measuring the degrees of
any angle.

Another mode of drawing a line at any required angle to
another line, is by using the scale of *chords* (and which will
be found on most scales supplied with instruments). Let *a b*

(Fig. 99) be the line. It is required to draw another line from the point *a* at an angle, say of 35°, to the line *a b*.
From the point *a*, as a radius, take the distance *always* of 60° from the scale of chords, and describe the arc *c d*; then take the distance 35° for the required angle from the scale of

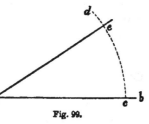

Fig. 99.

chords, and set it off from the point *c* on the arc *c d*, at *e*, and draw the line *a e*; *e a c* will be the required angle. In measuring an angle the same process can be applied.

*To bisect (or divide into two equal parts) a given straight line by a line drawn perpendicular to it.**

Let A B (Fig. 100) be the given straight line. 1. Set one foot of the compasses on the extremity A, as a centre; and with any convenient radius that is evidently

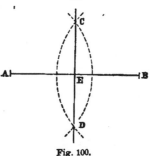

Fig. 100.

greater than half the line, describe the arc C D; similarly from the point B, as a centre, describe another arc with the same radius, cutting the first one at the points C and D.

2. Through the points of intersection. C and D draw a straight line C E D, this line will divide the given line A B into two equal parts, A E, E B, at the point E, and will also be a perpendicular to the line. It is not necessary in practice to draw the complete arcs. An experienced eye can readily anticipate the points of intersection of the arcs within small limits. Neither is it necessary to do more than apply a straight-edge to these points of intersection,

* In presenting methods of performing geometrical operations, the T-square, parallel rulers, &c., will, where applicable, assist considerably on many occasions in simplifying the solution of the problems, and with an accuracy generally quite sufficient for practical purposes.

and tick the point E, unless, indeed, the perpendicular itself be wanted, which is often the case.

The same process serves for the bisection of a circular arc ; for, supposing A B to be the chord of the arc, the perpendicular which bisects the chord will also bisect the arc.

To draw a perpendicular to a given straight line from a given point in that line.

FIRST, When the point is near the middle of the line.

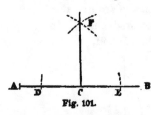
Fig. 101.

1. Let A B, Fig. 101, be the line, and C the point near the middle from which the perpendicular is to be drawn. On C as a centre, with any convenient radius, set off equal parts, C D and C E, on the line A B.

2. On D and E as centres, with a greater radius, describe equal arcs intersecting at F, and, if wanted, on the other side of the line also.

3. Draw the line F C—it will be a perpendicular to the line A B at the given point C.

SECOND, When the point is at or near one extremity of the line.

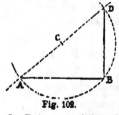
Fig. 102.

1. Take any convenient point C, Fig. 102, obviously within the perpendicular to be drawn from the given point B, place one foot of compasses on C, and extending the other to B, describe a circle A B D cutting the line A B at A.

2. Set a straight-edge to the points A and C, and draw a line cutting the circle at D.

3. Draw D B, which will be the perpendicular required.

Another method :—1. From the given point B set off on the given line a distance such as B A, equal to three of any units of measure, as 8 inches or 8 feet.

2. From B as a centre, with a radius of four of the same parts, describe an arc supposed to pass through D.

3. From A as a centre, with a radius of five parts, describe an arc cutting the other arc at D.

4. Draw D B for the perpendicular required.

This last method of solving the problem can be easily applied on a large scale for laying down perpendiculars on the ground. The numbers 3, 4, and 5 are, it is to be observed, taken to measure respectively the base, the perpendicular, and the hypotenuse of the right-angled triangle A B D. Any multiples of these numbers may be used with equal propriety, when convenient; as 6, 8, and 10, or 9, 12, and 15, whether inches, feet, or any other units of length.

To draw a perpendicular to a given line from a given point without the line.

FIRST, When the point is conveniently near the middle of the line.

1. Let A B, Fig. 103, be the line, and o the point without it. On o as a centre, with a convenient radius, describe an arc cutting the line A B at the points D E.

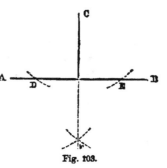

2. On the points D E as centres, and with equal radii, describe the arcs intersecting at F.

Fig. 103.

3. Set a straight-edge to the points o and F, and draw a straight line from o to the line A B. This will be the perpendicular required.

If there be no room below the line A B the intersections F may be taken above, that is between the point o and the line. This mode is not, however, so good as the one already described, because it is not likely to be so exact.

D

Second, When the point is near the end of the line.

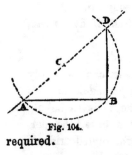

1. Let D, Fig. 104, be the given point, and A B the straight line. From D draw any straight line, D A, meeting A B at A.

2. Bisect A D at c, and on c as a centre, with c A as a radius, describe an arc cutting A B at B.

3. Draw D B for the perpendicular required.

Fig. 104.

To describe a square on a given straight line.

1. Let A B, Fig. 105, be the straight line, or the base of the proposed square. Draw A C and B D perpendicular to the base, from its extremities, and make each of them equal to A B.

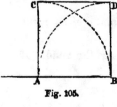

2. Draw the line C D; this will complete the square A B C D on the line A B.

Fig. 105.

To draw a line parallel to a given line.

First, To draw the parallel at a given distance.

1. Let A B, Fig. 106, be the given line. Open the legs of the compasses to the required distance, and from any two points C and D (the farther apart the better) describe two circular arcs on the side towards which the parallel is to be drawn.

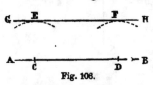

Fig. 106.

2. Apply a straight-edge tangentially to the arcs at E and F, and draw the straight line G H; this will be a parallel to the given line.

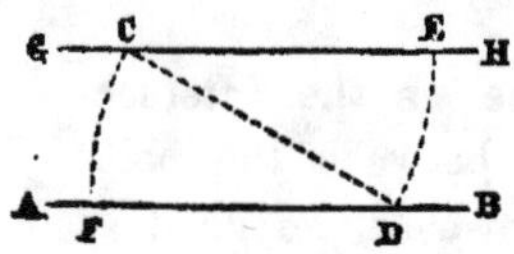

Second, To draw the parallel through a given point.

1. Let c, Fig. 107, be the point; from c draw any line C D to A B.

Fig. 107.

2. From o and d as centres, describe arcs D E and o F.

8. Make D E equal to o F, and through the points o E draw the parallel G H.   This is the line required.

The methods of describing squares and rectangles already given are also available for drawing parallels; though they are not so generally ready of application as the foregoing.

To divide a straight line into any number of equal parts.

1. Let A B, Fig. 108, be the straight line, to be divided

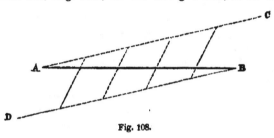

Fig. 108.

into, say, five equal parts.   Through the points A and B draw two parallels A o, B D, forming any convenient angle with A B.

2. Take any convenient distance, and lay it off four times (one less than the number of parts required) along the lines A o and B D, from the points A and B respectively, and join the first on A o to the fourth on B D, the second on A o to the third on B D, and so on.   The lines so drawn will divide A B into the required number of equal parts.

With the assistance of the straight-edge and the set square this process may be con- siderably expedited. Thus, having drawn an oblique line o B, Fig. 109, from the point B, lay off five equal parts on it; set the

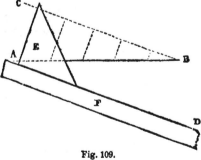

Fig. 109.

edge of the square E, to the point A, and the fifth divi-

sion on C B; slide the square parallel to itself on the
straight-edge F, in the direction A D, and draw parallels
from the points of division on C B to the line A B. The
latter will thus be divided into five equal parts.

Fig. 110.

To construct an equilateral triangle.

1. Let A B, Fig. 110, be the length of
the side of the triangle. On A and B as
centres, with radius A B describe arcs cutting each other at c.

2. Join A C and B C; the triangle, A B C,
thus formed is equilateral.

To construct a triangle, having its three sides of given lengths.
1. Let A B, Fig. 111, equal the base of the triangle.

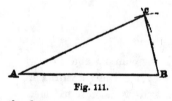

Fig. 111.

On A as a centre, with a
radius equal to one of the
sides, describe an arc.

2. On B as a centre, with
a radius equal to the third
side, describe an arc cutting

the former at c.

3. Join A C and B C. The triangle is thus completed as
required.

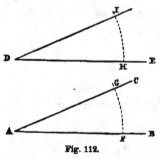

Fig. 112.

*To draw a straight line, so as
to form any required angle with
another straight line.*

1. Let B A C, Fig. 112, be the
given angle, and D E the line
upon which an equal angle is
to be drawn at the point D.

From the points A and D,
with any convenient radius,
describe arcs F G and H I.

2. Set off the length of the arc F G, contained between
the lines A B and A C, upon the arc H I, and draw D I. The
angle E D I will be equal to the given angle B A C.

To bisect a given angle.

1. Let B A C, Fig. 113, be the given angle. On A as a centre describe an arc cutting the sides of the angle at D and E.

2. On D and E as centres, describe arcs cutting each other at F. Through the point F draw the line A F, which will bisect the angle as required.

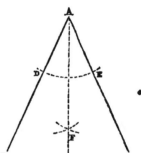

Fig. 113.

To find the centre of a circle.

1. Let A B C D, Fig. 114, be a circle of which the centre is to be found. Draw and chord A C.

2. Bisect the chord at E, and draw B D perpendicular to it, bounded both ways by the circumference. Then B D is a diameter.

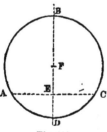

Fig. 114.

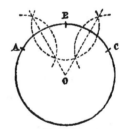

Fig. 115.

3. Bisect B D at F; this point will be the centre of the circle.

Or the following method may be adopted; and it is the more expeditious of the two :—

1. From any point B, Fig. 115, in the circumference, with a radius not greater than that of the circle, describe a circular arc.

2. From two other points, A and C, beyond this arc, one on each side, describe other arcs with the same radius, each cutting the first arc in two points.

3. Through the two points of intersection thus found

draw straight lines, meeting at the point o. This will be the centre of the circle.

To describe a circle that shall pass through three given points
Let A B C, Fig. 116, be the three given points.—1. From

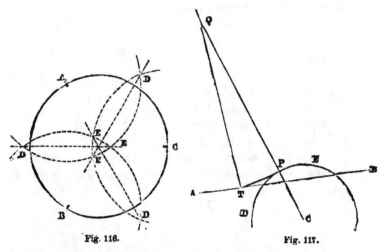

Fig. 116.   Fig. 117.

the points A, B, and C as centres, with the same radius, describe arcs intersecting each other at D E.

2. Through the intersections of any two pairs of arcs (two pairs being sufficient) draw straight lines; their intersection is the centre of a circle which will pass through the three given points.

To draw a circle which shall touch the given line A B, and also a given circle D E, in P, Fig. 117.

1. The centre of the required circle will be on C P produced.

2. Draw a tangent to the given circle at P, meeting B A in T. Then the required circle will touch the two lines P T and A B. Bisect the angle at T by a line T Q. Then the centre of the required circle will be on T Q. But it is also on C P; therefore it is at their intersection at Q.

To draw a number of radial lines upon the circumference of a circle, the centre being inaccessible.

If the radii are to be at equal distances, set off the equal parts on the circumference, as A B C, &c., Fig. 118.

On the points A B C, &c., as centres, with radii larger than a division, describe arcs cutting each other at *b c*, &c. Thus from A and C as centres describe arcs intersecting each other at *b*; and so on. Draw the lines B *b*, C *c*, &c., which will be radial lines, as desired.

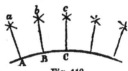

Fig. 118.

To describe a regular pentagon on a given line.

1. Let A B, Fig. 119, be the given line, bisect A B at C, and draw C F perpendicular to A B. Set off on this line a length C D, equal to A B, the given side of the required pentagon. Draw A D, and produce it indefinitely; make D E equal to half A B. From A as a centre, with the length A E as a radius, describe the arc E F, cutting C F in F.

2. From A F and B as centres, with A B as a radius, describe arcs cutting each other in G and H.

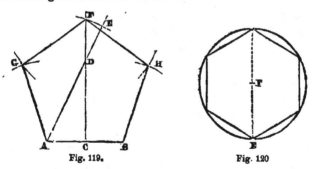

Fig. 119. Fig. 120

3. Draw the lines A G, B H, F G, and F H. A G F H B will be the pentagon required.

To describe a hexagon (Fig. 120).

Draw a circle, and with half its diameter, F E, in the compasses divide the circumference into six equal parts, and complete the figure by drawing the lines between the divisional points, as shown in diagram.

To describe a regular octagon in a given square.

Let A B C D, Fig. 121, be the given square. Draw the diagonals A D and B C intersecting at E. Upon A B C D as centres, with a radius E C, describe the arcs L E H, N E K, G E M, and F E I. Join K G, H I, M N, and F L, which will complete the octagon.

Or, let A B C D, Fig. 122, be the given square. Draw the

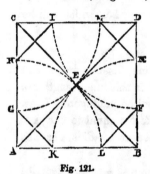

Fig. 121.

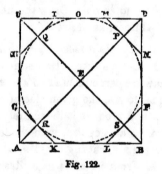

Fig. 122.

diagonals A D and B C, and from the point E, where they intersect, as a centre, and with the radius E O, describe a circle, and where it cuts the diagonals at the points Q P R S draw the lines H I and L F each parallel to the diagonal A D, and the lines M N and G K each parallel to the diagonal C B, which will complete the octagon.

If a circle is given in which to inscribe a regular octagon, it may be done in the following manner:—

1. Draw two diameters at right angles to each other.

2. Bisect the four arcs thus obtained, and draw chords to each—which chords shall form the octagon required.

To describe a duodecagon (Fig. 123).

If a circle is given in which to inscribe the required figure, it may be done in the following manner:—

1. Draw two diameters, A B and C D, at right angles to each other.

2. From the points A, B, C, and D, with half the diameter of the circle as radius, describe the arcs as shown.

3. Draw straight lines between the intersectional points of the arcs, as *e f*, &c., which will complete the figure.

To draw an ellipse.

Having given the two axes, set off from *c*, Fig. 124, half the major axis at *a* and *b*, which are the two foci in the ellipse, take an endless string, as long as the three sides in the triangle *a b c*, fix two pins or nails in the foci, one in *a*

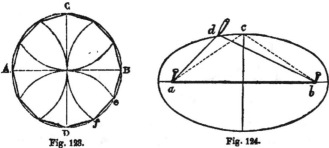

Fig. 123.   Fig. 124.

and one in *b*, lay the string round *a* and *b*, stretch it with a pencil *d*, which will then describe the desired ellipse.

A figure which is often substituted for the ellipse for practical purposes, but is decidedly inferior to it in point of regularity and beauty of contour, may be drawn by means of circles in the following manner :—

1. Let A B, Fig. 125, be a given transverse diameter; divide A B into three equal parts A O, O V, and V B. From O and V as centres, with O A or V B as a radius, describe the equal circles D V F and E G O, cutting each other in the points I and K.

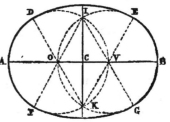

Fig. 125.

2. Draw the lines K O D, I V G, I O F, and K V E, cutting the circles in the points D E F and G.

3. From I and K as centres, with K D or I G as a radius.

describe the curvilineal tangents D E and F G, when the figure A D E B G F will be the ellipse required.

A common method of drawing such a figure is by placing a sheet of paper round a cylindrical object, and with the compasses describe the figure with the one radius at one operation from one centre.

Or by drawing it, as in subjoined diagram, Fig. 126, the ends *a b, c d,* being divided into the same number of

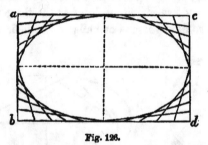

Fig. 126.

equal parts as the long sides *a c, b d,* which contain the larger equal divisions, and drawing the curve tangentially to the inner parts of the lines which are drawn between the several points.*

Cycloid.—A cycloid may be defined by supposing it to be formed by the motion of any given point on the float-boards

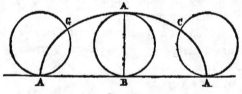

Fig. 127.

of a paddle-wheel running through the water (for finding the curve, see Chapter XIX.), or on the periphery of a cart-wheel rolling along a level road. Thus the circle A B, Fig. 127, may

* There are various methods of describing such curves geometrically and mechanically. The reader is referred to works on the subject.

be supposed to represent a cart-wheel rolling in the direction A B A, and A to be the given point in its periphery. Under these conditions the track of the point A during one revolution will be indicated by the curve line A C A G A, which is termed the cycloidal curve.

Epycycloid.—An epicycloid differs from the cycloid in this, that it is generated by a point in one circle rolling upon the circumference of another, instead of a level surface (Fig. 128).

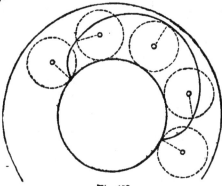

Fig. 128.

Catenary curve.—A curve assumed by a chain or cord of uniform substance and texture, when it is hung upon two points of suspension (whether those points be in a horizontal plane or not), and left to adjust itself in equilibrio in a vertical plane.

Sections.—If any object be cut through in any part, either of the two surfaces thus produced is called a *section*. If a cylinder be cut through the middle lengthwise, the section is a rectangle. If it be cut through parallel to its ends, the section will be

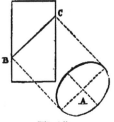

Fig. 129.

a circle. If, instead of cutting the cylinder parallel to its ends, it be cut obliquely, as at B C, Fig. 129, the section will be an ellipse, as shown at A.

To describe the ellipse produced by cutting a cylinder obliquely.

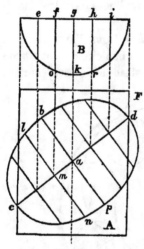

Fig. 180.

Let A, Fig. 180, be the elevation of the cylinder, and *c d* the angle at which it is cut. Draw a half-plan B, of cylinder, divide B by any number of vertical lines from *e f g h i*, and produce them to meet the line *c d*, and through the points *m*, *a*, &c., where the vertical lines intersect it, draw the lines *l n*, *b p*, &c., at right angles to *c d*, and on each of these lines set off the points *a b*, *a p*, each equal to *g k* on half-plan, and *m l* and *m n* each equal to *f o* or *h r* in half-plan B, and so on with the remaining breadths from plan. A curve line passing through the points thus found will be the form of curve or ellipse at the section *c d* of cylinder as required.

A conic section is the section obtained when a plane cuts a cone. Conic sections are of five different kinds, namely :—

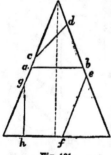

Fig. 181.

1. Triangle, when the plane cuts the cone through its axis.

2. Circle, when the plane cuts the cone at right angles to its axis, as at *a b*, Fig. 181.

3. Ellipse, when the plane cuts the cone obliquely, passing through the two sides, as at *c d*.

4. Parabola, when the plane cuts the cone parallel to one side, as at *e f*.

5. Hyperbola, when the plane cuts the cone so as neither to meet nor be parallel to the opposite side, as at *g h*.

To describe the curves in cone sections.

Of a parabola, or section parallel to one side of cone :—Let A, Fig. 182, be the cone and *d e* the section parallel to *f b*, a front view of which is required. Draw a centre line *n′ o*, parallel to *d e*, cut the cone by the divisional lines *g h i k* parallel to the base *b c*, draw a half-plan of cone B, and with radii equal to

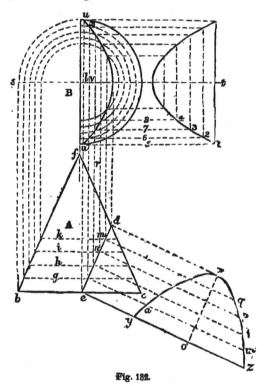

Fig. 182.

half-diameter of the cone at each of the horizontal sections *g h i k* describe the corresponding circles in plan B. From the points *m, n,* &c., in the horizontal lines *k, i,* &c., where the sectional line *e d* intersects them, draw the lines *m q, n p,* &c., at right angles to *e d*; and from the points *m, n,* &c., on sectional lines, draw vertical lines *r* to the plan, cutting their respective circles. Through centre of plan B draw the horizontal centre line *s t*, corresponding to centre line *o n'*, on which the curve points are to be laid off; take the distance *l u* from plan B and set it off equally on each side of centre line *n' o*—at *y* and *z*—this will represent the breadth on the base line of figure; then transfer the distance *v x* from plan equally to each side of the centre line *o n'* at *a* and *w*, and so on, transferring each distance on plan to each side of the centre line *n' o*, on their respective lines. A curve line passing through the points will give the form of curve required. To find the form of curve in the same section *e d*, when observed from points at right angles to axis of cone, draw the vertical lines 1, 2, 3, 4, &c., at right angles to centre line *s t* of plan B, and at equal distances to *g h i k* in cone A, and from each of the points in the circles in the plan

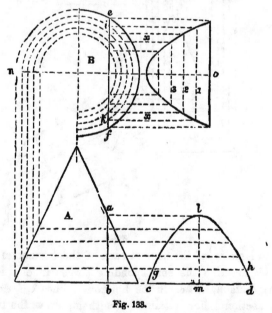

Fig. 133.

where the vertical lines *r* cut them, draw the horizontal lines 5, 6, 7, 8, &c., cutting their respective vertical lines 1, 2, 3, 4, &c. A curve line passing through the intersec-

tional points will give the curve required ; a curve line passing through the points in the circles in the plan where the
vertical lines *r* cut them, will also give a plan of the parabola at the sectional line *d e*.

In describing the curve of a hyperbola, or section of a
cone already referred to, the same process is gone through
as in the last example. Let A, Fig. 183, be the cone, and *a b*
the sectional line. Draw a half plan B, and sectional line
e f ; draw a vertical centre line *l m*, on each side of which
the curve is to be set off from the intersections in the plan
B ; make *c d* and *g h* each equal to *e f* and *i k* in the plan B,
and so on, transferring the half-breadths from the plan B
to each side of the centre line *l m* equally from it on their
respective lines. A curve line passing through the points
will give the form of hyperbola as required. Or, produce the
horizontal centre line *n* of plan B to *o*, and draw the vertical
lines 1, 2, 8, &c., corresponding to the horizontal lines on
side view of cone A ; and from the
points in the circles in plan B, where
the sectional line *e f* intersects them,
draw the horizontal lines *x* to the respective vertical lines 1, 2, 8, &c.
A curve line passing through the
intersectional points will be obviously
the same as that set off at the line *l m*.

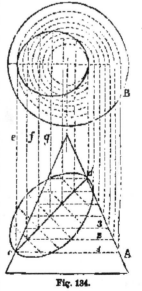

In describing the curve of an
ellipse, or the oblique section
of a cone, the same operation is
performed for finding the curve
points as in the previous examples, A,
Fig. 134, being the cone, B the plan,
and *c d* the oblique line of section,
through which the horizontal lines
1, 2, 8, &c., are drawn, and to
which the diameters of the circles

Fig. 134.

in the plan correspond, as shown ; the vertical lines *e, f, g,*

&c., from the points in cone A, where the section *c d* cuts
the horizontal lines 1, 2, 3, &c., are produced to the plan,
and intersect the respective circles ; the half-breadths at the
intersections are transferred to each side of the line of section
c d, on the lines which are at right angles to it. A curve line
passing through the points will give the form of ellipse as
required ;* a curve line passing through the corresponding
points in plan, where the vertical lines intersect the circles,
will give the plan of the ellipse.

ENVELOPES, OR COVERING OF SOLIDS.—*To find the envelope
for a given cone.*

Let A B C, Fig. 185, be a cone whose diameter is B C, and
slant side B A ; it is required to find the envelope.

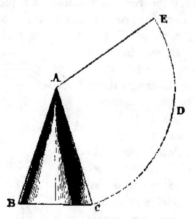

Fig. 185.

From A as a centre, with the radius A C, describe a circle
C D E, make C E equal in length to the circumference of the
base of the cone and join A E; the figure A C E will be the
envelope.

* It may be necessary here to remark, that though the upper part
of the section intersects the cone at a much less diameter in its length
than at the lower part of the section, nevertheless each half of the
ᵀllipse from the middle of its length is identical.

To find the envelope of a given frustrum of a cone.

Let F G B C, Fig. 136, be the frustrum of a cone whose base is B C, it is required to find the envelope.

Produce B F C G until they meet at the point A ; from A as

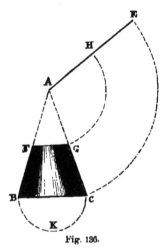

Fig. 136.

a centre, and with the distance A G as a radius, describe the circle G H ; and from A as a centre with radius A C, describe the circle C E ; make C E equal to the circumference of the base of cone and join A E ; the figure G C H E will be the envelope required.

The length of C E may be found approximately by describing a semicircle B K C and dividing it into minute equal parts, and making the length C E equal to twice the number of such minute divisions, as in B K C.

To find the envelope for a cylinder having one of the ends cut off at an angle to its sides.

Let A D B C, Fig. 137, be the given cylinder, having one of its ends A D at an angle to its sides ; it is required to find the envelope.

Upon the base B C draw a semicircle, which divide into any number of equal parts (the more parts the better), as at

1, 2, 8, &c., through these points draw the lines 1, 1; 2, 2; 8, 8, &c., parallel to the side A B of the cylinder; then mark off as in the right-hand diagram, the line H I K equal to the circumference of the base of the cylinder; or, otherwise, equal to twice the semicircle drawn on B C. Upon H I K set off on each side of I the same number of equal divisions as

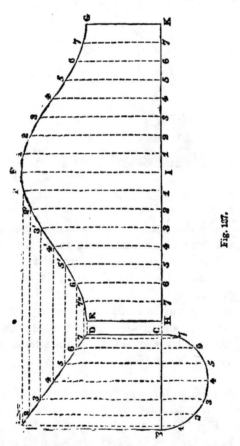

Fig. 117.

in the semicircle B C, and draw lines as I F, 1, 1'; 2, 2'; 8, 8'; &c., perpendicular to H I K. Make I F equal in length to B A, and H E and K G each equal to C D, also each of the perpendiculars equal to the lines in left-hand diagram, having the same figures, 1, 2, 3, &c. ; a line drawn through these points will be the form of the required curve for one side of the envelope, the whole of which is contained in the figure H E F G K.*

To cover a dome having the joints in vertical planes, supposing the axial section given, and also the breadth of the base of the envelope.

Let A B C, Fig. 138, be the axial section, and K f the base of the envelope; the length C E is made equal to the curve A B C, and divided into the same number of equal

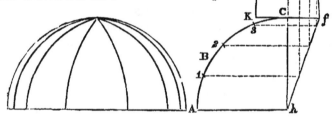

Fig. 138.

parts; join f h, and through the points of division, 1, 2, 3, draw lines parallel to the base A h, then the lines intersected between the axis c h and f h will be the half-breadth of the envelope at the corresponding divisions on C E, through which points draw the curve f E and K E, which will give the form of envelope required as E K f.†

* The foregoing is useful, practically, for making the elbows of pipes of sheet metal, saving much time and trouble, and avoiding waste of material.

+ Much the same process is used in the formation of the spherical ends of round boilers, allowance being made for a greater diameter at one side than the other for overlap of plate for riveting.

Geometry, as applied to drawing ordinary engineering details, will be found in Chapter XIII.

CHAPTER XII.

DRAWING FROM A COPY.

COPIES to be drawn from should either be drawn by hand, or engravings or lithographs, but *not* wood-cuts, as their lines are never so fine, or their shadows as distinct. A beginner especially should never use wood-cuts to copy from, unless they are very plain indeed.

If there are several copies of the engraving or lithograph from which a drawing is to be made, the same copy should always be used, as rarely any two impressions of the same plate are exactly of the same length and breadth, on account of the inequality of the moisture, and consequent unequal expansion of the different sheets when printed.

In drawing, *time* is not so much an object as correctness, though in actual business, the quicker a plain drawing is made the better, if correct.

Before drawing from the copy (original), a cutting-off line should be drawn all round the stretched sheet a little way inwards from the part adhering to the board; in a large sheet it should be at least one inch inwards from the outer edge of the paper, so as to be quite clear of the gum joint.*

Nothing detracts so much from the look of a good drawing as a too small margin. A drawing occupying a space of 1 foot or 15 inches square over all, should have at least a clear margin of 5 inches equally all round, with the border line from $1\frac{1}{2}$ to 2 inches from cut-off edge of paper; and other sizes in proportion.

By measuring, the middle of the sheet each way should be found; the centres also of all the views to be drawn should be put in from the copy.† Supposing there are to

---

* The space thus marked off is also useful upon which to try the drawing-pen before drawing a line when inking-in a drawing, or for trying the tint when colouring (when the drawing is not covered over in the manner described in a previous chapter).

† For a beginner, the drawing to be made should be of the same the copy (or original).

be three elevational views and a plan. It is usual in a properly got up engineering drawing to place the plan above the side elevation, and central on the paper if possible. End elevations, or sections, should be to the right and left of the principal elevation.

In copying from a tracing it is essential to put a sheet of drawing paper underneath the tracing ; it not only shows the lines to more advantage, but prevents the compasses tearing it while taking off measurements.

All measurements should be taken in the exact direction of the distance to be measured, or an obviously incorrect distance will be the result. The same rule applies when transferring the distance to the drawing about to be made.

In taking a measurement from the copy, it is better to first open the compasses and then close them to the distance, than to place the leg point on one extreme of the distance, and then open them to the other ; the right hand holding the compasses resting on the copy and also on the paper while transferring it. In making the mark, the compass point should never be pushed into the paper, a slight mark being all that is necessary ; a fine pointed pencil will render the mark more visible if required.

From the centre of the copy the distance of the base line of the elevations should be found by foot rule or slip of paper, transferring the same to the sheet to be drawn upon, and draw the base line, holding the pencil as directed in Chapter X., and not pressing too heavily, or superfluous lines will be difficult to rub out, and the fine point apt to break. Take, by the same process, the distances from centre of copy to the centres, right and left, of the several views, transferring them to the sheet, and drawing in these respective centre lines of the views required to be drawn. Find the distances from base line to all the principal working centres, and transfer them to the sheet, as well as their positions laterally ; and then general distances, and fill up between with the details, making it a rule to put in

centre lines for any objects which are to have both sides
equally distant from it.   Recourse must be had to light
pencil centre lines on the drawing to be copied from, where
necessary, to measure from.   Pencil lines should exceed
the proper length a good deal, so as to see where to terminate other lines meeting them.   In making a wrong
pencil line among finished pencil details it is better only to
scroll it out with the pencil than to rub it out with the
India-rubber, which is apt to obliterate more than is
wished.

The centre lines in all cases, in machinery drawing especially, must be correctly placed, as, in making a real machine
from a working drawing its correct working depends on that.
When an object has both sides alike the half of the whole
diameter, or breadth, should be taken from the centre line in
copy, observing also that the same distance agrees with the
other half from centre line before transferring it, thus proving
it correct for such whole breadth.   With the correct half of
diameter the distance is then transferred to each side of corresponding centre line on sheet to be drawn upon.   When
drawing by artificial light, measurements can be taken with
the fine point of the pencil of the compasses, which will
show a mark when transferring a size to the paper, though
this instrument should not be used if a mark from the compasses can be seen at all.

In drawing circular details, a little temporary pencil
mark, as shown at a, Fig. 139, should be put around the

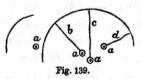

centre of a circle while the eye rests
on it, and arcs of circles which are
united, having different radii, should
have a temporary pencil line drawn
from each centre to its respective

Fig. 139.

arc, as shown at b c and d, so that when about to ink in the
drawing, centres of the required circles can be readily found.
In drawing large pencil circles with the large compasses,
and more especially with a lengthening bar attached, the

pencil end should never be touched while drawing the circle, the compasses being held by the top only.*

In copying a plain drawing in a hurry, it saves much time to place the copy at the right hand side of the sheet, fair and square to the board, and held by weights or pins at the corners. With the T-square placed at the horizontal lines of the copy, corresponding lines can be drawn on the new sheet. Having done these, the copy can then be placed at the top of the sheet, and the vertical lines or breadths similarly drawn in with the T-square. Of course this method cannot be so well relied on; for, should the copy be a little incorrect, there is not the advantage of finding the exact measurement on each side of a centre of a whole breadth, neither is it good practice for a beginner, who has to learn to take correct measurements. When only one view of a steam-engine has to be made from a drawing where two or three views are shown, the side elevation (or the view showing the crank breadth) is the most likely to explain on what principle it is constructed. The side elevation of most machinery other than the steam-engine, would generally give the best idea of the construction, when only one view is to be shown.

In a drawing having a front and side elevation and plan, the former two should agree in all points in the several heights, and the breadths of the plan should agree in all points with the front elevation above which it is placed; and in making such drawings one measurement should be sufficient for a height for either a front or side view, or a breadth in side view and plan, the T-square being used to draw the respective height across for the two former, and placed vertically for the breadths of the two latter.

If two views are to be shown of the same machine, with

* If a circle has to be made larger than the ordinary lengthening bar will admit of, and to save the expense of beam compasses, already referred to in Chapter IV., a piece of flat wood may be tied securely to the compasses, having the ordinary pencil foot at the other end, and at the proper distance.

the working parts in a different position, having once got
the centre lines in each view, one measurement by compasses should be applied to the corresponding part in each
of such views, and thus save time by not doing the same
thing twice over.

In making a full-sized copy of any irregular figure, it is
sometimes the practice to lay the copy over a blank sheet
and to prick it through with a fine needle * fastened in top
end of pencil, or with the pricker generally attached to
drawing-pen handles. This, however, is not so good as
tracing the figure from the copy, then turning the tracing
over, and retracing on the back of the figure first traced ;
lastly, laying the tracing in proper position on the drawing
paper and going over the figure with a hard pencil, there
will be left a sufficiently distinct line to ink in by.

The method of tracing is also useful in making an irregular figure, or combination of curves, when the same figure
is to be shown on each side of a centre line. Having traced
the figure on one side of the centre line by the pencil, draw
a centre line also on it, and transfer the tracing to the sheet
on which it is to be drawn—having also its centre line, with
which the line on tracing must correspond—and proceed as
before explained. In measuring an irregular figure from a
copy, such as is shown in subjoined diagram, Fig. 140, draw

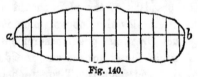

Fig. 140.

a line $a\,b$, and divide the line by any number of divisional
lines across and square to $a\,b$; make similar lines on the part
of sheet on which the figure is to be drawn ; then measure
from the line $a\,b$ to edge where the cross lines intersect,

* Pricking through is generally resorted to by shipbuilders in
making a copy of a drawing, but if frequently performed from the
same original, the latter becomes so full of little holes as to destroy the
wing.

which will give all the points through which the curve is to pass. In a regular curve, the line can be drawn with a baton and weights, as shown at Fig. 141, or by the moulds described in Chapter IV.

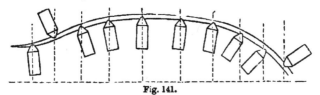

Fig. 141.

In measuring lines from a copy when they are not continuous, as shown at a, Fig. 142, draw a pencil line to b, in direction $f a$ in copy, and from a to c in direction $a e$. The measurement can then be taken from a given point, or centre line, d, in base line to c, and also from d to b. Producing $f a$ to b, mark off the length $b a$, join $a c$; then mark off the length $c e$, and if $e g$ is parallel to $a b$, take the parallel rulers, holding the bar of rulers next to you firm with the left hand, and set the edge of the other bar to $a b$, move back to $e g$ by the right hand, and draw the line.

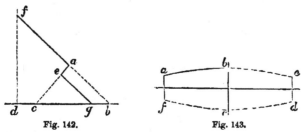

Fig. 142.   Fig. 143.

In drawing such objects as the side view of an oscillating cylinder, or anything similar, and inclined, a perpendicular should be raised for one line square to the centre line of the object, and any other lines which require to be so, made parallel to it.

In drawing the sides of any " barrelled " rod, those which are thicker at the centre than at the ends, such as connecting rods, the ends or necks $a f$ and $e d$, Fig. 143, and the diameter

E

at the middle, *b c*, are first marked off, and if a circle, and not too large for the compasses, the radius is found as already described in the last Chapter (XI.). But if too large, recourse must be had to a mould, being the segment of a circle large enough. If not a part of a circle, probably a parabolic mould for one half of the length (being a varying curve) would suit; and if so, the form must be drawn only as far as *a b*, a mark being put on edge of mould at the centre line *b* (which is always better than at the extremes, as at *a* or *e*), and the mould then turned over and the mark on edge of mould being made to coincide with centre at *b*, the other half, *b e*, can be drawn, making the two ends of the curve equal. The process is performed again for *f c* and *c d*. A stiff baton and weights, as described in Chapter IV., might do very well, marking more diameters in the length of the object.

REDUCING OR ENLARGING A DRAWING FROM A COPY.— To make a drawing half the size * of copy, the half of everything should be taken, keeping to the same rule in regard to drawing in base line, centre lines, and general heights as has been already described. If a drawing is to be made twice the size of copy, whole diameters, &c., are taken and transferred on each side of the several centre lines, doubling the heights, &c. Proportional compasses (reference to which will be found in Chapter IV.) are generally used for such purposes.

When reducing by scales, it is not essential to use the same scale as that to which the original is made: for instance, if a drawing is to be made half the size of another drawing whose scale is 1 inch to 1 foot, instead of applying an inch scale to the original drawing, and using a half-inch scale for reduced copy, any scale may be applied to the original, the reduced drawing being made to another scale in the proportion of 1 to 2 to the greater.

* Which means half the scale of copy, therefore covering only a quarter of the area.

The same remarks apply to drawings to be made to a larger scale * than an original, proportion between the two scales being all that is required.   When a drawing is to be enlarged to more than double, or less than half the size of the original, and if a scale or proportional compasses are not used for the purpose, it is better to take whole sizes from the original, and transfer such measurements to the margin of the sheet to be drawn upon, from which the desired proportion can be taken, as dividing by trial and error on a good drawing destroys its appearance by the numerous marks made by the compasses.

Before going into the process of inking-in a drawing, which will be treated of in Chapter XIV., preparation for drawing from a model or from large machinery, such as a steam-engine, requires some further instruction than in simply describing the making of a drawing from a copy.

CHAPTER XIII.

DRAWING FROM MODELS AND LARGE MACHINERY.

In drawing from a model, it is seldom necessary to make any sketch for marking the sizes on previously, a narrow strip of wood for taking off the heights, &c., compasses, external and internal calibers, being sufficient to transfer, as it were, the model to the paper.

In taking the measurements from a large engine or machinery to be drawn to a scale, more appliances are requisite ; though in drawing to a scale we proceed much in the same way as in drawing from a copy, as regards all the centre-line work, &c.   If a model is to be drawn to the

* If *twice* the scale of the original, it would be equal to four times the area.

E 2

same size, there is nearly as much merit in doing that well as when a greater or less size is wanted, correctness in either case being the principal thing. For large machinery it is necessary to be able to sketch well by hand, and this requires practice. Paper ruled down and across is frequently used—heavy lines showing feet, and light lines inches.* By rough measurements, a view can be sketched on the ruled paper bearing nearly the proper proportions of the parts, and on which the right dimensions are marked accurately after measuring more correctly. But the more common way is to make the sketches in a book having no ruled lines. The larger paged such book is, the better; and if less than half an inch thick it cannot comfortably be held flat for the operation. The following also are requisites :— a two-foot rule with slide, to go into narrow apertures, a straight-edge, a steel draw-point, a large workshop square, external and internal calibers, an ordinary pencil, and a tape line. In most cases an assistant is necessary; in others, a tape line with a hook (instead of a ring) will be found convenient; a light straight-edge, 10 feet long or so, with feet and inches marked on the side at edge, will also be found useful.

As it is necessary to have the entire arrangement of the machine before you when commencing to make your drawing to a scale, a complete sketch of side elevation or view to be drawn is to be made in the sketch-book. On this the principal lengths and heights over all are marked, and heights of working centres from a level line, such as the lower edge of bottom plate, if an engine, or bed plate of any machine; and, having found the centre of the machine, all the distances right and left from that centre to the working centres in feet and inches should be marked. In marking feet and inches, one tick above feet indicates feet, and two tinks above inches will indicate inches. The distances

---

* Price 1s. per sheet.

between two extremes are shown as in diagram, Fig. 144.
If inches only have to be
marked, a cipher and one
tick placed above it should
be put for *no* feet, and if
feet and *no* inches are to be

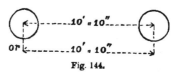

Fig. 144.

marked, a cipher and two ticks placed above it should
be put for *no* inches. By observing this rule a deal of
trouble will be saved; otherwise, when laying down the
drawing to a scale from the sketch sizes, it is sometimes
impossible to tell when only inches are intended; and, with
the tick or ticks absent, whether such figure is for inches
only, or for both feet and inches; for instance, 18, intended to be inches, may be taken for 1 foot three inches.

Having sketched in such different views in the manner
described, with the general distances and dimensions, the
different parts must then be sketched in detail, large enough
to mark the particular sizes upon, and this on a fresh page
of sketch book, placing all the different views of the one
object together, as is represented in diagram, Fig. 145, show-

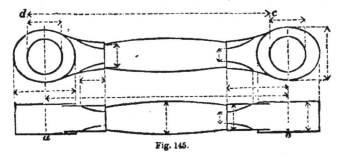

Fig. 145.

ing a common engine link,—the upper being the face, and
the lower the side views. The distance between the centres
a and *b*, if the eyes are of the same diameter, can be easily
found, by measuring from the inner part of the diameter of
one to the outer part of the diameter of the other, as at *c d*;
if both ends are alike, of course it will only be necessary to

mark the sizes once, though all the sizes may be distributed
in both ends and marked so in sketch.   In taking diameters
with the calibers, they should just touch, and never be
pressed on, or they would give the size inaccurately, in
consequence of their springing again inwards when removed
from the object.

In drawing an object like that described to a scale, the
centre lines in the long direction should be first drawn, then
the centre lines across at each eye, and from these centres
the other lengths follow as measured.   In a full-sized
working drawing on paper, the centre lines should be put in
in red ink, and iron and brass sections by their respective
colours.   In sketching circles from 2 to 6 inches diameter,
a very round one can be made by holding the pencil in the
same way as in writing, and placing the little finger in
position as a compass-leg and turning the paper round upon
a smooth surface by the left hand and holding the pencil
steadily with the right.

In measuring toothed wheels, the diameter is taken at the
pitch line, as shown at *a d*, Fig. 146, which coincides with the
line of contact of teeth when geared.   The pitch of teeth, or
distance from the centre of one tooth to the centre of tooth

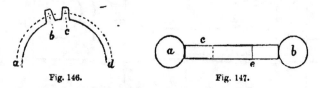

Fig. 146.   Fig. 147.

adjoining, as at *b c*, is also measured on the pitch line.   For
form and proportion of teeth see further on.

In measuring inconvenient objects and distances, as, for
instance, between two columns *a* and *b* (Fig 147), take two
pieces of convenient material, or straight-edges, *c* and *e*,
which, for obvious reasons, must be of greater length than
half the distance between the columns ; place the one above

the other, as shown in diagram, and their extremities in contact with the columns, and either measuring the distance on the straight-edges while so held, or by putting a mark with the draw-point or pencil at the end of upper straight-edge *c* at *e*, they can then be taken down and the length measured ; and adding half a diameter of each column for the distance from centre to centre, if such measurement is required, or if the columns are of the same diameter, add one diameter only. If the columns are tapered, care must be taken to mark the exact place on the columns where the distance was taken, so as to take the diameters at the same place.

The subjoined diagram, Fig. 148, shows another way of measuring objects similar to that which has just been described, though in this case some assistance is required. By placing a long parallel straight-edge against the two columns, and with

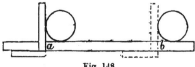

Fig. 148

a square placed in the positions as shown, and by making a mark on straight-edge at *a* and *b*, if the columns are of the same diameter, this one measurement will give the distance from centre to centre.

In taking the outside diameter of a large round object, such as a cylinder five or six feet diameter, when it cannot be measured across at either end conveniently, the easiest way is to place straight-edges, one on each opposite side of the cylinder, and so held as to be firm enough to measure the distance between the straight-edges by another straight-edge at their extremes. If the distance between is the same at each end, that will give the outside diameter. This is more in reference to a cylinder placed vertically. If lying horizontally, and the ends, from their surroundings, cannot be conveniently got at, a stout straight-edge should be set firmly across the top side and propped up below to keep it quite level, which it must be; a plummet can then be held against the straight-edge and one side of the cylinder, and the place of the string marked on the straight-edge; by repeating this process for the opposite side of cylinder, the distance between such marks will be the outside diameter. If a cylinder has a square flange at top or bottom it generally facilitates the measurement of the diameter, as the length of the sides is easily taken, and the distance measured from them to outer diameter of cylinder.

In measuring any irregular figure, as in the subjoined diagram, Fig. 149, place a straight-edge in a convenient posi-

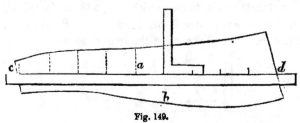

Fig. 149.

tion, and hold firmly by weights on the object, then mark off any number of divisions along the edge *c d* (the distances between which should be marked on the sketch in notebook), the lines *a* from divisions being drawn with a square by chalk or a draw-point; having completed these lines all along the length of object, the breadths can be measured on these lines from the straight-edge to the side of the object, and each marked on its corresponding divisional line in sketch. Having drawn a line at *c d* the straight-edge can then be removed, and the lines *a* produced across to the side *b* of the object, and the breadths measured on that side from the line *c d* to the edge.

It is hardly necessary to add, that the first thing to be done in making the drawing of such object to a scale is to draw the straight line *c d*, with the divisional lines following.

In taking the size of a six-sided nut of which a drawing is to be made, the measurement should be taken across its greatest diameter, as at *a*, Fig. 150.

Fig. 150.

Longitudinal sectional elevations (or objects cut through lengthways vertically), longitudinal sectional plans (or objects cut through lengthways horizontally), and transverse sections (or objects cut through across vertically), are necessary drawings at all times, and to get measurements from the actual engine to make such drawings is often an impossibility, however essential it is to show internal arrangements, often made in the casting of a piece of machinery and never seen again unless broken up. There is often no other way of showing the thickness of material than a section. If the object in question is in process of construction in the factory the only resort for what is required for the purpose is the large original working drawings which show the structure of the interior parts.

In drawings of machinery it is usual to place the plan above the side elevation and central on the paper if possible. End elevations or sections should be to the right and left of the principal elevation, and adjoining the end of the elevation which they severally represent.

When only one view of a steam-engine has to be made, the side elevation (or the view showing the crank breadth) is the most likely to explain on what principle it is constructed. The side elevation of most machinery, other than the steam-engine, would generally give the best idea of the construction, when only one view is to be shown.

If two views are to be shown of the same machine, with the working parts in a different position, having once got the centre lines in each view, one measurement by compasses should be applied to the corresponding part in each of such views, and thus save time by not doing the same thing twice over.

E 5

Different views of the same object on the same sheet should be equidistant from their several extremes, and if there are to be two or three sets of views of different objects on the same sheet there ought to be a greater space between each set than the distance between the individual views of each set. If on the same sheet of paper different details are to be drawn to different scales, the things of most importance and those most intricate should be drawn to the larger scale.

Sections surrounded by other views of the same object should have it stated where it is taken through, the letters having reference to the other views which have corresponding letters where such section is taken.

In finished *pictorial* sections, the parts that would be visible in the real machine, beyond and around the section, are generally shown, though in a sectional working drawing for the workshop the section only is all that is necessary, it not being intended to produce a pictorial view, but to show the actual thickness, &c., of material at the part sectioned.

In the little example of sections subjoined, Fig. 151, the

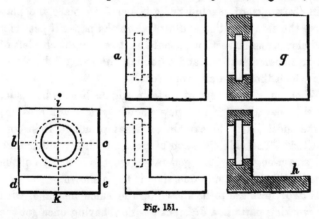

Fig. 151.

part *g* is seen projecting beyond the sectional part, being a plan of the base adjoining. In actual working drawings for factory use it would not be necessary to show it, if the sectional part only was required. If the dimensions of *g*

were really required, it can be got from the sectional elevation at *h*, and in front view from the breadth *d e*; the
sectional plan shown at *g* being through *b c*, and the longitudinal section at *h* through *i k*.

In some cases dotted lines suffice to show an internal part,
as in the three views of the objects shown at Fig. 151, if the
drawing is merely an outline; but it is more satisfactory to
have it in section, as shown at *g* and *h*. A pictorial drawing
should never have dotted lines.

When all the necessary dimensions are carefully noted
down in the sketch-book, and the paper stretched on the
board ready for drawing on, the scale must be chosen to
suit the number and size of the views to be drawn, and the
dimensions of the paper to be drawn upon (though the former
generally determines the latter). Find how much the entire
length and height will occupy to the scale, allowing for the
necessary space between each view to be drawn, so as to
place the whole in the middle of the sheet, leaving an equal
margin around, as described in the preceding chapter.

If instead of using the ordinary scales referred to in
Chapter V., it is found more convenient to make a scale
suitable for the required purpose, it is better, instead of
making the permanent scale at first, to make it on the margin
of the sheet on which the drawing is to be made, as it has to
undergo a good deal of tear and wear from the compasses;
and when the drawing is finished a scale can easily be copied
from the margin scale into its proper place on the drawing.
In making such scales to any part of a foot, for instance
a scale of a quarter of an inch to the foot, it would not be
so correct to take a quarter of an inch by the compasses from
the foot rule to divide the scale line into the number of feet
required. Supposing 20 feet are necessary to the scale line,
it is the more correct way to mark off the whole measure for
20 feet, or 5 inches, and to divide this into five equal parts,
and these again into four equal parts or quarters of an inch—
the whole will then be 20 feet as required. A scale for a

plain engineering drawing should be one fine straight line divided into the required number of feet, leaving the inches clear of the first foot and shown to the left, thus :—

Scale ½ inch = 1 foot.

Fig. 152.

The inch divisions at 3, 6, and 9, should project up a little beyond the intervening inches, as it facilitates taking a measurement in inches.

It is better to say how much the scale is to the foot, underneath it, when it is to any known part of a foot, which it is better to be, as the foot rule can be applied to any part of the drawing of greater length than the scale attached to it.

In taking a measurement by the compasses from the scale, they should be opened sufficiently wide, so that when one leg point is put on the division for feet the opposite leg is closed to the inches; this being more convenient than opening them to the exact divisions of the scale. (See Scales, Chapter V.)

To find the centre line of cylinder and fly-wheel shaft in a beam engine.

Let the horizontal line *c e c*, Fig. 153, be the centre line of beam or lever when at half stroke—and *e* the centre. With the half length of beam *e c*, and from *e* as a centre, describe the radius *f c g* at each end, as shown ; set off the extremities of the stroke or *vibration* of beam at *f* and *g*, a half on each side of centre line *c e c*, and join *f g* by a vertical line, intersecting the horizontal line *c e c* at *i* ; bisect *c i* at *d*, and through the point *d* draw the vertical line *d k*, which will be the centre lines of cylinder and crank shaft.* To find the position of crank at half stroke.—With half stroke (or distance *i f*) as a radius, and on the line *d k*,

* The centre of shaft is sometimes placed vertically from the end *e* of lever.

from l as a centre, describe the circle n—indicating the path of crank. The length of the connecting rod is taken from the point c to the centre of shaft l. With the radius $o\,l$

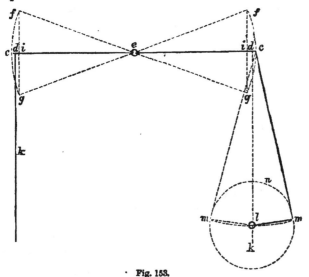

Fig. 153.

describe the arc $l\,m$, cutting the circle n at m, and join $l\,m$ by a straight line, which will be centre line of crank at either side of the shaft, when the lever is at half stroke.

In condensing engines the centre of air-pump is found by describing an arc from e as a centre, through the given centre for working the pump, on lever between e and c, in the same manner as for the cylinder centre line. In marine side-lever engines the annexed diagram applies equally, the lever being placed below the crank being the only difference. The position of the crank of an oscillating, or of any description of connecting rod engine at half stroke is the same.

The civil architecture most frequently adopted in framework and columns for engineering purposes are the Tuscan, Grecian. and Roman Doric orders.*

Regular mouldings are eight in number, and are named—

* For examples of which, with their proportions, see Appendix, Part I.

the Fillet, or Band, the Torus, the Astragal, or Bead, the Ovolo, the Cavetto, the Cyma-recta, the Cyma-reversa, or Talon, and the Scotia.

The Fillet, *a*, Fig. 154, is the smallest rectangular member

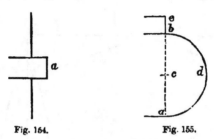

Fig. 154.   Fig. 155.

in any composition of mouldings. When it stands upon a flat surface its projection from the surface is generally made equal to its heigh⁺   It is frequently employed to separate other members.

To describe the Torus, Fig. 155, let *a b* be the vertical diameter from which the Torus projects ; bisect *a b* in *c* ; from *c*, with the radius *c a* or *c b*, describe the semicircle *b d a*, which will be the profile of the Torus. This is surmounted by a fillet *b e*, and being of a rope-like shape (like the Astragal) is intended to bind and strengthen the parts to which it is applied.

The Astragal is described in the same way as the Torus, the only distinction between them being that, when employed in the same order, the Astragal is smaller than the Torus. The latter is generally employed in the bases of columns, the Astragal both in bases and capitals.

The Roman Ovolo consists of a quadrant or a less portion of a circle, and is described at ʌ, Fig. 156, the height and projection being given. First, let the height be equal to the projection, draw *a b* equal to the height, and *b c* at right angles with, and equal to, *a b*, for the projection. The quadrant *a c* described from the centre *b*, with a radius *b a*, or bc, is the contour of the Ovola. But when the projection is less than the height, as in B, draw ab and bc as before, at right angles, ab being the height, and bc the projection. From the point a draw an arc of a circle bd, with the radius

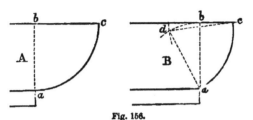

Fig. 156.

ab, and from the point c, with the same radius, describe another arc, cutting the former arc at d; the point d is the centre from which the Ovolo is to be described, with the radius da or dc.

The Greek Ovolo, Fig. 157, unlike the Roman Ovolo, cannot be described by means of circular arcs, but must be described by finding a number of points in it. For this purpose draw the line ac from the lower extremity a, indicating the inclination of the curve at that point; draw also the vertical line dbc through the extreme point b, or projection of the curve. Draw be parallel to ca, and aef parallel to

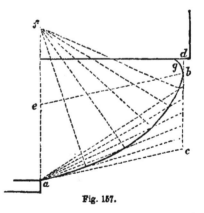

Fig. 157.

cb; make ef equal to ae; divide the lines eb and bc into the same convenient number of equal parts; draw straight lines from the point a to the points of division in bc, and similarly, draw straight lines from the point f, through the points of division in be, meeting successively the lines drawn from *a* to *b c*; the points of intersection of the pairs of lines thus drawn will be as many points in the contour of the moulding, and a curve line drawn so as to embrace these points will be the greater part of the contour.

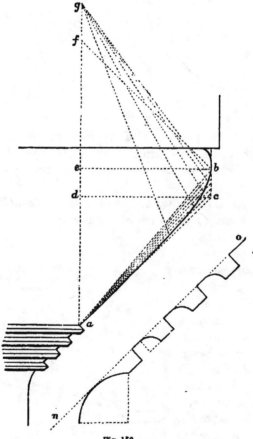

Fig. 158.

The remaining part *b g*, if required to be determined in the same manner, may be found by drawing lines from *a* instead of *f*, through the points in *b e*, and from *f* to *b d*, instead of from *a* to *b c*; of course this will give a good deal more of the curve than is necessary. The curve drawn in this manner is a portion of an ellipse, somewhat greater than a fourth of the whole circumference. The recess of the moulding, *b g d*, at its projecting point is denominated a *quirck*. Fig. 157 is from its great projection relatively to its height, adapted for capitals of Doric columns. With less projection it would be suitable for entablatures.

To describe the hyperbolical Ovolo, Fig. 158, as employed in Doric capitals; having given the projection *b* of the curve and the lower extremity *a*. Draw the line *a c* in the direction of the lower end of the curve, and *b c* vertically through the point *b*; draw *a g* vertically from *a*, and *b e* and *c d* perpendicular to *a g*; set off *e f* equal to *a d*, and *e g* equal to *a e*; join *b f* and divide *b f* and *b c* into the same convenient number of equal parts; draw straight lines from *a* to the points of division in *b c*, and also straight lines from *g* through the points in *f b*; the successive intersections of these lines, as in the foregoing case, are the positions of as many points in the contour. This is the general form of the Ovolos in the capitals of the Grecian Doric. It will be seen that the lower part towards *a* is nearly straight, and is succeeded by four fillets, shown in section on a large scale, and rounded away on the under sides into the fundamental line *n o*.

The Cavetto, Figs. 159, 160, 161, is the reverse of the

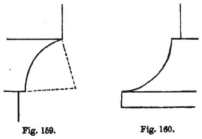

Fig. 159. Fig. 160.

Ovolo, and both in regard to form and to the weakness of the extreme parts, is well adapted for purposes of shelter for the other members. It is always employed as a finishing, and i·

applied where strength is required. It is never used in bases or capitals, but frequently in entablatures; thus, in the Roman Doric order, it forms the crowning member of the cornice, and is evidently employed to overhang and shield the under members.

The Cavetto is described in the same way as the Roman Ovolo, by arcs of circles, which may be either full quadrants

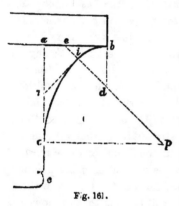

Fig. 161.

or less. The Greek Cavetto, Fig. 161, is somewhat elliptical, and may be described by a combination of two circular arcs, thus: Let $a\,b$ be the projection of the moulding, and $a\,c$ the vertical line; from the point b draw $b\,d$ vertically from b, and make it equal to $b\,e$, which is two-thirds of $b\,a$; from the centre d describe the arc $b\,i$; draw $i\,n$ perpendicular to $e\,d$, make $n\,o$ equal to $n\,i$, draw $o\,p$ perpendicular to $a\,c$, and meeting $e\,d$ produced in p, and from the centre p thus found describe the arc $i\,o$. The contour $b\,i\,o\,c$ will represent the Greek Cavetto.

The Conge or Scape, Figs. 162 and 163, is a species of Cavetto, and is not recognised as a distinct moulding. In section it is partly concave and partly straight, the latter being vertical. It is employed in the columns of some of the orders, for joining the capitals and bases to the shafts. Let $a\,b$, Fig. 162, be the projection of the moulding from the vertical line $a\,e$, which it is required to touch; and first, if the projection $a\,b$ is equal to the height of the curve, make $a\,c$ equal to $a\,b$; and from the points b and c as centres, with $a\,b$ or $a\,c$ as a radius, describe the arcs intersecting at d; from d with the same radius describe the arc $b\,c$, which will complete the contour of the Conge. Or the centre d

may likewise be found by drawing $b\,d$ vertically, and making it equal to $a\,b$.

If the Conge contains less than a quarter of a circle, as in Fig. 163, let $b\,e$ be the tangent to the curve at the point b; on the vertical $a\,f$, set off the distance $c\,d$ equal to $c\,b$; draw

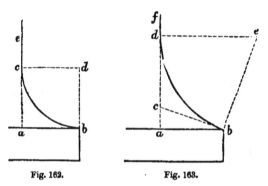

Fig. 162.   Fig. 163.

$b\,e$ at right angles to $b\,c$, and $d\,e$ at right angles to $c\,d$; from the point e, as a centre, describe the arc $b\,d$, which will complete the contour of the moulding $b\,d\,f$.

To describe the Roman Cyma-recta, or Ogee, Fig. 164, join the point of recess a to the point of projection b by the line

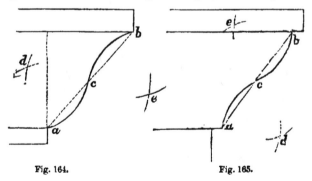

Fig. 164.   Fig. 165.

$a\,b$; bisect $a\,b$ in c; with the distance $b\,c$ from the points c, b, describe the intersection e; and from the points a, c, with the same distance, describe the intersection d; from d, with th‑

distance da or dc, describe the arc ac; and from e, with the distance eb or ec, describe the arc bc; and acb will be the contour of the Cyma-recta required. The projection of the upper end of the curve over the under, as nb, Fig. 164, is generally equal to the height of an of the moulding. If the curve is required to be made rounder, we have only to use a less radius than that of ac or cb, in order to describe the two portions of its contour.

The same description applies to the Cyma-reversa, Fig. 165, letter for letter.

The Greek Cyma-recta is little different from that just described, except that its projection over the under fillet is less than that of the latter, and that its curvature is also less.

The nature of the Greek Cyma-reversa, or Talon, is represented in Fig. 166. To construct the moulding, join the

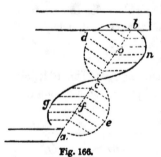

Fig. 166.

points ab, the extremities of the curve; bisect ab at the point c; upon bc, as a diameter, describe the semicircle cdb, and on ac describe the semicircle aec; draw perpendiculars do and ef from any number of points in bc and ca, meeting the circumferences of the semicircles; from the same points draw a series of horizontal lines, as represented in the figure, equal in length to the corresponding perpendiculars, on equal od, fe equal to fg, &c. The curve line $bncga$, drawn through the extremities of the lines, will be the contour of the moulding.

The curve might be made flatter by using arcs of circles of a greater diameter than ac or cb, as the height, od, of the arcs would not be so great as it is in the figure. This will be exemplified in describing Fig. 169 following. If the ~er part bnc be required to be larger than the under part *c a*, of the contour, this may be effected by shifting the point *c* nearer to *a* before drawing the circular arcs.

The Cyma, like the Cavetto, is always used as a finishing, and never applied·when strength is required.

To describe the Scotia, Fig. 167, *the extremities* a˙ *and* b *of the curve being given.*—Draw the perpendicular *a c*, then *b c* is the projection of the curve or moulding; draw the perpendicular *b e;* add one-half of *a c* and two-thirds *b c* into one length, which set off from *b* to *d*; from the centre *d*,

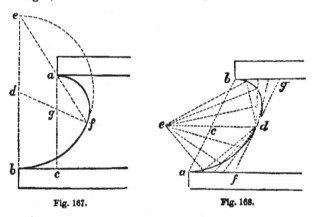

Fig. 167.   Fig. 168.

with the radius *b d*, describe the semicircle *b f e*; join *e a*, and produce it to *f*; then join *d f*, cutting *a c* in *g*; from *g*, as a centre, describe the arc *a f*; this arc, in conjunction with *b f*, forms the contour, *a f b*, of the Scotia.

Another mode of describing the Scotia is shown in Fig. 168. Join *a* and *b*, and bisect *a b* in *c*; draw *e c d* horizontally, and make *c d* equal to the required recess of the curve, and *c e* equal to *c d*; draw *f d g* parallel to *a b*; divide *a f* and *a c* into the same convenient number of equal parts, and to the points of division in *a f* draw straight lines from *d*; draw also straight lines from *e* through the points in *a c* till they meet successively the lines drawn to *a f*. Having performed the same operation on the upper side, the series of intersections thus found are points in the curve, and by drawing a line through them the contour will be obtained.

In Fig. 169 a method is given somewhat similar to that used at Fig. 168. Join *a b*, upon which describe the semi-circle *a d b* from the centre *c*; draw a series of lines perpendicularly from *a b*, meeting the circumference *a d b*; draw also a series of horizontal lines from the same points in *a b*, as shown in the figure, making these lines equal to the corresponding lines in the semicircle, *c e* equal to *c d*, &c.

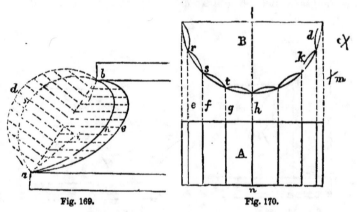

Fig. 169.   Fig. 170.

The extremities of these lines will be as many points in the curve. If the recess of the curve is required to be less than *e c*, as, for instance, *c n*, then set off *c o* equal to *c n*, and describe an arc *a o b* from the centre *i*. By the method in the former case we find the contour *a n b*.

The mode first described, to produce a graceful contour, should be confined to medium proportions. For example, in Fig. 167 the projection is two-fifths of the height.

To find the gradation of the flutes on the elevation of fluted columns.

FIRSTLY. When the column is parallel.

Let A, Fig. 170, be the elevation, having its opposite sides parallel. On its centre line *n*, and with a radius equal to half diameter of column, draw a half-plan B, (a half being sufficient for the purpose). Divide this semi-circumference into the required number of flutes, *r*, *s*, *t*, &c., and from these flute points draw the vertical lines *e*, *f*, *g*, &c., in elevation of column A. In making the plan of the flutes, describe the arcs as at *c*, *m*, &c., with the same requisite radius from each division on the circumference, and from the intersections *c*, *m*, &c., describe the circle of flute as at *d*, *k*, &c., between each of the divisions.

SECONDLY. When the column is tapered, Fig. 171.

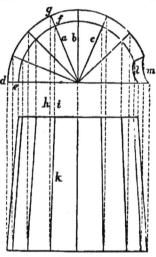

Draw the half-plan of top and bottom of column as at *e* and *d*, divide the larger semi-circle *d* into the required num-ber of equal parts for the flutes, and from which divisions draw to the centre the radial lines *a*, *b*, *c*, &c., and which will divide the lesser semicircle *e* at the same time, and from the points *f* and

Fig. 171.

g, where the radial lines intersect the circles, draw vertical lines as at *i* and *h*, &c., which will give the points on top and bottom of elevation, between which, when the lines *k*, &c., are drawn, will be obtained the elevation of the flutes as required. A plan of a tapered fluted column, when divested of initial circles *e*, *d*, and radial lines *a*, *b*, *c*, &c., will be as represented in part at *l m*.

THIRDLY. When the column is barrelled, Fig. 172.

The process is somewhat similar, only the elevation A must be divided into a number of horizontal parallel lines *a*, *b*, *c*, &c., to represent the different diameters, and which are necessary for intersectional points. In the half-plan B draw the semicircles equal to the diameters *a*, *b*, *c*,

&c., on elevation, and as indicated by the dotted vertical lines *d, e, f,* &c. The lines at *g h* being squared down from

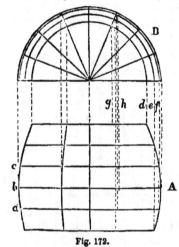

the points where the radials cut the respective circumferences to the horizontal lines *a, b, c,* &c., on elevation A, give the several points for the curve. The process is the same at each radial line, giving the curve points for each flute in elevation. The curves are drawn in by the moulds described in Chapter IV.

In the diagrams just described the figures are exaggerated in their proportions

Fig. 172.

in order to render the process more distinct.

Wheel Work.—In drawing the plan or end view of a spur wheel, Fig. 173, the process is the same as at Fig. 170.

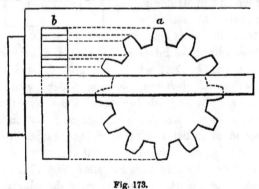

Fig. 173.

The T-square is placed at the several points of the teeth in view *a,* and the horizontal lines drawn in the end view *b,* as shown in diagram. In spur wheels and pinions the diameter (as has been said elsewhere) is always taken at the *pitch line, a,* Fig. 174, which line runs through the broadest part of the upper halves of the teeth, and is coincident with the line of contact with the wheel or pinion with which it is intended to work. The distance between the centres of each pair of teeth *b c, c d,* &c., is measured on this line, and is called the *pitch.* The form of tooth, though variable, is usually similar to that shown in diagram Fig. 174. Having divided the pitch line into the number of equal divisions for number of teeth, and the half breadth of the tooth having also been marked off on each side

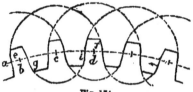

Fig. 174.

of its centre on the pitch line, with the radius *c g,* and from *c* as a centre on every tooth, describe the arcs *g* and *i,* which give the form of the lower part of the teeth; then with the radius *c e,* with *c* as a centre on every tooth, describe the arcs and *f,* which give the form of the upper part of the teeth. The pitch line being kept nearer the outer edge than the middle of depth of tooth, gives a broader base to them for strength. In proportioning the teeth of wheels, the application of the following rule has been found in practice to work well:—

Depth from point to pitch line . . 5¼ parts.
   ,, pitch line to root of tooth 6¼ ,,
Whole depth of tooth . . . . 12 ,,
Working depth . . . . . . 11 ,,
Thickness of tooth . . . . . 7 ,,
Width of space . . . . . . 8 ,,

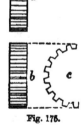

If a plan *a* as well as a front view *b* of a spur wheel is required (Fig. 175); having once found the front view of the teeth at *b* from a face view *c;* it is unnecessary to repeat the process by drawing a temporary face view of wheel opposite *a* for again finding the lines of teeth, the lines can be easily

Fig. 175.

F

márked off from *b* on the straight side of a slip of thin paper and transferred to the view at *a*.

Bevel wheels and pinions and mitre wheels, the latter being two of the same diameter working together, are simply frustrums of cones, the line of contact of teeth of either class terminating in the same centre or apex, as shown in Figs. 176 and 177, the former showing wheel and pinion, greater and

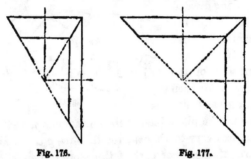

Fig. 176.   Fig. 177.

less, and the latter mitre wheels. In either case a good deal of care has to be exercised in projecting the teeth properly.

It is easier to draw a pair of mitre wheels in gear, than bevel wheel and pinion, as one face view of one of the former serves to project the teeth for the other of the same size working into it; but in the latter a face view (or half, which is sufficient) has to be drawn of both wheel and pinion. In every case where side views only are shown, the teeth can only be projected from a face view, even though it has to be effaced again after the operation. As the process is the same for each of these classes of wheels, the explanation of the subjoined diagrams, Figs. 178 and 179, of mitre wheels will be sufficient.

1. Having determined the diameter of pitch line, draw a vertical line—on which set off the diameter A B, Fig. 178, bisect A B in *c*; from *c* as a centre, and with radius *c* A or *c* B, draw the circle or pitch line A *d* B *e*.

2. Through *c* draw the centre line *d e* at right angles to A B.

3. Draw the vertical tangent line *fg* of a length equal to A B, and which will be one pitch line of side view.

4. Join, by straight lines, *fc* and *gc*, which will form the

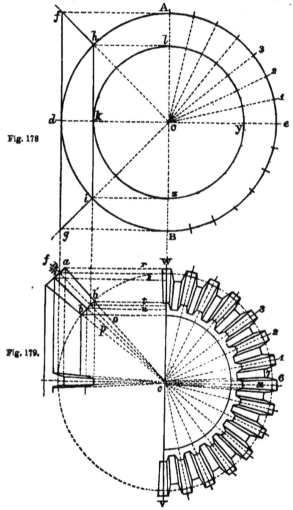

Fig. 178

Fig. 179.

sides of the cone, or the angle of line of contact of the teeth.

5. Having fixed on the length of teeth *fh*, draw the line

F 2

$h\,i$ parallel to $f\,g$.   This line will be the pitch line of teeth at inner diameter of side view of wheel; and through the point k, where it cuts the centre line $d\,e$, and with radius $c\,k$, draw the inner pitch line circle of face of wheel $k\,l\,y\,z$.

6. Having fixed on the dimensions of teeth, space, and pitch; on the greater pitch line A d B e pitch off the centres of teeth as at 1, 2, 3, &c., and through these centres draw the radial centre lines of teeth c 1, c 2, &c.

7. On line $f\,c$, Fig. 179, corresponding to the line $f\,c$ in Fig. 178, mark off the length of tooth $a\,b$, draw in the ends at right angles to the line $f\,c$, on either side draw in the depth of tooth $m\,n$, and from the top and bottom points draw the radial lines p, o, to the centre c; from the same points draw the horizontal lines r, s, and also the lines t, u, from the points $b'b$ to the vertical centre line w v of face of wheel, and from c, as a centre, describe the semicircles corresponding to these half-diameters $c\,r, c\,s, c\,t$, and $c\,u$, which will give the face view of the line of top and bottom of teeth.

8. On face view, from radial line mark off the half thickness of tooth on each side at pitch line,* and at top and bottom of outer end of each tooth at 6 and 7, Fig. 179, on the circles corresponding to r and s.

9. From these points draw in the radial lines towards the centre c, into which centre, with great advantage, a fine needle may be put to bear the front of straight-edge, and thus complete the sides of teeth as at x.   The points for the smaller ends of the teeth will be found from the radial lines cutting the respective inner circles.   The side view of tooth at m being simply drawn in to assist in finding the diameters of the circles in face view, will be almost hidden by the other teeth when all are projected back from face view.

Having drawn in the body of side view of wheel on which the teeth are to be projected from face view, and the line of top and bottom at each end of teeth as at $a\,b\,c\,d$, Fig. 180,

---

* When of the curved form to a large scale.

square the points *e f* and *p o* on face view to *g h* and *i k* on the vertical lines of side view, and join *g h* and *i k*. The lines

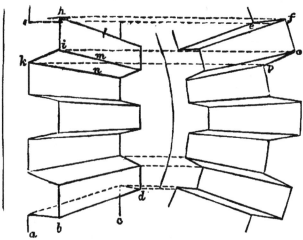

Fig. 180.

l m n, drawn from the points of large end of tooth *h i k*, and from the corresponding points on every tooth, are all radiated to the same centre, as were the centre lines and sides of teeth in face view, the points for the inner ends of the teeth, as already referred to, finding themselves both in face and side view. As the process is the same in each tooth as in that just described, the one definition, with the aid of the dotted lines as shown in Fig. 180, and with an example drawn in fully as at Fig. 181, will be found sufficient. If a face view is not required, but only a side view, then the four points *e f o p*, Fig. 180, of each tooth are all that are necessary in a temporary face view from which to draw in the teeth of the side view.

If the face view is to be shown in conjunction (or *geared*) with a side view, and not two side views, then the teeth which were first drawn in on the face view for projecting the side view must be drawn in where the spaces were between each tooth for the finished drawing of such face view; if drawn in as at first projected for finding the points for the teeth in the side view, it would not present the spaces for the teeth of side view of wheel to work in. The relative change in position of teeth will be observed in the diagram of mitre wheels at *a*, Fig. 181, they having the same diameter and number of teeth as in diagram Fig. 179.

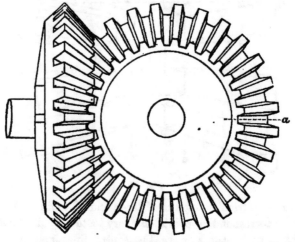

Fig. 181.

If only two side views and no face view is required, having found one side view from the points on the latter (temporarily drawn for the purpose), such points from the one finished side view can be transferred on the straight edge of a strip of thin paper to the other side view to be drawn. It would look more uniform to have a tooth exactly in the centre, which must be arranged at the beginning of the process. In projecting the teeth on side view as in Fig. 180, the points should be found and the teeth drawn in on each side from the centre outwards, as they gradually conceal each other in receding from the centre. By observing this, much rubbing out of useless lines will be avoided.

drawing mitre or bevel wheels in an oblique position,

ınuch the same process as that just described is applicable; with this difference, that the circles when viewed in their obliquity are ellipses, and which the following diagram, Fig. 182, will further explain.

A is a side view of the wheels (the teeth being drawn in complete in each, from a face view, as previously described). Directly over A is the required view B. (To find the ellipses, see diagram following, Fig. 188.)

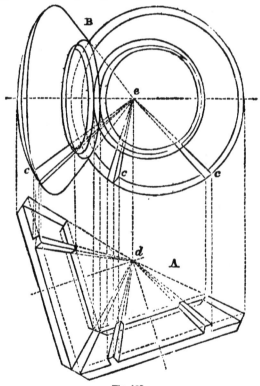

Fig. 182.

The several points of the teeth as at c, c, in view B, on their corresponding circumferences (the ellipses) are set off vertically from the several points of the teeth in view A; vertically, also, over the point d on horizontal centre line of wheels B is the point *e*, to which all the lines are drawn from the several points on the ellipses in both wheels, and as described at Fig. 179.

It is a convenient and more correct method, where the teeth points come closer together towards the edges of the wheels A, to have the side view of the wheels set off vertically at either side of view B (or a face view would be equally suitable) for laying off the points horizontally on the right and left sides of the ellipses.

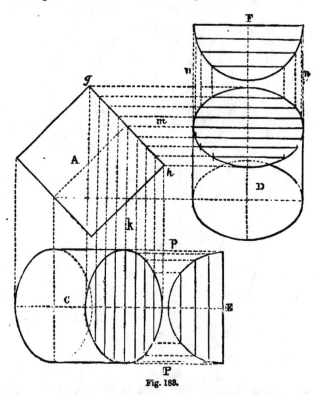

Fig. 183.

To draw the plan, or front view of the end of a cylinder lying obliquely, such as in those of oscillating engines.

Draw a side view A of the cylinder, Fig. 183, at its required inclination, and at a convenient distance from the required position of the plan o or front view D.

To find the points of the ellipse ; on the centre lines of o and D, draw semicircular plans E and F equal to diameter of cylinder opposite each view o and D ; divide the line g h on side view A into any number of equal parts, and divide E and F into the same number of equal parts of equal widths with the other, as represented by the parallel lines in each ; from the points on the line g h on side view A draw the vertical lines k to o on plan, and from the points where the parallel lines intersect the semicircle E draw the horizontal lines p p, cutting the vertical lines k. A curve line drawn through the intersectional points will give the plan of end lying obliquely as required.

From the same points on g h, on side view A, draw the horizontal lines m to D, or front view, and from the points where the parallel lines intersect the semicircular plan F draw the vertical lines n n, cutting the horizontal lines m. A curve line drawn through the intersectional points will give the front view of end lying obliquely as required. The curves at the opposite ends in each view are the same. In drawing the lower ends of such cylinder, a pencil tracing of the curve found for one end can be transferred to the other end of the same view by turning the tracing upside down, taking care that the centre lines, which must be put on such tracing, come exactly over the centre lines of the curve to be drawn. If the back of the pencil curve on the tracing is gone over with a fine-pointed pencil, it will leave a sufficiently clear line to ink it in by, and save repeating the process just described twice over. Indeed, in all curves where both sides are alike, if one-half only is found and traced, this method saves time by rendering points for both sides unnecessary.

NOTE.—In any diagrams such as that described, it is not absolutely necessary that the parallel lines referred to in the semicircular plans E·F should be equidistant, only that they should agree in each relative view or plan. It is usual to make them equidistant, as it is more symmetrical, and in one sense easier, one width in compasses serving for the whole.

It frequently occurs that in oscillating engines the slide valve casing is to the right or left of centre of front of the cylinder. The projection in a front view for an inclined position is found in a similar manner to that when such object is in the centre of the cylinder.

Let A, Fig. 184, be the front view of the cylinder on which the object is required to be projected. Draw a plan B, of

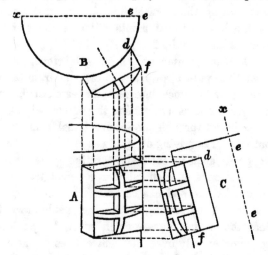

Fig. 184.

the object in its position, also a side view c, of the object at its required inclination, the distances *e d* and *e f*, &c., in such side view c, corresponding to the distances *e d* and *e f*, &c., in plan B, each being measured from and set off at right angles to the respective centre line *x e*. From the several points of the object in side view c draw the horizontal lines as shown (dotted) to front view A; also the vertical lines as (dotted) from the several points of the object in plan

B, to front view A. Their intersections with the horizontal lines from C will give the points of projection for the object on front view as required. If the cylinder and casing were in a vertical position, the plan B only would be necessary, as the heights of required object would be set off on the front view, instead of on a side view, as at C, when inclined.

Other objects under similar circumstances would be projected in the same manner as that just described.

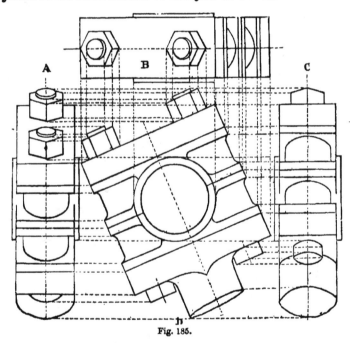

Fig. 185.

In drawing the front or back view, or plan of the engineering detail, shown in accompanying diagram, Fig. 185, when the object is lying obliquely, the points for such views have to be projected, as in similar cases, from another view than any of those named, even though it has to be effaced again after such process, if not required for the drawing. The view required for finding the points of those in Fig. 185, at

A, B, or C, would be a side view, as shown at D. Such views
as A, B, and C have their right breadths or thicknesses put
exactly on them throughout. The dotted lines will be quite
sufficient to show without further explanation how the
oblique positions of the parts in the several views are found,
the lines from the central figure D to the views on right and
left of it being horizontal lines, and those upwards to the
plan B being vertical lines, or at right angles to the right and
left horizontal lines.

To find the curve at either end of the side view of a crank web.

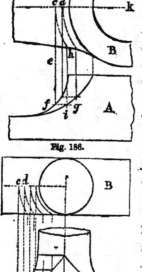

Fig. 186.

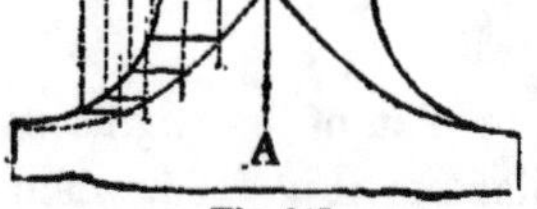

Fig. 187.

Let A, Fig. 186, be a part of
the side view of a crank. Draw a
corresponding part B, of plan of
crank. From the centre K of crank
eye, with any radii (so that it is
on the curved part of web), describe the arcs, as at *c h*, &c. ; from
c draw a vertical line, cutting the
profile of curve at *f*; from the
point *f* draw the horizontal line
f g ; and from the point *h*, where
the arc *c h* cuts the side of the
crank web, draw down a vertical
line, cutting the line *f g* in *i*; *i* will
be one point for the required curve.
Repeat the process from any other
arcs, as from *d*, &c., which will
give other points for the curve
required. The same process is
applicable to the ends of rods
where they change from the circular into the flat butt, as
shown at B and A, Fig. 187, giving plan and side view.

In projecting rivets of the conical form on the side
view or plan of a round boiler, the process is similar to
that for finding the points at Fig. 173. The rivets, other

than those immediately in front of the observer, where the diameters are seen equally, as they recede, appear elliptical; the horizontal diameters * are all of the same breadth, their diminishing diameters being in the vertical direction.

Let A, Fig. 188, be a side view of the object referred to. Draw part of an end view B, of outline of boiler, on which to pitch off the rivets at their required distances; also a longitudinal section, C, on which to project the heads of the rivets in interior view, each view in a direct line with exterior side view A.

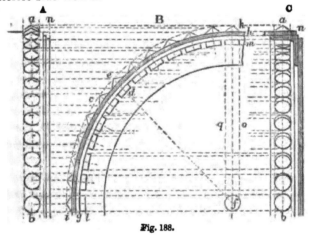

Fig. 188.

The rivets on end view (or section) B having been equally divided from centre to centre, draw a centre line through each point as shown at *e f*, the point *f* being the centre of the circle or quadrant *g h*. Set off the height of a rivet outside, and thickness of a rivet head inside of section B, and draw the circle *i k* passing through the point of height of rivet, and which, cutting all the radial centre lines, will set off the height of each rivet at one operation for outside, and the inner circle *l m* for the thickness of heads inside. Take the half diameter of bottom of rivet (or the base of the

* Supposing the views referred to are drawn horizontally as in diagram.

cone), and lay it off on each side of its centre line.   Draw
the sides of each rivet from these points of its diameter at
base to the point of its height already found by the circle
$i\,k$ cutting the radial or centre lines.   For the head, lay off
each half diameter, $a\,c$ and $a\,d$ (as shown on a larger scale
at Fig. 189), from their centre lines $i\,k$.   Draw lines $c\,e$ and
$d\,f$ through these points and parallel to the centre line $i\,k$,
or, in view B, from f as a centre, describe a circle equal to
the diameter of rivet or head ; and having set the parallel
rulers to the centre f and centre line of rivet, draw the outer

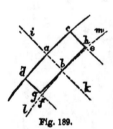

Fig. 189.

diameter of each rivet, as at $q\,o$, equal
to the diameter of circle at f.   The point
b, Fig. 189, through which the circle
passes (as already referred to), being the
thickness of head from a.   Set the
parallel rulers to the points where the
circle $l\,m$ cuts the side lines of diameter
of head $e\,f$, and draw the line $g\,h$ through
the point b parallel to $e\,f$, which will complete the head of
rivet.

In views A and c, Fig. 188, the centre line $a\,b$ having been
drawn in vertically at its proper distance from the end n,
set off the lines for the half breadth of rivet on each side
of it, and square across the points from the top, bottom,
and centre of each rivet from outside of view B, as indicated by the dotted lines c, to side view A, and from
the heads inside at d to interior view c.   For a drawing
to a small scale it may suit the purpose to draw in the
ellipses through the four points thus found for each rivet head
by hand; but for a full-sized rivet, the process of drawing
in the ellipses correctly requires further explanation, as more
than one vertical and one horizontal diameter is requisite.

In Fig. 190 the process for finding the points of the ellipses
(or bases) of the rivets as they recede is shown more distinctly by using a larger scale.

Let A be the side view, B the end view, and c the interior

view of the iron plating, of which the lines *d e* and *f g* in end view B represent the outer and inner surface.

As in the previous instance, draw in the form of rivet *l m n*, on end view B, and draw the lines for breadth (or horizontal diameters) of rivets *h i* on side view of plating A. Draw the semicircle *h k i* equal to the horizontal diameter, or breadth of rivets; divide *t h* and *t i* into two parts, it may be equal, or if nearly so, will suit the purpose, *t p* and *t r*

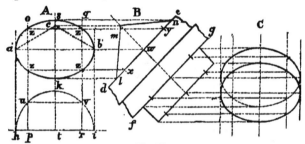

Fig. 190.

being equal; draw the vertical lines *p o* and *r q* (which will be parallel, of course, to the vertical centre lines *s t*), cutting the semicircle at *u* and *v*.

On end view B mark off the points *w y* and *w x* equal to *r v* on side view A; from the points *y* and *x* draw the horizontal parallel lines to side view A, and where the vertical lines *o p* and *q r* cut the horizontal lines from *y* and *x* at *z*, will give four more points through which to draw the ellipse than could be given in the small scale of the first diagram. The dotted lines *c a'* and *c b'* in view A indicate the centre line of the object viewed obliquely, and are found by drawing the horizontal lines from *m* and *w* respectively; no such lines, however, should appear in a finished drawing, the apex only being indicated by a point at *c*.* In each rivet the same process is applied. What has been already

* The natural form of such objects in a similar position is best shown by shading, in a shaded drawing. The same remark applies to the front view of the lower part of the stuffing-box of a cylinder cover, &c., lying obliquely.

explained in regard to the top of the rivet is equally
applicable to the head, as shown at o, the dotted lines being
presumed a sufficient guide, and the whole process being
somewhat similar to that described at Fig. 188.

In the view B the lines *d e*, &c., are assumed for such
short length of curve having a large radius to be straight
lines, and which for all practical purposes would be sufficient; but in a *quick* curve, as in diagram D, Fig. 191, the
following rule is observed:—

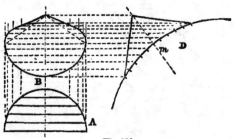

Fig. 191.

Divide the half diameter A by any number of horizontal
divisions (equal being convenient), and with the same distance in the compasses from the centre line *m*, and on each
side of it, on the curve, set off an equal number of divisions,
proceed as shown in diagram, Fig. 188. The curve line B
passing through the intersectional points will be the view
required.

NOTE.—The curve is simply that of a circle bent round a
cylinder; were it the curve produced
by a regular cone (which that described is not), intersected by a cylinder at right angles to axis of cone,
the process would be as follows:—

Through any point, *x* or *y*, Fig. 192,
draw a straight line at right angles to
centre line of cone *m*, intersecting the
sides of cone at *a b*. At any con-
venient distance on centre line *m* draw a circle of corre-

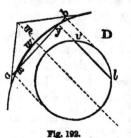

Fig. 192.

sponding diameter to $a\,b$ in section of cone; from the point y draw a straight line $y\,l$, parallel to centre line m, intersecting the circle at $u\,l$; $u\,l$ will be the distance horizontally between two points of the curve relatively, as z in view A, Fig. 190.

To find the horizontal diameter at w.—Through the point w draw a line parallel to $a\,b$; the diameter will be the distance between the points of its intersection with the sides of the cone.*

In making a drawing of a six-sided nut, the half of diameter a, Fig. 193, is taken as a radius from the scale with the

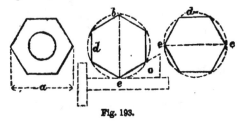

Fig. 193.

pencil-bows, and a circle drawn of the proper diameter. A vertical line $b\,e$, or horizontal line $e\,c$, is next drawn through the centre of the circle and depending on the position the angles of the nut are required to be shown; then, with half the diameter in the compasses, the circumference of circle is divided from b, c, or e into six equal parts, and between the points, the straight lines, as at d, &c., are drawn, completing the hexagon; or the T-square and angle of 80° may be employed (as indicated in the diagram at o), without dividing the circumference by the compasses.

The side view of the nut is completed as in subjoined diagram, Fig. 194, the dotted lines sufficiently explaining the different radii for the curves.

In drawing a side view of any object where a front view

* For a similar object on a larger scale more intersectional points than those given, as at z and y, would be necessary to insure correctness, and may be chosen anywhere in the curve.

is also given, as, for example, in Fig. 195, *a* is the proper position for the side of the nut, of which *b* is the front view. In the diagram adjacent to it the side view *c*, should never be drawn as shown, with its back turned on its front view *d*.

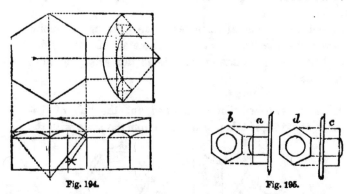

Fig. 194.   Fig. 195.

This principle holds good in all larger objects of the same kind, especially in finished drawings, and referred to previously in this chapter in regard to end views with elevations.

NOTE.—If a temporary plan, &c., is necessary simply for finding points in an intersection or other view, it is quite immaterial where it is placed, if it is in a position suitable for the required purpose.

INTERSECTIONS.—In the details of machinery there are numerous instances where one part appears to be fitted or mitred upon another, and sometimes one portion seems to be penetrated, or completely passed through by another. All such appearances of the interruption or penetration of parts by one another may be called the penetration of solids, and the lines of intersection where these solids meet and run into one another are the intersection of solids.

In a side view of such a common object in engineering as a round pipe joined at right angles, or square to another round pipe of the same diameter, the formation of the joining is an operation simple enough to perform, as it will be a straight-line joint, as at *a* and *b* in each of the sub-joined examples shown in Fig. 196, and of which *d e f* are the respective plans. The diameters being alike, the points *c* terminate vertically and horizontally in the centre. But,

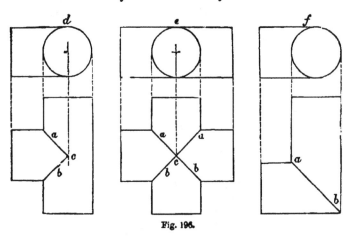

Fig. 196.

when a smaller cylindrical object is joined at right angles to a greater, as in Fig. 197, the operation is not performed with so much facility, as the joining in the side view is a curved line.

To find the intersectional curve of two cylinders of unequal diameters joined together at right angles.

Let A and B, Fig. 197, be the side elevation of the objects on which the curve is required to be drawn, and of which *c d* and *e f* are their respective centre lines. Draw a half-plan G, of the objects. On centre line *e f*, with radius equal to the half diameter of smaller cylinder B, and at any convenient distance from it, describe the semicircle H.

Divide the half diameters *e p* and *n m* into the same number of corresponding divisions as at 1, 2, 3, 4 and *l, k, i, g*. From the points *g, i, k, l*, draw horizontal lines to the circumference *z* of larger cylinder; from the points in the semicircle H, where the vertical lines 1, 2, 3, 4, intersect it, draw

the horizontal lines as at *w*; from the points where the
horizontal lines from *g, i, k, l* intersect the circumference *z* of
larger cylinder, draw vertical lines *x* intersecting the horizontal lines *w* at 5, 6, 7, &c., through which points draw the
curve line *y*, which will be the intersectional curve required.

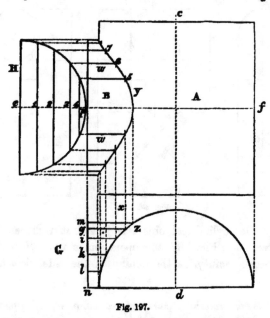

Fig. 197.

*To find the intersection of a rectangular object with a cone,
central and at right angles to the axis of cone.*

1. Draw a vertical centre line, Fig. 198, on which set off
the height of the object A; draw the horizontal lines for the
ends of object, and on these lines set off the half of each
diameter for each end from the centre line, as at *a b* and *c d*
(as described in Chapter XII.), and join *a c* and *b d*. Draw
in its position, the depth of the rectangular part of the object
e f g h.

2. At any convenient distance draw a horizontal line
v w, as a centre line for the plan B of the object, and on
which the halves of whole diameters or breadths are to be

laid off on either side of it. (An inverted plan will be more convenient for the required purpose.)

3. At the central point *z*, and with a radius equal to half of *a b*, draw the circle *n*, and with radius equal to half of *c d*, draw from the same centre the circle *o*—corresponding severally to greatest and least diameter of conical object.

4. From *z* as a centre, draw the dotted circles *q* and *r* of diameters corresponding to *l m* and *i k* of side view.

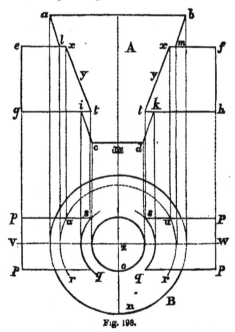

Fig. 198.

5. On plan B draw the breadth, or plan, of passages *p p*, and where the lines *p p* at inner ends cut the lesser circle *q* at *s*, it will give the point *t* on line *g h* on side view; and where the lines *p p* cut the greater dotted circle *r* at *u*, it will give the points *x* on line *e f* on side view.

6. Join *x t* by the lines *y*, which will be the termination or intersection of the inner ends of rectangular passages v

conical object, as required.* These points can be measured
from their respective centre lines on either view, applying
such measurement to the other ; or by squaring them up or
down with the T-square.

In engineering objects of a similar description to the foregoing, the object intersecting the cone is more frequently
cylindrical than rectangular, and joined to the cone as in the

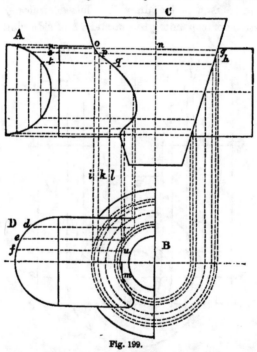

Fig. 199.

former case at right angles to its axis. The cone in accompanying diagram, Fig. 199, is enlarged, to render the process
of finding the intersection, which is a curve, more distinct.

To find the curve.

1. Let o be the side view on which the curve is to be

* On a small scale the lines *x t*, for all practical purposes, may be
drawn straight, the curve (which is hyperbolic) is so slight. See
Chapter XI., Fig. 133.

drawn. Draw a half of front view A, of cylinder, also a half-plan B, of conical object inverted (the half of each of these being sufficient for the purpose).

2. Proceed exactly in the same way as in the case of the two cylinders (described at Fig. 197), but extend the horizontal parallel lines r, s, t, &c., from the points where the vertical lines intersect the circumference of front view of cylinder A, right across the diameter of cone to g h, &c.*

3. With the half n g, &c., of each of these diameters as a radius, draw the dotted circles in plan B.

4. For convenience, transfer front view of A to D.

5. Produce the parallel lines d, e, f in view D to the plan B, and from the points where they intersect their respective circles draw the vertical lines i, k, l, &c., cutting the corresponding lines of the diameters g and h, &c., at o p q, &c.; and having similarly found all the points on the respective diameters of the cone from the plan B, a curve drawn through them will be the required line of intersection.

In inverted plan B, a curved line m

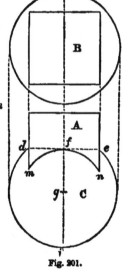

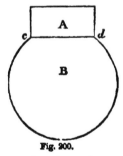

Fig. 200.   Fig. 201.

passing through corresponding points as those already found

* Or the lines in cylinder A may be drawn horizontally across, in which case, when transferred to position D, they would be vertical, or the reverse to that shown, the intersections producing similar results to that described.

on opposite side of centre line at *u*, &c., will be the inverted
plan of intersectional curve.

In Fig. 200, the side view of a cylindrical object A joined
vertically to a sphere B, the intersection is represented by a
straight line *c d*.

In Fig. 201, the side view of a rectangular object A (and
of which B is a plan) joined vertically to a sphere C, the
intersection is represented by a part of a circle. To find
which—

1. Draw in a centre line *h i*, and from the points *d* and *e*,

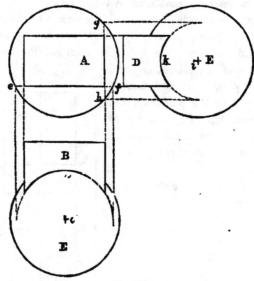

Fig. 202.

where the sides of rectangular object cut the circumference
of the sphere, draw a horizontal line *d e*, cutting the centre
line at *f*.

2. From *g*, the centre of sphere, and with the radius *g f*,
describe the required circle *m f n*.

In Fig. 202, the side and end views of a rectangular object,
of which A is a plan, B a side view, and D an end view,

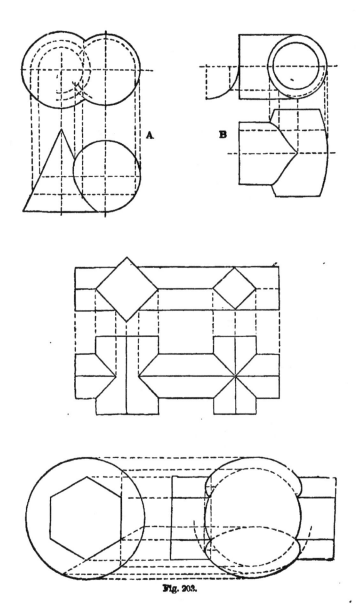

Fig. 203.

G

joined to a sphere E, and central on its axis, the intersection at such side and end view will each be part of a circle.

In side view B, the diameter of the circle required, of which *e m* is the radius, is equal to the diameter *e f*; and in the end view D, the diameter of the circle required, of which *i k* is the radius, is equal to the diameter *g h*, each described from the respective centres *c* and *i* of spheres E.

From what has already been described in the foregoing diagrams, it is presumed that in those which follow, in Fig. 203, the dotted lines will explain sufficiently. In the first diagram A (which is a cone intersected by a sphere), and in the second diagram B, additional sectional lines to those shown may be made, to render the curves of the intersections more accurate.

HELIX (OR SCREW).—*To find the points for drawing in the curve of a common square-threaded screw.*

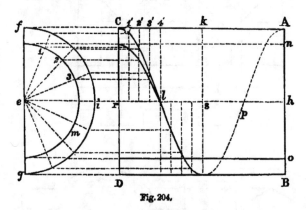

Fig. 204.

Let A B, Fig. 204, be the diameter outside the thread, and *n o* the inner diameter, O A the pitch (or the distance passed through by one revolution of screw, which for distinctness is here shown to be greater than it would be for an ordinary screw). Draw a vertical line *f g*, equal to diameter of screw, opposite its side view O D, the centre line *e h* being common to both. On *e* as a centre, with the radius *e f*, or *e g*, describe the semicircle *g i f*, which will represent the outer circumference of thread, and on *e* as a centre, and with radius *h o* or *h n* describe the semicircle *m*, which will represent the inner circumference of thread; bisect the pitch *c A* in *k*, which will be the distance of half a revolution of screw—one half being sufficient for the purpose—and the part really visible to the eye of the observer, the other half being represented by the dotted line P; divide the quadrants *g i* and *f i* into any number of equal parts represented by the radial lines 1, 2, 8, &c. Bisect *r s* in *l*, and divide *r l* and *l s* into equal divisions as at 1', 2', 8', &c., corresponding to the number of the radial lines with similar figures in semicircle (and which semicircle corresponds to the half revolution *c k*). Draw vertical lines through these divisions, and from the point where the radial 1 intersects the larger semicircle draw a line parallel to *e h*, cutting the vertical line 1' of its corresponding division; this will be one of the points for the curve.

From the points in the larger semicircle intersected by the radials 1, 2, 8, &c., draw lines parallel to *e h*, cutting their respective vertical lines 1', 2', 8', &c., and a curve passing through these points will give one quarter of the curve. The points in the lower part, completing the half revolution, are found exactly in a similar way from the lower half *i g* of semicircle or quadrant. Having found one half thus, for practical purposes, when the remaining half is required to be drawn, it is easy to trace it, turn over the tracing, and prick it through, or rub the back of tracing, leaving the pencil mark, which will complete the curve for a whole revolution.

The curve of the inner part of the thread is constructed precisely in the same manner. From the points intersected by the radials 1, 2, 8, &c., in the inner semicircle *m*, lines drawn parallel to the others for the outer part of thread, and cutting the same verticals 1', 2', 8', &c., as in the other, will give the required curve, as shown in diagram. It may be mentioned that the same semicircle with its divisions is the same for any pitch, the diameter being the same. For triangular-threaded and internal screws, as in sections of nuts, the process is exactly similar.

In a series of threads, as in Fig. 205, for the outer part, the

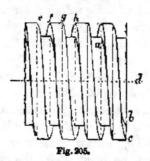

Fig. 205.

outlines of each side of each thread are exactly alike, and the curves of the inner part *a b* on each side are also alike. In making a drawing of a screw such as that represented in accompanying diagram, the simplest way is, after having found (by the process described at Fig. 204) the part of the curve from *c* to *d*, to trace this half diameter and prick through the traced line to a piece of cardboard or thin wood, and having cut the curve out as a mould, by reversing it and turning it upside down, it will be suitable for drawing in both sides, and both edges of every thread, the centres of each thread and space being drawn in previously as represented by the vertical lines *e, f, g, h*. It will be found the easiest way to pursue the same method for the curves *a* and *b*. In drawings to a small scale, the front view of the threads is generally drawn straight and at an angle.

NOTE.—For drawing in the proper number of threads to the inch to a given diameter of screw the following table will be found useful for the two kinds of threads in common use :—

V-THREADS.				SQUARE THREADS.	
Diameter in Inches.	Threads per Inch.	Diameter in Inches.	Threads per Inch.	Diameter in Inches.	Threads per Inch.
$\frac{1}{8}$	20	$1\frac{7}{8}$	$4\frac{1}{4}$	$\frac{5}{16}$	9
$\frac{3}{16}$	18	2	$4\frac{1}{2}$	$\frac{3}{8}$	9
$\frac{1}{4}$	16	$2\frac{1}{4}$	4	$\frac{7}{16}$	8
$\frac{5}{16}$	14	$2\frac{3}{8}$	4	$\frac{1}{2}$	7
$\frac{3}{8}$	12	$2\frac{3}{4}$	$3\frac{1}{2}$	$\frac{9}{16}$	7
$\frac{7}{16}$	11	3	$3\frac{3}{4}$	$\frac{5}{8}$	7
$\frac{1}{2}$	11	$3\frac{1}{4}$	$3\frac{1}{2}$	$\frac{11}{16}$	7
$\frac{9}{16}$	10	$3\frac{1}{2}$	$3\frac{1}{4}$	$\frac{3}{4}$	6
$\frac{5}{8}$	10	$3\frac{3}{4}$	3	$\frac{13}{16}$	6
$\frac{11}{16}$	9	4	3	$\frac{7}{8}$	6
$\frac{7}{8}$	9	$4\frac{1}{4}$	$2\frac{7}{8}$	$\frac{15}{16}$	6
$\frac{15}{16}$	8	$4\frac{1}{2}$	$2\frac{3}{4}$	1	5
1	8	$4\frac{3}{4}$	$2\frac{1}{2}$	$1\frac{1}{8}$	4
$1\frac{1}{8}$	7	5	$2\frac{1}{2}$	$1\frac{1}{4}$	4
$1\frac{1}{4}$	7	$5\frac{1}{4}$	$2\frac{5}{8}$	$1\frac{3}{8}$	3
$1\frac{3}{8}$	6	$5\frac{1}{2}$	$2\frac{5}{8}$	$1\frac{1}{2}$	3
$1\frac{1}{2}$	6	$5\frac{3}{4}$	$2\frac{1}{2}$	$1\frac{5}{8}$	$2\frac{1}{4}$
$1\frac{5}{8}$	5	6	$2\frac{1}{2}$	$1\frac{3}{4}$	$2\frac{1}{2}$
$1\frac{3}{4}$	5				

The angle of the V-thread is generally 55°, and the depth of the nut equal to the diameter of the bolt.

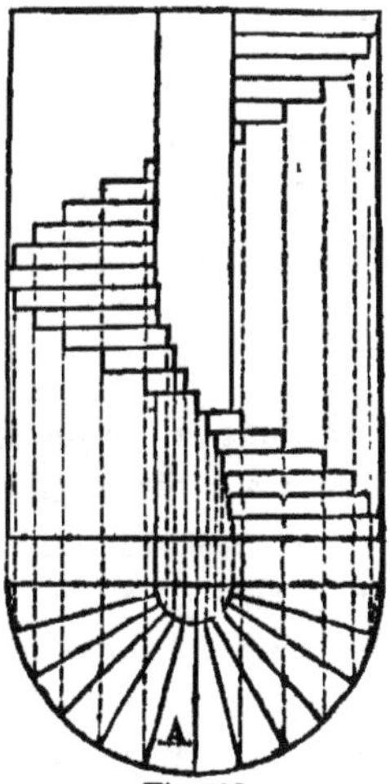

In drawing the elevation of a circular staircase turning either to the right or left, of which Fig. 206 is a view of the latter, A being a half-plan, the same process is applied as in drawing the thread of a screw, Fig. 204, and will be understood by the dotted lines.

To draw a front view or plan of a worm, or screw wheel.

The first part of the process consists in simply drawing a portion of the thread of a screw, its full diameter

Fig. 206.

being cut off at each side, at *a* and *b*, Fig. 207, by the breadth of wheel *c d*—*c d* being less than the diameter *e f* of screw.

Let g *oh* d be the profile of worm wheel, and I the end
view of screw, or *worm*, draw a half-face view K of the
wheel, having the same centre line common to both views;
draw the centre line lm through the side view of wheel and
screw, and when required to be very accurate for the process
on a larger scale then mc and md may be bisected, and
lines drawn through the bisection parallel to lm, making
semicircles in half-plan K to correspond; one line lm is

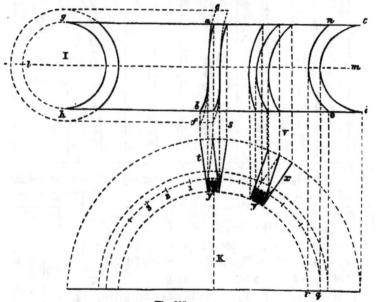

Fig. 207.

sufficient in the present instance to show the process. The
line no is the bottom line of tooth, the dotted semicircles
rq representing the same in face K. Complete one tooth
in centre of wheel as at ef, in the same manner as in
drawing the threads of a screw from an end view I, and as
described at Fig. 204; from the points where the curve
cuts the centre line lm and side lines gc and hd, draw
down vertical lines s to face view K. The position of
middle part of tooth requires to be shown distinctly (for

the process only) as in sectional lines in к at *y*. This process will give all the points for the end view of the curved tooth as shown at *t*. Having previously divided or pitched off the centres of the teeth as shown at 1, 2, 3, &c., transfer the identical form of the tooth at *t*, to each division at 1, 2, 3, &c.; from the corresponding points in each tooth, as at *t*, draw vertical lines up to profile view, which will give points for the proper form of each tooth, as it recedes to the right or left of centre of wheel, and as shown by the dotted lines v, drawn from a tooth *x* placed in its position at one of the divisions. Of course, no two curves of the teeth on profile are alike. These varying forms are drawn in with the moulds referred to in Chapter IV., and when thus completed such representative lines as the dotted ones *n o*, being only pencil lines for finding diameters in the face к, are not retained. Fig. 208 is a finished view of a worm wheel made according to the process just described.

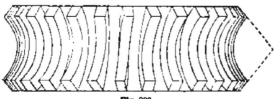

Fig. 208.

The delineation of screw threads, &c., just described naturally leads to the subject of screw-propellers, which is simply the common screw with a flat thread, the body or inner diameter of which is necessarily small in proportion to those in the examples already described.

If it is required to find the sections at two or three places in the length of arm or blade of a screw-propeller, and to show the same in plan, proceed as before by drawing a half end view, as at A E B, Fig. 209, and make C D half the length of pitch, having the same number of divisions, 1, 2, 3, &c.,

as in the semi-circumference A E B.   From the points H and I
draw the horizontal lines F H and G I, intersecting the semicircle at F and G, which will be the end view breadth of
blade of screw.   Complete the sides of blade to inner
diameter M and N, to which also the points K and L correspond.   If the section is in the position O P or Q R produce
the horizontal lines as shown from the points O Q and P R

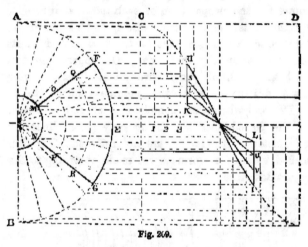

Fig. 209.

to s t, u v, in the sides of blade H K and L I in plan, and complete the curves between s v and t u, which will give the
section at the parts required.   These sections are found as
before, from the points where the radial lines in end view
cut the sectional arcs O P and Q R, by producing horizontal
lines from such points, cutting the corresponding vertical
lines 1, 2, 3, &c., in plan, which are common also to any
diameter of thread less than A B, having the same pitch.

In the subjoined diagrams, Figs. 210, 211, 212, are represented front and side views of screw-propellers having two,
three, and four blades respectively.   The dotted lines from
the front views showing the corresponding points in the side
views of each.

In any long objects, such as shafting, when too long to

admit of full length to the scale on which the drawing is
being made, the ordinary way is to show it as if broken

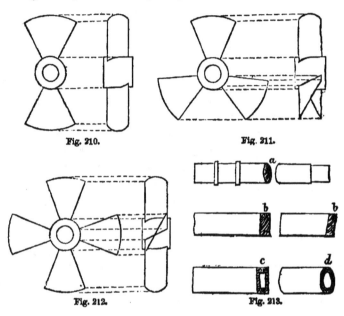

Fig. 210.   Fig. 211.

Fig. 212.   Fig. 213.

through. For iron work, it should never appear too ragged
at the break. The break is made in the middle of the length
shown, as at *a* in diagram, Fig. 213, or at any other convenient place, depending on its surroundings. If it is a
round shaft, it is better to show the section as in adjoining
diagram—of an elliptical form, and more especially so if the
drawing is only to be an outline—the extreme ends being
finished similar to the object represented. If it is a square
shaft, or any other square object,—as at section represented at *b b*; if a hollow beam, or square pipe,—as at *c*;
or a round pipe, or cylindrical object,—as at *d*; greater
thickness of material should be shown at the top and
bottom than at the sides, in the two latter instances, thus
showing a little perspective. Breaks in wood, and graining
to represent oak, as in subjoined diagram, Fig. 214, a-

executed by the drawing pen ; and in doing more than one
plank, as shown in diagram, Fig. 215, at *a b c*, where they are

Fig. 214.

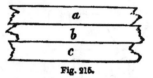

Fig. 215.

joined at the sides, the break at the ends should be such as
to show each distinct from the one adjoining it ; and in

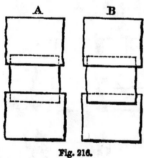

A   B

showing a portion of iron plates,
where two or three are joined
together, the distinction of each
plate at the ends should be clear,
as in diagrams A and B, Fig.
216.

In any object where the full
length is not to be shown, it is
better to represent it broken off
than squared off, as the latter

Fig. 216.

course would indicate the termination of its length.

CHAPTER XIV.

INKING-IN A DRAWING.

As a drawing is a series of boundary lines, the lines should
be as fine as possible, especially for a drawing which is to
undergo the process of shading. The ink should not be so
black for the latter purpose as for a drawing that is to be
only an outline, so that the light lines may blend into the
colouring. Lines for such drawings should be as nearly as
possible "length without breadth." * Summer is the best

* Lines should never be drawn of such a thickness all over as to
suggest the question, Whether the right size is to be obtained from
the outer or inner side of line ?

for outlines ; for the paper being more dry, a clearer line can be drawn. In winter the paper will get damp under the best circumstances. A clean sponge, a tumbler of clean water, and a sheet of clean white blotting-paper, should always be within reach, in case of any accident happening to the drawing.*

Before rubbing down the Indian ink, it is necessary to have the palette quite clean and free from dust.†

In not inking-in a drawing of an intricate kind until all pencilled in, the first pencil lines are apt to get obscure and cause confusion, to obviate which it is better to ink-in such a drawing as the pencilling proceeds, taking care always to put in the parts of the object supposed to be nearest you first. This method is especially advisable when the drawing has to be in hand for a lengthened period

The ink should be at least a quarter of an inch up the pen or compass ink-foot. If a little brush is used, with which to supply the pen, it is better to keep it exclusively for such purpose, as it will be almost useless for any other after. A little slip of paper may be used, but the common plan (*not the most cleanly*) is to moisten the ink-foot in the mouth, so that capillary attraction will cause the ink to ascend. The mouth should be well washed out with water after meals, as, if the pen is the least greasy, the ink will not flow freely. The superfluous ink should be wiped clean off from each side of the pen, or it will probably blot the drawing. It is

---

* Should a drawing get an ink blot, the blotting-paper should be applied first, and if clear of any lines on the drawing the place sponged immediately after, and if among lines, the part should be washed with a small hard brush instead of using the sponge, and the line renewed with very thin Indian ink, or with a hard fine-pointed pencil, or it will never be one with the other lines owing to the roughness of the part after the process named.

† A common card, bent up half an inch at one end, will be found useful upon which to place the Indian ink cake immediately after using, otherwise it is likely to soil everything with which it comes into contact.

Note.—A little ox-gall mixed up with the ink assists it to flow more freely from the pen. It is sold in little pots at 8*d*. each.

better always to try the pen or ink-bows on the margin of
the paper, taking care not to come within the cutting-off line
of paper referred to in Chapter XII., before drawing the
required lines or circles, so as to regulate the pen to the
proper fineness. All ink circles or curves should be put in
before any lines,* and any parts of circles inconveniently
small for ink-bows should be put in with a fine-pointed
metallic *crow-quill.*

In using the ink compasses, the lower part of the legs
should be as nearly vertical as possible. If it is attempted
to draw too large a circle, the legs being at a great angle, a
large hole will be made in the paper at the centre of the
circle; in a proper drawing the compass centre marks should
hardly be seen. The ink leg, especially for small circles,
should be shorter than the other. In drawing a circle the
compasses should be held by the top, by the right hand
(without holding the centre leg during the process in its
position by the left hand); and in inking, the ink leg should
be made to bear as lightly on the paper as is necessary to
produce the circle. It is always necessary to see that the
radius of ink compasses fits the pencil circle all round before
touching the paper with the ink point. The reason for
drawing in the circles before the lines is, it is easier to
join the lines to circles the least thing " *out* " than to join
circles to lines a little out of the right place.

In drawing a series of concentric circles, when not of
large diameters, it is better to make the smallest first;
for if the compass leg enlarges the hole in the centre,
which it is likely to do after describing many of them,
it would be more difficult to draw in the lesser circles
correctly.

---

* If a larger circle has to be made than the ordinary lengthening
bar will admit of, and to save the expense of beam compasses already
referred to in Chapter IV., a piece of flat wood tied securely to the
compasses, and having the ordinary ink-foot tied at the other end at
the proper distance for the required radius, will be found to answer
the purpose.

The drawing-pen should be held as nearly vertical as possible; but to get the point close to the lower part of the edge of the square—the top of the pen should be held with the least inclination outwards. The pencil line should just be visible; the square should be held firm in position to the board by the left hand, as in pencilling; and in drawing the line, if the points of the drawing-pen are not held in the direction to be drawn, it will leave the edge of the square (supposing the forward edge of points are inclined *outwards*). As a safeguard against such mistakes, some pens have the holder made with a part of it square. The pen should not be pressed unduly on the paper, or it will make a rough line. The line should be drawn always from left to right, and never in the opposite direction. After having got in all the circles, it will be found convenient while the square is on the board in one direction to draw all the horizontal lines first, beginning at the top, until the lowest is reached; and then, with the T-square shifted to the bottom edge of the board, beginning at the extreme left, draw in all the vertical lines.

A wrong line should never be scraped out with a knife, neither should an ink eraser be applied, especially in a drawing to be coloured. It is best to wash out a wrong line with a small hard brush, and slightly sponge over the place, through a hole of the requisite size cut in a scrap of drawing-paper to save the other parts of the drawing. A needle point will take out a short line in a way which leaves little trace of the error. If a line has to be drawn after washing out, it should be with thin Indian ink, or a hard fine-pointed pencil, as before stated.

In sections of boilers, &c., where the thickness of iron plate is shown in section to any scale under three-eighths of an inch, it is better to make it a thick black line, a little thicker than any shade line, if any, in the drawing. Sections of the same material, when the scale is above three-eighths of an inch to a foot, should have a double line.

In office outline drawings for reference, it is frequently
the custom to outline the cast iron in Indian ink, the
malleable iron in blue, the brass in yellow, and the copper
in red.

A drawing to be coloured should never have any dotted
lines indicating parts of the machine not visible to the eye,
as those parts are made visible by the lines. A highly-
finished coloured drawing may not be a perspective view,
but still it is intended to be a picture. Dotted lines, therefore, should only appear in common or working drawings
intended for reference, where they are very useful.

Sections of end wood should be circular, especially if the
drawing is only to be outline, to distinguish it from iron or
other section, which should be straight and at the angle of
45°. The wood can be done with the ink compasses and
Indian ink if for outline drawing only, and with wood colour
if a coloured drawing. In drawings to about one inch to a
foot, if the grain circles are to be equidistant, spring bows
are the best for the purpose, as one whole turn of the nut
will open the ink foot to the required distance after drawing
each circle. If more than one beam end is shown, the
centre of the grain circles should be in a different position in
each section; and there is more need for this variety when
the ends are joined close together, as at *a*, *b*, *c*, Fig. 217.

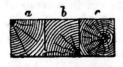 Sometimes wood sec-
tions are shown by alter-
nate thick and thin straight
diagonal lines, as at *d*,
either in Indian ink or

Fig. 217.

wood colour. These can be made with either parallel rulers,
or with a little wooden angle of 45° moved along the edge
of T-square, kept firm on the board by a weight on each
end, and which is more to be depended on than the former,
or with T-square set at the proper angle by shifting the
stock, drawing all the lines fine in first process, and making
each intermediate line thicker after. It frequently happens

that beginners cannot do these lines very equally apart, and when two lines are much wider than they should be they fall into the second error of bringing the next line closer than all the rest to make up for the wide space, instead of gradually coming to the proper width again. When two sections or more of end material come close together, it is better to reverse the angled lines of section, leaving a clear little space at top and left side (or side the light is sup-posed to come from), as shown at *a* and *b*, Fig. 218.

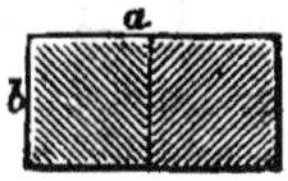

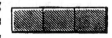

Fig. 218.

In every section of the same kind this should be observed. The light space should not be shown where they join when flush or straight across. This will be more par-ticularly referred to in Chapter XVI., on shading and colour-ing. In engraved work of machinery, &c., where there are sections across material like that already referred to, it is a common thing to have the angled lines in the same direction throughout, as shown at Fig. 219 ; and it seems to look better thus in an engraving than in a drawing owing to greater regularity. This process is called hatching. It is almost needless to remark that no such sectional lines on

Fig. 219.

transverse sections are ever pencilled in before inking in drawings under one inch to a foot, though large sections with the distance between each sectional line being ⅛th or ¼th of an inch, would, to look symmetrical, be divided by the compasses.

A drawing gone over in the manner described, with fine ink lines, may be considered for some purposes a finished drawing, without shade lines, colouring,* or printing,† the superfluous pencil lines being rubbed out previously to cutting off the sheet.‡

---

* If the drawing is to be shaded, and should the lines not be so fine as they ought to be, a slight sponging over them will take off the superfluous ink, which would be apt to *run* in shading.

† For which see Chapter XVII.

‡ For cutting off see Chapter XXIII.

*Shade lines.**—Shade lines, especially in an outline draw-ing, are considered by competent judges of such matters to be an improvement. They seem to throw out the projecting objects, as well as give effect to a recess, the line thicker than others adjoining showing apparently the side of the object very much foreshortened;† for which reason it is not correct to put a shade line on the side of anything cylindrical, though for uniformity's sake a line a little thicker than the fine lines of the drawing, but not so thick as on the objects with a square side, is necessary. If they are to be put on an outline drawing it is better to finish the drawing first by the ordinary fine lines than altering the pen for thick and thin lines every minute. Shade lines are frequently objected to in either outline-finished, or coloured drawings; they are a matter of taste. When coloured drawings are to have such dark lines they should never be put on till after colouring, otherwise the brush in coming over them would cause them to *run* and blot. The ink for such purposes should be as thick as it will flow from the pen. A single shade line put on the wrong side of any part of a drawing by mistake would

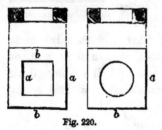

Fig. 220.

destroy the effect of the whole, whether for an outline only or a coloured drawing.

In engineers' drawings the shade lines are generally put on the right and bottom sides of projections, as shown at *a* and *b*, Fig. 220 (the same as the sha-dows in their shaded drawings), the tops and left sides being opposite the light.

In drawing a shade line on a circular projection, as at *c*,

---

* If a drawing is to be varnished, the shade lines should not be put on until after the sizing; and in all shade-line work indigo should never be used instead of Indian ink.

† Shade lines are therefore not suitable for isometrical or perspec-tive drawings, the sides, &c., of the objects in such drawings being fairly represented. Drawings for working to should never have them.

Fig. 221, or on a circular recess, as at *d*, the thick lines should gradually terminate at a line drawn through the centre of the

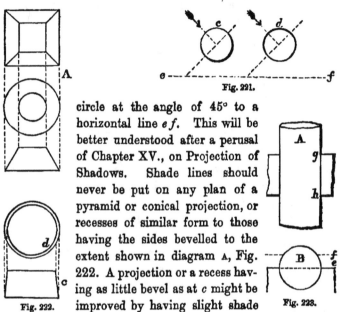

Fig. 221.

circle at the angle of 45° to a horizontal line *e f*. This will be better understood after a perusal of Chapter XV., on Projection of Shadows. Shade lines should never be put on any plan of a pyramid or conical projection, or recesses of similar form to those having the sides bevelled to the extent shown in diagram A, Fig. 222. A projection or a recess having as little bevel as at *c* might be improved by having slight shade

Fig. 222.

Fig. 223.

lines. In drawing the shade line on a circle a fine line should be made first, the ink points should then be opened a little after each time, and coming two or three times over where the line is to be thickest. The thickness ought to lessen gradually to the points already described, and should never exceed the half circle.

In shade lining a cylindrical object, as A, Fig. 223 (of which B is an end view), if the plane *e* was in a line with the centre, as shown in view B, or above it, as at *f*, there should be no shade line from *g* to *h*, where the plane intersects; but if the plane was below the centre of cylindrical object the shade line should be continuous on it.

In a figure such as a hexagon or six-sided nut there would be three different thicknesses of shade lines, that at *a*, Fig. 224, furthest from the light, being the thickest; the line *b*, ·

approaching nearer to the light, being finer, *c* finer than *b*, and *e, e, e,* more or less nearly opposite the light than the others, being ordinary fine lines. Each individual straight shade line should be of uniform thickness. Every shade line

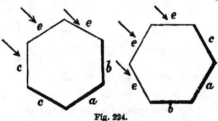

Fig. 224.

should be of a thickness regulated by its being more or less from the light side, as shown in the last and adjoining diagrams, Fig. 225.

In making a shade line on a short length of a segment of a circle, of large radius, a mould will be found more convenient than any compasses.

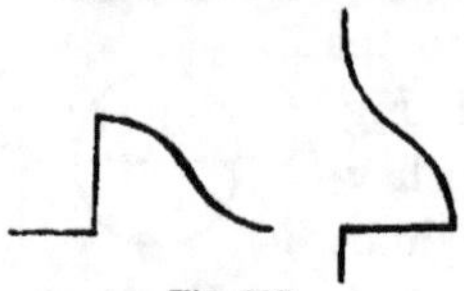

Fig. 225.

The shade lines on *breaks* of wood or iron should have as much care as the shade lines on any piece of machinery adjoining. It is by attention to the details of apparently little things as well as of the apparently greater, that makes an effective whole. There should never be a shade line as a base line for any elevation supposed to be standing on any thing.*

CHAPTER XV.

PROJECTION OF SHADOWS.

THE rays of an artificial light placed near to any object at right angles to a plane and of itself parallel, project a radiated

* Before laying aside the pallette it should be washed clean, as old dried ink when moistened again is apt to *run* in the colouring, and for an outline only it will not flow from the pen so freely.

shadow, as shown in diagram, Fig. 226, *a* being the position of the light, *b* the object, and *c* the shadow of the object

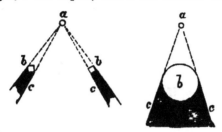

Fig. 226.

projected by the light, the sides of the shadow being in a direct line with the light.

In projecting shadows in mechanical drawings the light is supposed to be at such a distance as to come in apparently parallel rays; and assuming for our purpose that they are so, it is obvious that the projection of the shadow will be in parallels, as at *e f*, Fig. 227; or let *e*, Fig. 228, be a cylindrical object, and *a b* a plane placed at right angles to the rays of light *d h* or *c i*, the exact diameter of the object *e* will be projected on such plane at *l m*, and the sides of the

Fig. 227.

shadow will be parallel to each other whether the plane is or is not parallel to the cylinder. If the plane be oblique to the rays of light as shown at *f g* the shadow is increased on the plane to the breadth *h i*, the shadow having its sides parallel whether the plane *f g* is or is not parallel to the cylinder.

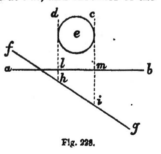

Fig. 228.

In engineering drawings the shadows are generally understood to be projected at the angle of 45°, and inclined also at that angle from a projecting object towards the right hand.

The angle of inclination at 45° is projected with facility

by setting off equal distances on the base and vertical lines of any rectangular part in a drawing. The length of the shadow is measured from the object on the diagonal (or angle of inclination), and is equal to the projection of the object from the plane.*

It is impossible to project the shadows of any object correctly on any drawing of which there is only one view, and which is to be shaded, if the several projections on such view are not exactly known. In such instances the only alternative is to make undefined shadows as to their length or breadth at the ordinary angle from any of the parts obviously known to project, and to soften them off with the water brush. In intricate drawings of machinery, even where all the projections are known, if every shadow were projected and put in distinctly with a hard edge of the proper outline (as would be done in a plain drawing having few parts and details), it would have much the same effect, when shaded, as a well-used sheet of blotting-paper; in such cases it is better to soften off most of the shadows.

PROJECTION OF SHADOWS.—FIRST SERIES.—The plans and elevations being given, in all cases the plans are invariably understood to be directly opposite their elevations, and their side views opposite their front views. In projecting the following shadows the angle of 45° is that in which the parallel rays of light are supposed to come.

In the following examples the plane on which the shadow is projected may be considered either horizontal or vertical, the shadows (according to the ordinary system) being identical.† In drawing the angular lines the T-square and little wooden set square, having an angle of 45° bearing on it, as

---

* Frequently in architectural and other drawings the shadow, measured from the object on the angle of inclination, is of greater length than the projection of the object from the plane; neither is the angle of inclination in such drawings always 45°. See also note, Fig. 260.

† The process in the Second Series of the Projection of Shadows is also applicable to the examples given in this First Series; but the shadow being projected on a horizontal or vertical plane, renders such ation less necessary.

indicated in position in the following diagram at *e*, Fig. 229, should be used throughout as being best calculated to facilitate the operation.

To project the shadow of a square column, having its opposite sides parallel, on a plane at right angles to it.

Let A, Fig. 229, be the plan, and B the elevation of column. From the points *h, m, k,* draw the lines *h i, m n,* and *k l* at the aforesaid angle ; on the line *h i* from the point *h,* set off the height of column *c d* at *o* ; repeat the same from *m* at the point *p,* and from *k* at the point *r* ; join *o p* and *p r* ; *h o p r k* will be the projection of shadow required. It will be obvious that the termination of the shadow is a fac-simile or counterpart of the plan of column.

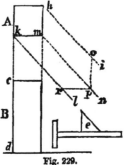

Fig. 229.

The process described is given as being more explanatory, but in the examples which follow it will be quite unnecessary to repeat it. In actual practice, having first found the length *h o,* equal to the length of column *d c,* the point *o* would be quite sufficient for finding the other points at *p* and *r,* for *o p* being parallel to the sides of column *m h,* the right-angle side of set square bearing on the T-square and placed at the point *o,* would, by drawing the line *o p,* find the point *p,* and since *p r* is also parallel to the side of column *m k,* the T-square placed at the point *p* already found would draw the horizontal line *p r,* thus completing the required shadow without setting off the lengths at *p* and *r,* as in the first process shown.

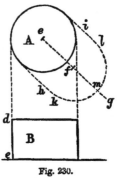

Fig. 230.

To project the shadow of a cylinder on a plane at right angles to its axis.

Let A, Fig. 230, be the plan, and B the elevation of cylin-

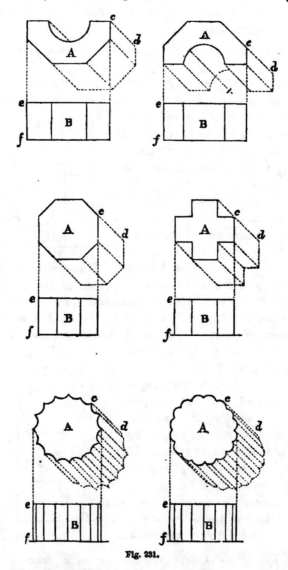

Fig. 231.

der. From the point *e*, the centre of cylinder A, draw the

diagonal *e g* ; from the point *e* set off the distance *e f* equal to the height *e d* of elevation B ; from the point *f*, with a radius equal to half the diameter of cylinder, describe the semi-circle *k l m* ; from the points *k* and *l* draw the lines *i* and *h* parallel to *e g*, which will be the projection of shadow required.

In the preceding examples, Fig. 231, the projections of their shadows are found in a manner similar to those already described, and will be understood by the dotted lines. A are the plans, and B .are the elevations of the several objects, which are at right angles to the plane on which their shadows are projected ; and in each case the length *c d* in plans A is equal to the height *f e* of elevations B.

To project the shadow of a square tapered column on a plane at right angles to it.

Let A, Fig. 232, be the plan, and B the elevation of column.

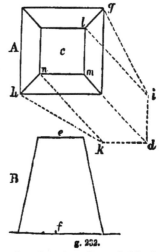

From the three points *l, m, n*, in top of column o, draw the diagonal lines—as if the column were parallel ; on these lines, from the points *l, m, n*, set off the distances *l i, m d*, and *n k*, each equal to the vertical height *e f* in elevation B. Join *g i*, *i d, d k*, and *k h*, which will be the projection of shadow required.

Fig. 232.

To project the shadow of an obelisk on a plane at right angles to it.

Let A, Fig. 233, be the plan, and B the elevation of object. As in last example, Fig. 232, set off the length of the sides at *h* and *i*, equal to the vertical height *l k* in elevation B, and from the centre *o* of plan A set off the distance *o g* on central diagonal line equal to entire height *f e* of elevation B from base line. Join *d h, h g, g i,* and *i n,* which will be the projection of shadow required. The projection of the shadow at the side of the pedestal in plan A is equal to the heights *a* &c., in elevation B set off on the diagonals *r s t* and *u v y*.

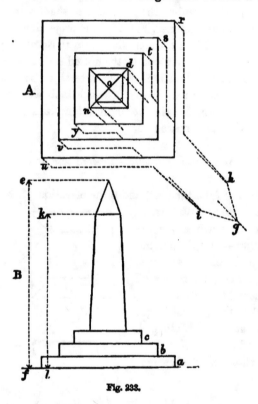

Fig. 233.

To project the shadow of the side of a cylindrical recess between two planes at right angles to it.

Let A, Fig. 234, be the plan, and B a section showing the depth of the recess. It is required to project the shadow of the upper part *f g k* on the inner plane c.

Through the centre *h* of circle, or recess, draw the diagonal; from the centre *h* set off the distance *h i* on the diagonal equal to the depth *d e* of recess in section B; from *i* as centre, and with a radius equal to half the diameter of recess, describe the circle *l m n*, which will be the projection of shadow required.

To project the shadows in a series of square recesses, the planes of each being parallel.

Let A, Fig. 235, be the plan of the object, and B a section

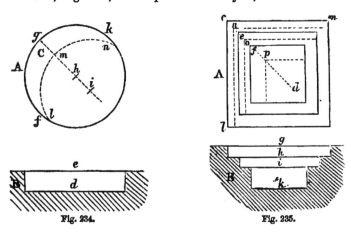

Fig. 234.   Fig. 235.

showing the several depths. Draw the diagonal *c d*; set off the distance *c n* equal to the depth *g h*, in section B, *e o* equal to the depth *h i*, and *f p* equal to the depth *i k*; from the points *n*, *o*, and *p* in plan A draw lines parallel to *c m*, and also from the same points lines parallel to *c l*, which will be the projection of shadows required.

To project the shadow of a vertical square parallel column into a parallel plane recess, and upon the plane adjacent.

Let A, Fig. 236, be the plan, and B an elevation of the object. Proceed as in Fig. 229, making the distance *c d* in plan A equal to height *e f* in elevation B; *c d g h i* will be the projection of shadow required.

H

To project the shadow of a vertical square parallel column into an adjacent parallel plane recess.

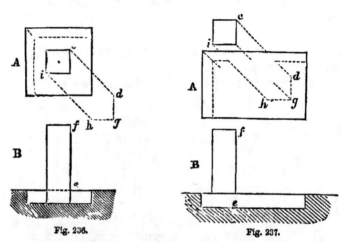

Fig. 236.   Fig. 237.

Let A, Fig. 237, be a plan, and B an elevation of the object. Proceed as in Fig. 229, making the distance *c d* in plan A equal to the height *e f* in elevation B; *c d g h i* will be the projection of shadow required.

To project the shadows of square parallel columns lying obliquely to a plane.

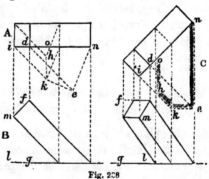

Fig. 238.

t A, Fig. 238, be the plans, and B the elevations of the

objects. From the points d and i in plans A draw the diagonals, set off the distance $d\ e$ equal to the height $g\ f$ in elevations B, and $i\ k$ equal to the height $l\ m$, and join $k\ e$, $k\ h$, also the sides $n\ e$ and $h\ o$; $n\ e\ k\ h\ o$ will be the projection of shadow required.

NOTE.—When the object is at the angle of 45° with the plane, and also inclined in the plan at that angle, as in the diagram at o, the sides of the shadow will be vertical as shown.

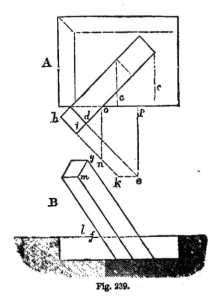

Fig. 239.

To project the shadow of a square parallel column on two parallel planes recessed, the column being oblique to the planes at an angle of 45°, and also inclined at 45° in its plan.

Let A, Fig. 239, be the plan, and B the elevation of the objects. In plan A the dotted lines $c\ c$ will represent the shadow as projected on the inner plane (as in last example, Fig. 238). For the projection of the shadow on the upper or outer plane, set off the distance $d\ e$ on the diagonal equal to the vertical height $f\ g$ in elevation B, and the distance $i\ k$

H 2

equal to the vertical height *l m*; also set off the same distance *h n* from the point *h*; from the points *e* and *n* draw the vertical lines *n o* and *e p*, which, with those at *e k n* and *c c*, will be the projection of shadow required.

To project the shadow of a square parallel column on two parallel planes recessed; horizontal in plan, and inclined between 90° and 45° in its elevation.

Let A, Fig. 240, be the plan, and B the side elevation of the objects. Set off the length *c d* on plan A equal to the vertical height *e f* on elevation B; draw *g h* in the direction *g d*, and

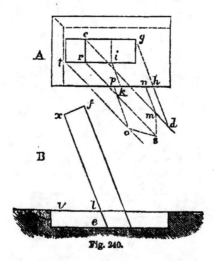

Fig. 240.

draw *i k* parallel to *g h*; *g h* and *i k* will be the projection of the shadow on inner plane. On first diagonal line *c d* set off the distance *c m* equal to the vertical height *l f* in elevation B, draw *m n* parallel to *g d*, also set off the same distance *l f* from *r* at *s*, and the distance *t o* equal to the vertical height *v x*; draw *o p* parallel to *m n*; and join *m s* and *s o*; *n m s o p* will be the projection of the shadow on the outer ~lane, which with that on the inner plane will be the shadow
   both as required.

To project the shadow of a square parallel column on a pedestal, being a plane, also on a plane adjacent and parallel to it; the objects being horizontal in plan, and the column inclined between 90° and 45° in its elevation.

Let A, Fig. 241, be a plan, and B the elevation of the objects. Draw the diagonals from *c*, &c., on which set off the distances *c d* and *c′ w*, each equal to the vertical height *e f* in elevation B, and the distance *v x* equal to the vertical height *b z*, and join *d w* and *w x*. In plan A produce the line *c l* to *k*; *k* being the point on base of column if produced to lower plane (corresponding to the point *i* in side-view B). From the point *d* in plan A draw *d n* in the direction *d k*, and from the point *x* draw *x o* parallel to

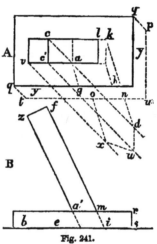

Fig. 241.

d n; this will complete the projection of shadow on lower plane, which will terminate at *n o*, being its intersection with the line of shadow of pedestal *t u*. From the point of intersection of column with upper plane at *l* (corresponding to *m* in elevation B) draw *l h* parallel to *k d*, and from the point of intersection of column with upper plane at *a* (corresponding to the point *a′* in elevation B) draw *a g* parallel to *l h*. *l h* and *a g*, on upper plane, and *n d w x o*, on lower plane, will be the projection of shadow required.

The projection of the parallel shadow of pedestal at *y y* is found by setting off the height of pedestal *s r* in elevation B, on the diagonals *q p* and *q t* in plan A.

NOTE.—The projections of the shadows of inclined objects of various cross sections are found in a similar manner to the preceding; that of an inclined cylinder is found by completing the ellipse (see Chapter XI. Fig. 180) at its intersection with the plane, and drawing lines tangentially (as at Fig. 230) for the two sides of the shadow to the projection of its upper end, which will be at 45° from the top of the object; the shadow will be broader than the diameter of the cylinder if inclined otherwise than directly from, and towards the light.

To project the shadow of a square knee—in its section square, on a plane at right angles to it.

Let A, Fig. 242, be the front and B the side view of the

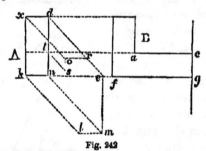

Fig. 242

object. On the diagonal from *d* set off the distance *d e* equal to length *f g* from the plane in side view B, set off the same distance from *n* at *m* and from *k* at *l*, join *e m* and *m l*. Also with the length *a c* in side view B set off the distance *d r* and *x o* in front view A, and join *o r*; from the point *o* draw a vertical line, and from the point *t* (corresponding to the upper edge *a c* in side view) draw a diagonal parallel to *d e*, intersecting the vertical line drawn from *o* at *s*, completing the projection of shadow required.

To project the shadow of a square parallel object, inclined, and projecting from the side of a plane at right angles to it.

Let A, Fig. 243, be the side view, B the front view of the object, and F the plane upon which the required shadow of the object is to be projected. From the points *d* and *h*, where the vertical line (or side of plane) *c e* intersects the side view of object A, draw the horizontal lines *d g* and *h i*; and from the points *k, l, m,* in the end of front view B draw the diagonals; with the horizontal distance *r s*, in side view A, from the point *k* in front view B, set off the length *k n*; and with the horizontal distance *t u* from the points *l* and *m* set

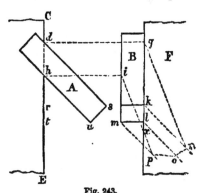

Fig. 243.

off the length *l o* and *m p*; join *g n*, *n o*, *o p*, and *p i*, the latter intersecting the side of plane at *x*. *g n o p x* will be the projection of shadow required.

To project the shadows of parallel objects radiated from a common centre, whose lengths are equal from the centre, and projecting from the side of a plane at right angles to them.

Let A, Fig. 244, be the side, B the front views of the objects, and F the plane upon which the shadows are to be projected. From the point *k*, corresponding to the point *s* in side view of object A, draw the diagonal; from the point *h*, where the side of the plane *c e* intersects the radial line *w s*, draw a horizontal line *h g*, intersecting the line of plane *i x* at *g*; from the point *k* set off on the diagonal the length *k l*

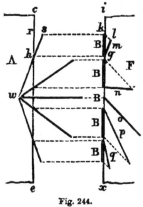

Fig. 244.

equal to the horizontal distance *r s* in side view A, and join *g l*. *g l* will be the projection of the shadow on the plane *r* of the radial *h s* in side view A. Proceed in the same way with the other radials; *m n o p q* will be the projections of the shadows required.

NOTE.—When these radial lines or arms have a periphery, as shown in Fig. 245, of which A represents the side and B the

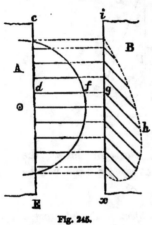

front views; if lines, as at *d f*, at any distance apart be drawn at right angles to o E (instead of being radiated as in the other), and produced horizontally to *i x*, and diagonal lines, as *g h*, &c., be drawn from the several points of intersection, and the horizontal lengths *d f*, &c., be set off upon the respective diagonals, it is obvious that they would give points for a curve coincident with a curve projected from a periphery,

Fig. 245.

on the extremities of the radiated lines as in Fig. 244, the position of plane, centre of circle, and radius being the same in either diagram.

To project the shadows of semicircular objects on the three sides of an octagon at right angles to the plane bounded by the three sides.

Let A, Fig. 246, be the plane upon which the shadows are to be projected, *f* the plans of the objects (supposed to be of imperceptible thickness). On each plan of object *f* draw their elevations B, C, D: divide them by any number of equally distant lines *f e*, and at right angles to the sides of the octagon. (Equally distant lines, though not quite essential, are convenient, for when each of the objects is similarly divided from its centre, one measurement on one divisional line on either side of its centre line will set off six of the

equal lengths required on the diagonal). From each of the
intersectional points on the lines f draw the diagonals; set off
the lengths $f\,g$, &c., equal to the corresponding heights $f\,e$,
&c., a curve line passing through the points will be the
projection of shadow required.

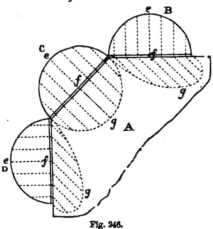

Fig. 246.

NOTE.—It will be obvious that the shadow projected from
the semicircular object c will also be a semicircle, and the
curve projected from B and D also similar to each other but
in different directions. For any figures of irregular form the
process would be the same.

*To project the shadow of a half cylinder on a plane at right
angles to its ends.*

Let A, Fig. 247, be the plan
of the object, and D the plane
upon which the shadow is to
be projected: draw a semicircular elevation B and c on
each end of object, and proceed exactly as in Fig. 246,
with the divisional lines on the
elevations, drawing diagonals from their intersectional points,

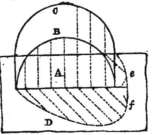

Fig. 247.

H 3

and setting off the heights on the respective diagonals. It will be observed that the inner circle в is chiefly that which is required, only a part of the upper semicircle o being requisite for projecting the part of its shadow towards the right hand; curved lines passing through the points, joined at their extremes by the vertical line *e f*, will be the projection of shadow required.

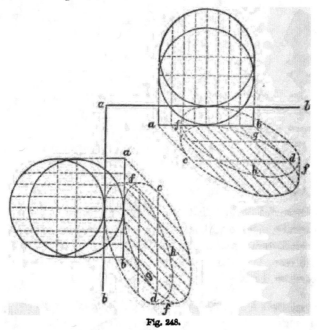

Fig. 248.

To project the shadow of a cylinder on a plane parallel to its axis. *

From the preceding examples, the shadows projected by entire discs or cylinders, as in the accompanying example, Fig. 248, will be easily understood by the dotted lines, much further explanation being unnecessary: the lengths in the elevations of the objects being set off on their respective diagonals as

* Another method of projecting a similar shadow will be found in second series of shadows, Fig. 276.

heretofore, either from a base line *a b*, or the half breadths of
the circles at their divisional lines, may be set off on a projected centre line *c d* on the corresponding diagonals. Having
thus found the several points and drawn in the curves, the extremes of each pair are joined by the straight lines *f*, vertical
and horizontal in the two diagrams respectively. As in a
previous example (Fig. 247), it is only a part of each circle
that is required for projecting the entire shadow, that, as
projected at *g h*, drawn simply to show the process, being
discarded. To prevent confusion the diagonals are omitted
from the outer circles, the process being the same as for the

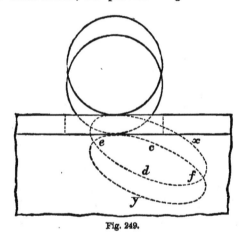

Fig. 249.

inner circles. Having found the several points as indicated,
the outer curves passing through them will be the projection
of shadow required.*

NOTE.—In drawing the curves projected by the rays of
light through a circular aperture having its sides parallel, in
any material object of parallel thickness at right angles to a
plane, as shown in the diagram, Fig. 249, the process for

* In projecting such shadows in a drawing where there are a
number of curves similar to each other, having projected one correctly, the simplest way is to trace it and transfer it to any other
positions where requisite. Such process is referred to in Chapter XII.

finding the points of projection would be similar to that just described at Fig. 248 ; the difference being in the retention of the part of the ellipses *c d* in the present instance, discarded in the last example, and also the discarding of the parts *x* and *y* ; neither would there be straight lines at the extremes of the curves. *c d e f* would be the projection required.

To project the shadow of a bracket on a plane at right angles to it.

Let A, Fig. 250, be the front view of the object from which the projection of shadow is required. Draw a side view B of

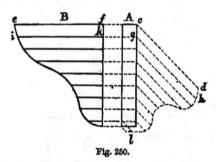

Fig. 250.

the object; divide it by any number of horizontal lines as shown; produce them to the right-hand side of front view A ; from the points of intersection draw the diagonals; set off the length *c d* equal to the distance *e f*, *g h* equal to *i k*, and so on. A curve line passing through the points *d h*, &c., will be the required curve for the right-hand side of the object. As the projection of a part of the lower left-hand side of bracket is required, repeat the process, using the intersections of the horizontal lines on left-hand side of bracket, join the lower extremes of the curves by a horizontal line *l*, which will complete the projection of shadow required.*

In *ogee* mouldings the projections of their shadows are

* In actual practice, having found the shadow of lower part of bracket for right hand side, transfer by tracing for the left hand side, and join them by the horizontal line *l*. Process explained in Chapter XII.

similarly performed, as shown in subjoined diagram, Fig. 251,
A being end views, and B plans of the objects referred to.

Transfer the end views A to the
plans B, as shown by the dotted
curve lines e; divide e by vertical
lines as shown, draw the diagonals
from the intersectional points in
the lower lines c c, set off the
several heights on their respective
diagonals (if each of the dotted
end views at ee are equally divided,
the same lengths on the corre-

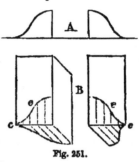

Fig. 251.

sponding diagonals are applicable in each); curved lines
passing through the points will be the projection of the
shadows required.

To project the shadow of a straight flange on a plane, being
parallel and at right angles to it.

(NOTE.—The flange may be either horizontal or vertical, as
in subjoined diagrams.) Let A, Fig. 252, be the front view of

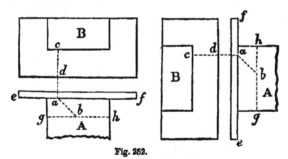

Fig. 252.

the plane on which the shadow of the flange $e f$ is to be projected, and B a plan of the objects; draw the diagonal on
front view A, on which set off the length $a b$ equal to the
distance $c d$ in plan B, and through the point b draw the
straight line $g h$ parallel to the line of flange $e f$; $g h$ will be
the projection of shadow required.

Note.—A plan is not required as far as regards the projection of the shadow on a front view, when the projecting part of the object is straight and parallel to the plane on which the shadow of the vertical or horizontal object is to be projected, if the projection is known. For instance, if the distance of the projecting part *g h*, Fig. 253, is known to be 6 inches, then 6 inches taken from the scale to which the drawing is made and set off on the diagonal at *c d* would give the point through which to draw a line *e f* parallel to the projecting part *g h*, as explained at Fig. 252, the projection of shadow required on the plane A.

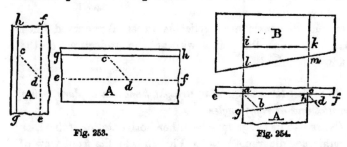

Fig. 253.   Fig. 254.

To project the shadow of a bevelled flange on a plane at right angles to it.

Let A, Fig. 254, be the front view, and B a plan of the object. From the points *a* and *c* on the lower line of flange *e f* in front view A draw the diagonals, from the same points *a* and *c* draw the vertical lines *a i* and *c k*; with the distance *l i* in plan B set off the length *a b* on the diagonal, also the distance *m k* on the diagonal *c d*. Through the points *b* and *d* draw the line *g d*, intersecting the side of plane at *h*; *g h* will be the projection of shadow required.

To project the shadow of a circular flange on a plane at right angles to it.

Let A, Fig. 255, be the front view, and B a plan of the object. Produce the line *c d* in plan B to *i*, divide the line *i d* into any number of parts by vertical lines, as shown at

$h\ n$, &c.; produce them to the lower line of flange $e\ f$ in front view ᴀ; from the points of intersection draw the

diagonals; with the distance $h\ g$ in plan ʙ set off the length $l\ m$, also with the distance $n\ c$ set off the length $o\ p$, each on their respective diagonals, and so on with the other distances in plan ʙ on the diagonals in front view ᴀ. A curve line $m\ k$ passing through the points will be the projection of shadow required.

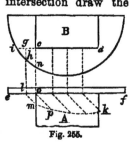

Fig. 255.

To project the shadow of a ring on a plane at a given distance from and parallel to it.

Fɪʀsᴛʟʏ, having its section rectangular (upper diagram.)

Let ᴀ, Fig. 256, be a plan, ʙ a side view of the object, $c\ d$ the line of plane, and $f\ e$ the distance of the object from the plane. Through the centre of ring i, in plan ᴀ, draw the diagonal; from the centre i set off the length $i\ k$ on the diagonal equal to the distance of ring $e\ f$ from the plane $c\ d$; also from the point i set off the length $i\ l$ on the diagonal equal to the distance $h\ g$ (the distance from the plane $c\ d$ to the top of the ring ʙ); from the point k in plan ᴀ, with a radius equal to the radius of outer part of ring, describe the semicircle $m\ n\ o$, and from the point l, with the same radius, describe the semicircle $p\ q\ r$; join with straight lines $o\ r$ and $m\ p$, the two semicircles described. From the point l on the diagonal in plan ᴀ with a radius equal to the radius of inner part of ring describe the part circle $s\ t\ u$, and from the point k with the same radius describe the part circle $s\ v\ u$, which, with the outer part already described, will be the projection of shadow required.

Sᴇᴄᴏɴᴅʟʏ, having its section circular.

Let ᴀ (lower diagram) be a plan of the ring. Through the centre w of the ring draw the line $x\ y$ in the direction of the light, also through the centre w draw a line $z\ a$ at right

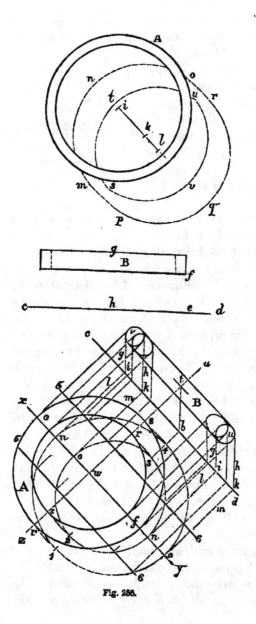

Fig. 256.

angles to xy. At any convenient distance draw a line of plane cd parallel to xy. On za, as a centre line, draw a side view, B, of the ring at its distance from the plane cd. At each end of the side view B draw sections v and u of the ring corresponding to the sections e and f in the line xy. To these draw tangentially, at the angle of 45° to the plane cd, the lines g and h, intersecting the line of plane cd at i and k. From the points i and k draw lines l, m, each parallel to the line za, intersecting the line xy at n, o, which will be points for the shadow. From each side of the thickness of ring r and s, on either side of the diameter of ring in plan A, draw lines parallel to xy, and from the corresponding point t in the centre of the thickness of the ring in side view B, draw the diagonal tb intersecting the line of plane cd in b, from which point draw a line parallel to za intersecting the lines drawn from r and s at 1, 2, 3, 4, which will also be points for the shadow. Take any other sections in the plan of ring A, as at 5-6, and draw corresponding sections (see subjoined note) in side view B as shown, and proceeding as before for additional points, curve lines passing through which will be the projection of shadow required.

NOTE.—To find the points for describing sections such as that referred to, let A B, Fig. 257, be the outer and inner circumferences of a ring, circular in section, and cd the line of section in plan of ring. Through any points e, f, g, in cd,

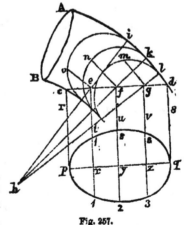

Fig. 257.

draw the radial lines hi, hk, and hl from h, the centre of the ring. On each of the radial diameters draw semicircles as shown, and from the intersectional points e, f, g, draw the lines $e\,o$, $f\,n$, and $g\,m$, at right angles to the respective radial diameters. Let $p\,q$ be the centre line of the figure to be described. From c and d draw the lines r and s at right angles to the line $p\,q$ (Fig. 103, Chapter XI.), giving intersectional points for the length of the figure. From the points e, f, g, draw lines t, u, v, each parallel to r or s, intersecting the line $p\,q$ at x, y, z. From the point x with the distance $e\,o$ set off $x\,1$ equally on each side of the line $p\,q$. From the point y with the distance $f\,n$ set off $y\,2$, and from the point z with the distance $g\,m$ set off $z\,3$. A curve line drawn through 1, 2, 3, and the points of extreme length already found, will be the figure required.

To project the shadow of a sphere on a plane.

Let A, Fig. 258, be a plan of the sphere from which the shadow is to be projected. From the centre of sphere b draw the diagonal $c\,d$, and through the same centre b draw a line $e\,f$, at right angles to $c\,d$. At any convenient distance draw a line $g\,h$, parallel to $c\,d$, which will represent the side view of the plane upon which the shadow is to be projected. From the point i, as a centre, draw the side view B of sphere tangentially to the line $g\,h$; divide the diameter of sphere A equally on each side of centre line $c\,d$, and draw the lines $l\,m$, &c., through the divisional points, and parallel to $c\,d$. From the centre i, in side view B, with half the diameters of $n\,o$, $p\,q$, &c., in plan A, as radii, draw the circles r, s, &c. At the angle of $45°$ to the line $e\,f$, and tangentially to the circles or diameters r, s, &c., draw the lines u, v, &c., to the line of plane $g\,h$, and from the points of intersection 1, 2, 3, &c., draw the lines 1-4, 2-5, &c., parallel to $e\,f$. Through the points where these lines intersect their corresponding diagonals, $c\,d$, $l\,m$, &c., a curve line z (ellipse) passing, will be the projection of shadow required.*

* The shadow may also be projected by the process described at Fig. 294.

NOTE.—The shadow of a sphere projected at the same angle as at Fig. 258, just described, is identical with the ellipse produced in a cylinder cut through at an angle of 45°. If the sphere were placed in a tube of the same diameter, and at the angle named (or in a direct line with the light), the tangential line of the sphere with the tube would be as indicated by the dotted line 6-7 in plan and side

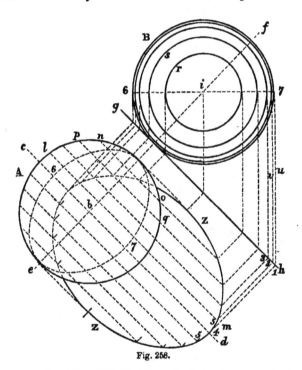

Fig. 258.

views A and B, Fig. 258, dividing the light from the dark side of object; and which tube, if produced and intersected by the plane, would be coincident internally in every point with the projection of the shadow of the sphere.

Objects such as that described will only project a shadow identical with their outline when the plane is at right angles to all the rays of light from the several points of the object.

To project the shadow in a hollow half sphere (or semi-circular cup) of its side.

Let A, Fig. 259, be the plan of the object in which the shadow is to be projected. Through the centre *k* of the object draw the diagonal *b c*; divide the object equally on each side of centre line *b c* by any number of lines as at *l v*, &c. Through the centre *k* draw a line *f r*, at right angles to *b c*. At any convenient distance from plan A draw a line *d e*, parallel to *b c*. On the line *d e*, and from the intersectional point *y*, with radius equal to radius of plan A,

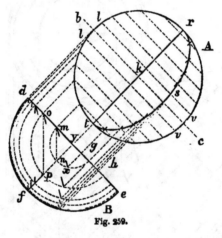

Fig. 259.

draw the semicircle *d f e*, which will represent a side view B, of the object. From *y*, as a centre, and with radii equal to the half diameters of the lines *l v*, &c., describe the semicircles in side view B, and from each of the points of intersection, *o, m*, &c., on the line *d e*, draw the diagonals *m n*, *o p*, &c., each at an angle of 45° to the line *d e*. It will be seen that the points *n, p*, &c., where the respective diagonals intersect their respective semicircles, are also the intersectional points of the centre line *f r*; the projection of the shadow required will therefore be the straight line *t r*.

NOTE.—If the angle of the light were greater or less than

45°, as shown at *m x* in side view B, the shadow would be a
curved line in each instance, the greater angle projecting a
concave and the lesser a convex shadow, as represented by
the line *s* in diagram, the process being the same for finding
the points in the curve as in that already described, and as
indicated by the dotted lines *g h*, &c.

PROJECTION OF SHADOWS.—SECOND SERIES.—In the examples of the projection of shadows in the first series, the
angle of 45° only has been employed, as from the nature
of the projections it alone was requisite; but in the projection of shadows of a more intricate sort, as of those
which follow, there are required in addition a plan and side
views of the angle in its inclination, the relative angle of
light in such views being similar. Suppose the object A, in
diagram, Fig. 260, to be the front view of a little set square
at the ordinary inclination of 45°, and also having the

requisite angle of 45°, the side of
which would be as represented by
the dotted lines *f c g*. In looking
from a position *e*, above it (supposing it possible to look in parallel
lines at every point, as is supposed
in mechanical drawings), it would
present the angles as in plan B. It
would also present similar angles
viewed from the positions *l* or *p*.
To project the angle—from a point

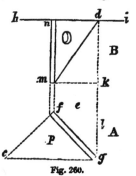

Fig. 260.

f draw the diagonal, on which set off any length, *f g*; at
any convenient distance draw a horizontal line or plane *h i*;
from the point *f* draw a vertical line *f n*, intersecting the
line *h i* at *n*; on the line *f n* from the point *n* set off the
length *n m* equal to the length *f g*; and from the point *g* draw
a vertical line *g d* intersecting the line *h i* at *d*, and join *m d*,
which will be the plan of the angle of 45° as required.*

* In projecting shadows at any other angle or other inclination in a
front view, it is obvious that the relative angle in the plan or side

As an application of what has just been explained to a mechanical object, and an illustration of the necessity of the projection of the plan or side view of the angle already referred to, let A, Fig. 261, be a cylindrical object or shaft (horizontal or vertical), and B a plane parallel to axis of shaft. The projection of the shadow of shaft is required on the plane B. Draw an end view c of the shaft,* and also

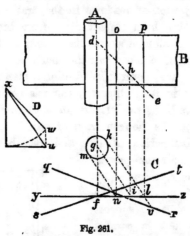

Fig. 261.

the horizontal line of plane $y\,z$ at its distance $f\,g$ from centre of shaft. In plan A from any point d (shown in this instance on centre line of shaft) draw the diagonal of 45°, which is the direction of the light; from the point d, with the distance $f\,g$ in end view c set off the length $d\,h$; from the point h draw the vertical line $h\,i$ intersecting the plane $y\,z$ at i, and join $g\,i$, which will then represent a side view of the angle of

view of the object must correspond to it, and is found in a similar manner. In some drawings the relative angle of light in plan or side view is as great as 45°, and the angle of inclination of shadow in front elevation also 45°, resulting in the projection of a longer or broader shadow than that described (Fig. 260). The latter is generally considered preferable, is more easily understood, and has therefore been adopted throughout this chapter.

* If A were a vertical view, c would be a *plan* as well as an end view. If A were a plan or horizontal view, then c would be an *ena* view only.

45°, whose length of base is *d h* in plan A. Set the parallel rulers to the line *g i*, and from the diameter *m k* of the shaft, draw the lines *k l* and *m n* parallel to *g i*; and from the intersectional points *n* and *l* in plane *y z*, draw the vertical lines *n o* and *l p*. The vertical lines *o* and *p* will be the projection of shadow required on the plane B. If the plane were placed obliquely, as at *q r*, the breadth of shadow would be increased on it, as shown by the line *k l* produced to *v* ; or if placed as at *s t*, it would have less breadth than in position *y z* in the first instance. At whatever angle the plane is placed the same process would be applicable, a horizontal and vertical line being always necessary* on which to erect the side view of the angle from its plan as at *d h*, and as explained at Fig. 260. The line of plane in example *y z*, as also the centre line of shaft, is taken advantage of in such instances, being ready drawn to hand, and being convenient lines; though in this and in many of the examples which follow, the angle may be projected anywhere in close proximity to the place where it is required, so that the requisite lines from the points of the object can be drawn with facility parallel to the plan, end, or side view of the angle of 45° referred to. In the example given, Fig. 261, the height *g f* is taken in the end view C from the plane *y z* to the centre of the shaft *g*. There is no other reason than that given why this height should be taken ; any height would do equally well, so that the same distance is set off on its corresponding view of it as at *d h*. It may be projected in the position shown at D, Fig. 261, and by drawing *k l* and *m n* in end view C, parallel to *x u*, it will render the diagonal *d e* in plan A unnecessary, being drawn at *x w* for projecting the line *x u*.

To facilitate such process in the projections of shadows, where there are many lines to be drawn parallel to each other at the given angle on the plans and side views of the

---

* In the absence of a little set square having the proper angle, to bear on the edge of T-square.

several objects, it will be found convenient to use a little set square of the proper angle (and which would be as represented in Fig. 260 at *d m k*) to bear on the edge of the T-square in the several positions shown in the following diagram, Fig. 262, and which are also indicated in all the

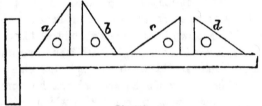

Fig. 262.

diagrams which follow, in the position suitable for drawing the lines of the relative angle of the light in the plans and side views of the objects, those in the front elevations being always at 45°.

The position of the set square *a*, Fig. 262, is suitable for drawing in the relative angle of the light in a plan placed either above or below the front view of the object on which the shadow is to be projected.

That in position *b* for the angle of light in projecting the shadow of a horizontal line on an inclined plane, &c.

That in position *c* for side views placed to the left of the object on which the shadow is to be projected.

That in position *d* for side views placed to the right of the object on which the shadow is to be projected.

In drawings of an engine, or other machinery containing different views of the one object, representing plans, elevations, side and end views, &c., it is the common practice to project all the shadows at the same angle as a matter of convenience. The shadows thus projected in one view have no relation whatever with the shadows of the view next to it, and on the same sheet of paper. In which case, each view must be considered as belonging to another object of similar construction and size, and all placed in the same light. It

would be quite unsatisfactory otherwise, as the following explanation will show. Let A, B, and C, Fig. 263, be the plan,
front, and side elevations of three walls of parallel thickness
at right angles to a plane. The shadows shown are projected
in the ordinary manner in engineering drawings, all being at
the angle of 45°, and also inclined at that angle. If the
shadow in the front elevation B had any relation to the

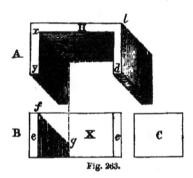

Fig. 263.

shadow in the plan A, the part x in front elevation B would
be all dark to correspond with the shadow from line of wall
H in plan A, the front elevation of wall e e would also be correspondingly dark; the side view C would also be dark,
corresponding to the shade side l d in plan A. The shadows
thus carried out would never make a desirable drawing, and
if left to choice, it would look better to produce an outline
drawing only.

In Fig. 264, the shadows of the three views of the same
object are projected in relation to each other, the diagonal
f g being the same (45°) as in last diagram, and made equal to
the length x y in plans A in each diagram, Figs. 263 and 264.
It will be observed that the relative shadows in the plan A,
Fig. 264, are at the opposite side of object, and at a different
angle from that at Fig. 263 (that in the present example being
the same angle as the one referred to at Fig. 260), and the
end view C is dark, or in the shade, to correspond with the
shadow projected by l d in plan A; and though it might be

I

convenient to have the shadows in plan to correspond thus with the front elevation, still, if o was also made to correspond, it would be as represented, all dark.

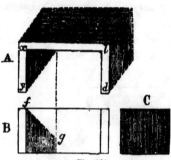

Fig. 264.

In the plans and front views of the following projections of shadows, though each series of diagonals in their respective views must be drawn parallel to each other, the distances between one couple and the couple next to them are not of necessity the same, except for uniformity of appearance, but they must agree relatively, those in the plan or side view with those in front elevation.

To project the shadow on a vertical cylinder of a circular flange which is at right angles to the axis of cylinder and projects equally around its circumference.

Let A, Fig. 265, be the front view of cylinder upon which the shadow of the flange *ef* is to be projected.

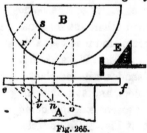

Fig. 265.

1. Draw a plan B of the cylinder and flange on a centre line common to both views, A and B.

2. With the set square bearing on the T-square in position E draw the relative angle of light in plan B as at *r s*.

3. From the point *r*, where the line *r s* cuts the outer circumference of flange in plan B, draw the vertical line *r x*.

4. From the point *x*, where the vertical line *r x* intersects the flange *e f*, draw the ordinary diagonal in front view A.

5. From the point *s* in plan B, where the line *r s* intersects the cylinder, draw a vertical line intersecting the diagonal from *x* at *u* ; *u* will be one point for the shadow.

Proceed in the same manner for finding other points as at *n*, *o*, &c., through which a curve line passing will be the projection of shadow required.

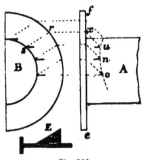

NOTE.—In objects such as that described, when horizontal, as at Fig. 266, the process is almost the same, the only difference is, the shadow is at the opposite side to that at Fig. 265.

The following examples, Figs. 267 and 268, will be found useful for reference. The shadows being projected similarly to that at Fig. 265, further explanation will be unnecessary.

Fig. 266.

The plan of each object is above its respective front view, or elevation.

To project the shadow of a square flange on an inclined plane, the flange being at right angles to the plane and parallel to it.

Let A, Fig. 269, be the front view of the object on which the shadow of the flange *c d* is to be projected, and B the side view at the required inclination. From the point *e* in side view B draw the relative angle of light intersecting the line *f y* at *h* ; from *h* draw the horizontal line *h k*, intersecting the side of front view A at *l* ; from the point *c* in front view A draw the diagonal intersecting the line *k l* in the point *i* ; from any other point *n* in side of flange in front view A draw another diagonal line *n o* parallel to *c i* ; from *n* draw a horizontal line intersecting the under side of flange in side view B at *p* ; from *p* draw a line parallel to *e h* intersecting the line *f g* at

2

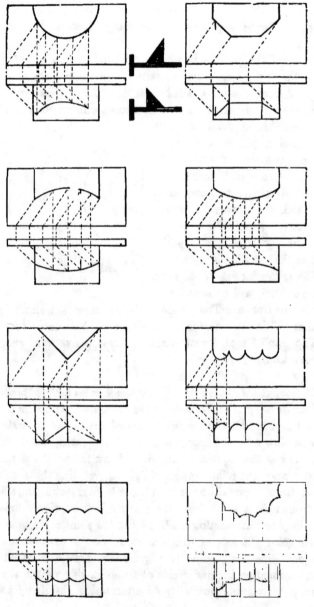

Fig. 267.

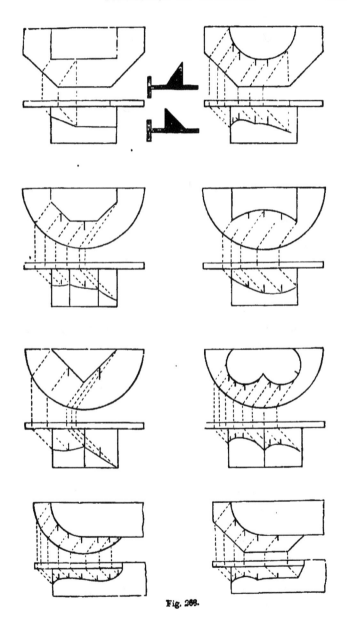

Fig. 266.

r ; from *r* draw a horizontal line intersecting the line *n o* at *s*, and join *s i*, intersecting the side of object at *t* ; *t i l* will be the projection of shadow required.

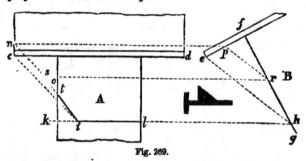

Fig. 269.

To project the shadow of a circular flange on an inclined plane, the flange being at right angles to the plane.

Let A, Fig. 270, be the front view of the object on which the circular flange *c d* is to be projected,* and B the side view at the required inclination.   On front view A from any points *k, i, g,* on flange *c d,* draw the diagonals, and from the same points on flange *c d* in front view A draw the horizontal lines *k m, i n,* and *g o,* intersecting the side view of flange

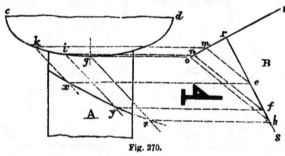

Fig. 270.

o t in side view B at *m, n,* and *o* ; from the points *m, n,* and *o,* draw the relative angle of light towards the line of inclination *r s,* and from the points of intersection *e, f, h,* draw the horizontal lines intersecting their respective diagonals in

* To find the curves in this, and those which immediately follow, ~~he~~ Chapter XIII., Fig. 183.

front view A from k, i, and g, at $x y z$; through which points a curve line passing will be the projection of shadow required.

To project the shadow of a circular flange on an inclined cylinder, the flange being at right angles to the axis of the cylinder and equidistant from it.

Let A, Fig. 271, be the front view of the object on which the shadow of the flange $n y$ is to be projected, and B a side view at the required inclination. Draw a plan o of the object on a centre line common to both views, A and o, as if it were a plan of a vertical cylinder, or as viewed in the direction ef in

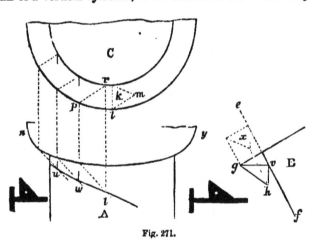

Fig. 271.

side view B. From the point g in side view B draw the relative angle of light; and (to render the process more explanatory) let the triangle $g v h$ represent the side view, inclined, of a set square having the angle of 45°. Draw a plan of the triangle as shown at x, and transfer it to position k, in plan o; $l m$ will be the relative direction of the light. Draw any number of lines p, r, &c., parallel to $l m$, and proceed in the same manner to find the points of the shadow as in example, Fig. 265. A curve line passing through these points, u, w, t, will be the projection of the shadow required.

NOTE.—The direction of the light, *l m* in plan o, is the same relative angle as in the other examples; it is observed in this instance in the same direction as the inclination of the cylinder, instead of being observed from a position vertical to the object as in the other examples.

To project the shadow of a round flange on a tapered (or conical) stuffing-box, the flange being at right angles to the axis of the cone and equidistant from it.

FIRSTLY, when in a vertical position, Fig. 272. Let A be the front elevation of the object on which the shadow is to be projected.

On a centre line common to both views, A and B, draw a plan B of stuffing-box and flange, on which draw the relative angle of light from any points on the circumference of flange, as at 1, 2, 3, &c. It is then required to draw lines on elevation A coincident severally with the relative angle of light, 1, 2, 3, &c., in plan B, and which lines will be curves in their front view. On elevation A, at convenient distances apart, draw the horizontal lines *d*, *e*, also their plans as indicated by the dotted circumferences in plan B. From the intersectional points of the angle of light with the several circumferences, as at *g*, *f*, &c., draw vertical lines intersecting their relative horizontal lines in elevation A at *h*, *i*, *k*, *l*, through which points draw the curve line. From the point 1 on circumference of flange in plan B draw a vertical line intersecting the lower edge of flange in elevation at *m*, from which draw the diagonal intersecting the curved line *l h* at *n*, which will be a point for the shadow; proceed in the same manner to find other points from the relative angle of light, 2, 3, 4, &c., as at *o*, *p*, &c., through which a curve line passing will be the projection of shadow required.

SECONDLY, when inclined, Fig. 273. Let c be the side view of the object at the required inclination, from which is drawn a corresponding front elevation A and plan B; proceed exactly as in the other, Fig. 272, and, as shown by the dotted lines, a curve line passing through the points *n, o, p,* &c., will be the projection of shadow required.

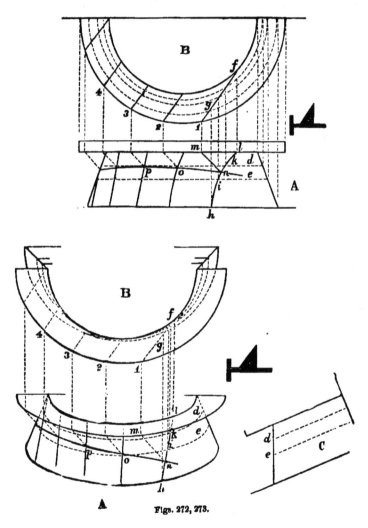

Figs. 272, 273.

To project the shadow of a bracket on a convex or a concave surface.

I 8

Let A in Fig. 274 be a convex, and in Fig. 275 a concave surface. (As the same process applies to both Figs. the reference letters are the same in each.) Draw plans B and side

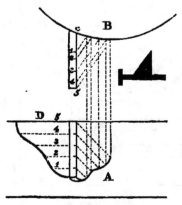

Fig. 274.

views D of the bracket, the latter adjoining the front view. Divide the side view D by any number of horizontal lines. On the right-hand side of bracket in plan B, from the point c, set off the lengths of the dotted divisional lines of bracket,

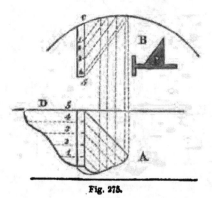

Fig. 275.

making c-1 equal to the length of the line 1 in side view D, c-2 equal to the length of the line 2 in side view D, and so on with each line on D. From the points opposite the divisional lines on D, on the right-hand side of the bracket in front view A, draw the diagonals, and from the points 1, 2, 8, &c., on bracket in plan B, draw lines for the relative angle of light; from the points where they intersect the curved surfaces in plan B draw vertical lines intersecting their corresponding diagonals on front view A. A curved line passing through the points of intersection will be the projection of shadow required.

NOTE.—The same process may be repeated for the lower part of left-hand side of bracket; though to trace the lower part already projected, and to transfer it to the part required, is a quicker process, and the one generally adopted in actual practice.

To project the shadow of a cylinder on a plane parallel to the axis.

Let A, Fig. 276, be the elevation of cylinder, and B the plane on which the shadow is to be projected. Draw a plan c d of the plane; on the centre line of cylinder A produced to h, with half the diameter of cylinder A as a radius, and at its required distance i h from the plane, draw a plan c of the cylinder. On plan c draw the relative angle of the light, as shown by the parallel lines l t, &c. From the points l x, &c., where the lines t l, w x, &c., intersect the circumference of the cylinder c, draw vertical lines intersecting the top k e of cylinder A at o, y, &c.; from the intersectional points o y, &c., on the line k e, draw the diagonal lines; from the point t in the line of plane c d draw a vertical line intersecting the diagonal line drawn from o, at r, and from the point u in line of plane c d draw a vertical line intersecting the diagonal drawn from the point n at s; r s will be the breadth of the shadow of the cylinder on the plane B. From w, in the line of plane c d, draw a vertical line intersecting the diagonal drawn from y in the line k e at z, which will be a point of projection of the shadow of the top of the cylinder. Proceed

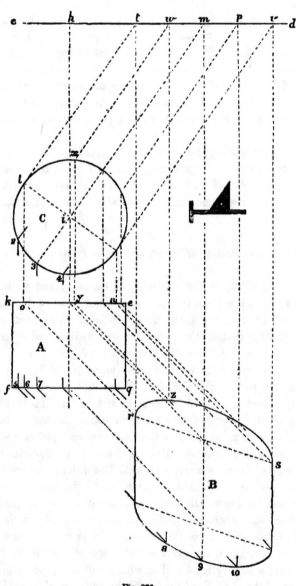

Fig. 276.

in a similar way for finding the other points, as shown by the dotted lines ; a curve line passing through the points will be the projection of shadow of top of cylinder.

To project the shadow of lower end of cylinder.

Produce the lines *w x*, &c., in plan o, so as to intersect the circumference of cylinder at 2, 3, 4. From the points 2, 3, 4, draw vertical lines intersecting the lower line *f g* in elevation A of cylinder at the points 5, 6, 7 respectively, and from these points draw diagonal lines parallel to *o r*, &c. From the points *w, m, p*, in the line of plane *c d*, draw vertical lines, intersecting their corresponding diagonals drawn from the points 5, 6, 7, at 8, 9, 10, and a curve line passing through the points will be the projection of shadow of lower end of cylinder, completing the projection of shadow required.

NOTE.—In projecting shadows such as that described on a larger scale than that shown in diagram, Fig. 276, more points for the curves would be required to insure accuracy ; these are obtained by multiplying the diagonals, &c.

To project the shadow of a horizontal on a vertical cylinder.

Let A, Fig. 277, be the horizontal cylinder in its position, and B the vertical cylinder, upon which the shadow of horizontal cylinder A is to be projected. Draw a side view o of the vertical cylinder, and an end view D of the horizontal cylinder, at its required distance from o. Draw the ordinary centre lines in each view of the vertical cylinder. Divide the lower part of each view of the vertical cylinder B and o by any number of horizontal lines 1, 2, 3, &c., identical in each view. (It will facilitate the process if the lines are equidistant.) From the end view D of the horizontal cylinder, tangentially to its circumference, draw the relative angle of the light *e* and *f*, intersecting the horizontal lines 1, 2, 3, &c., at *k l* and *m n*. Draw a half plan E of the vertical cylinder o. From the points *k* and *l* draw vertical lines intersecting the

half plan ʙ at *q* and *s*. From the points *g* and *h*, where the
relative angle of the light *e* and *f* intersects the cylinder ᴄ,
draw the horizontal lines *g v* and *h u*, intersecting the centre
line of cylinder ʙ at *v* and *u*, which are the upper and lower
points of projection of shadow. On the horizontal lines 1
and 4 in view ʙ set off the distances *o p* and *o w* on each side
of centre line, each equal to the length *r q* in half plan ʙ;
and on the horizontal lines 2 and 5 in view ʙ set off the dis-

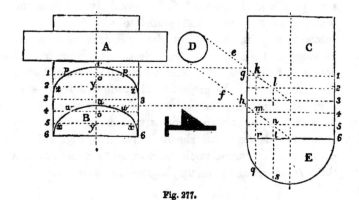

Fig. 277.

tances *y z* and *y x* on each side of centre line, each equal to
the length *t s* in half plan ʙ. As the lines *e* and *f* terminate
at the centre line in view ᴄ at the horizontal lines 3 and 6, so
in front view ʙ the extremities of the lines 3 and 6 will be
points for the shadow, and a curve line passing through the
points 3 *z p v* and 6 *x w u* will be the projection of shadow
required.

Another method.—On the centre line *k*, Fig. 278, in
vertical cylinder ʙ, with radius equal to half of the diameter
of cylinder, describe from *p* as a centre the semicircle *f m g*;
and with the same radius, on centre line *l* in side view ᴄ, from *i*
as a centre, describe the quarter circle *h n*. Draw the relative angle of the light *e*, *f*, as in previous example, from the
horizontal cylinder ᴅ.

Divide the quarter circles *f m*, *m g* in front view ʙ, and also the quarter circle *h n* in side view o, each into the same number of equal parts, and from the divisional points in each quarter circle draw the vertical lines as shown in views B and o; from the points in view o, where they intersect the

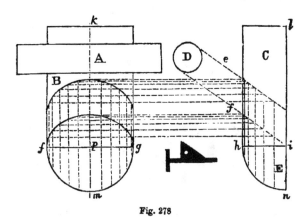

Fig. 278

relative angle of the light *e* and *f*, draw horizontal lines, intersecting their corresponding vertical lines in view B; a curve line passing through the points thus found will be the projection of shadow required.

To project the shadow of a less on a greater cylinder, both being vertical.

Let A, Fig. 279, be the small cylinder, and B the greater, upon which the shadow is to be projected. Draw a half plan o of the larger cylinder, and a plan D of the small cylinder at its distance from the greater.

From the point *l* draw the relative angle of the light *l m* tangentially to cylinder D. From the point *l* draw a vertical line *q*, intersecting the lower line of smaller cylinder A, at *r*; from *r* draw the diagonal; and from the point *m*, which is the intersection of the relative angle of the light with the circumference of larger cylinder o in half plan, draw a vertical line *m g*, intersecting the diagonal from *r* at *n*; *n g* will

be the projection of the shadow of the side of smaller cylinder A.   On plan of cylinder D draw lines parallel to *l m*, as

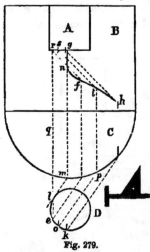

Fig. 279.

at *e, o, k*; from *o*, &c., draw a
vertical line intersecting lower
line of cylinder A at *s*; from *s*
draw the diagonal, parallel to
r n; from the intersectional point
p, in half plan C, draw a vertical
line, intersecting the diagonal
drawn from *s* at *t*; *t* will be a
point in the projection of shadow.
Proceed in a similar manner to
find other points, as at *f* and *h*
on cylinder B; a curve line passing through *n, f, t, h*, with the
vertical line *g n* will be the projection of shadow required.

NOTE.—It will be observed that the shadow from the
smaller cylinder when placed in such position as given in
example, does not show a boundary line to the right of the
larger object; if the smaller cylinder were placed more to
the left side of the larger one the shadow would have a
defined line to the right.

In cylinders of various diameters adjacent, the process
for projecting the shadow of any one upon the next is similar
to that already described, whether vertical or horizontal.   In
the latter, the only difference would be in the shadow being
towards the opposite side to that in Fig. 279.

*To project the shadow of a disc on a cylinder; the former in
a vertical and the latter in a horizontal position.*

Let A, Fig. 280, be the side view of the cylinder upon which
the shadow is to be projected, and B the disc.   Draw an end
view C and D of the objects at their distance.   From any point *e*,
on circumference of disc B, draw the horizontal line *i* to the edge
view D of disc, intersecting it at *t*; from the point *e* in disc B

lraw the diagonal; from the point t, in edge view of disc D, draw the relative angle of light, intersecting the circumference of cylinder c at u; from the point u draw the horizontal line f, intersecting the diagonal drawn from e at the point x, which will be a point in the projection of the shadow.

From any other points, as at k and p, in edge view of disc D, draw lines parallel to t u, intersecting the cylinder c at h and q, and from k and p draw the horizontal lines m and n,

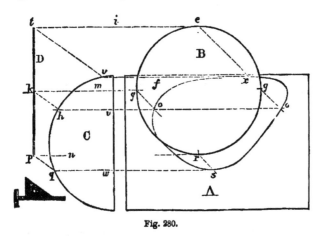

Fig. 280.

intersecting the disc B at g and r; from g and r draw the diagonals parallel to e x; from h and q draw the horizontal lines v and w, intersecting the diagonals drawn from g and r in disc B, at o and s. A curve line passing through the points x, o, s, o, will be the projection of shadow required.

NOTE.—As in other examples, if the cylinder were placed vertically, with the disc in the same relative position to it, the process would be similar, the shadow being on the left-hand side of disc.

To project the shadow of the square thread of a common screw on the inner surface, the position being vertical.

Let A, Fig. 281, be the body of screw on which the shadow

is to be projected.   Draw a plan B of the object.   From any point d, on lower edge of thread in front view A, draw the diagonal; also from d draw a vertical line, intersecting the plan of the thread at e; from e draw the relative angle of the light, intersecting the inner circumference at f; from f draw a vertical line, intersecting the diagonal drawn from d in front view A at g, which will be a point in projection of shadow.

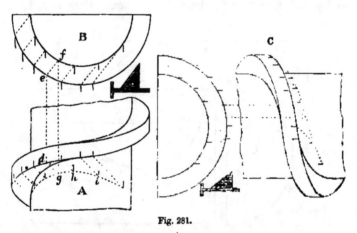

Fig. 281.

Proceed in a similar manner to find other points as at h, i, &c., through which a curve line passing will be the projection of shadow required.

NOTE.—When the screw is in a horizontal position, as shown at C, the process is the same, the shadow being projected towards the opposite end, the diagonals being in the opposite direction relatively to the thread shown at A and B just described.   The light is in the same direction, but the thread being more directly opposite the light, the curve of shadow, as will be observed, is not the same as when the object is vertical.   The process in either position is the same as at Figs. 265, 266.

To project the shadow in a vertical half cylinder, having its upper end at right angles to its axis.

Let A, Fig. 282, be the front view of the object on which the shadow is to be projected.

Draw a plan B of the object; from the point c, in front view A, draw the diagonal; from the corresponding point h in plan B draw the relative angle of light, intersecting the inner circle at n; from n draw the vertical line n p, intersecting the diagonal drawn from c at o in front view A; o p will be the projection of the shadow of the side c d of cylinder.

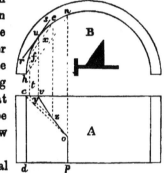

Fig. 282.

In plan B draw a tangential line r s, parallel to h n, the point of contact being u; from u draw a vertical line, intersecting the upper end of front view A at v; draw any other line, as at x, parallel to h n; from the point of intersection f draw a vertical line t; from the point of its intersection with upper line of cylinder A draw the diagonal y parallel to c o; from the point of intersection of x at e in plan B draw a vertical line, intersecting the diagonal y at z; v, z, o, p will be the projection of shadow required.

NOTE.—The process is the same when the object is horizontal, the shadow being in the opposite side to that at Fig. 282.

To project the shadows in vertical half cylinders having flat, convex, or concave covers, at right angles to the axis of cylinders.

(As the process is similar in each example the reference letters apply to either.)

Let A, Fig. 288, be the front view of the object on which the shadow is to be projected.

Draw a plan B of the object.

From c in front view A draw the diagonal c d; from the

corresponding point *m* in plan B, draw the relative angle of the light; from the point *n* in plan B, where the line *m n* intersects the inner circle, draw a vertical line *n p*, intersect-

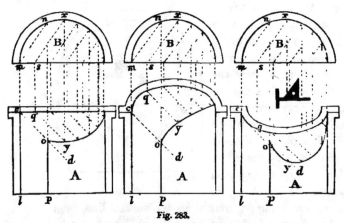

Fig. 283.

ing the diagonal *c d* in *o*; *o p* will be the projection of the shadow of the side of cylinder *c l*.

In plan B draw any number of lines, as *s x*, parallel to *m n*; from the point *s* in plan B draw a vertical line, intersecting the lower line of cover at *q*; from *q* draw a diagonal parallel to *c d*; from the point *x* in plan B draw a vertical line, intersecting the diagonal drawn from *q* in view A at *y*, which will be a point in the projection of shadow of the cover; find other points similarly, through which a curve line passing will form, with the shadow of side of cylinder already found, the projection of shadow required.

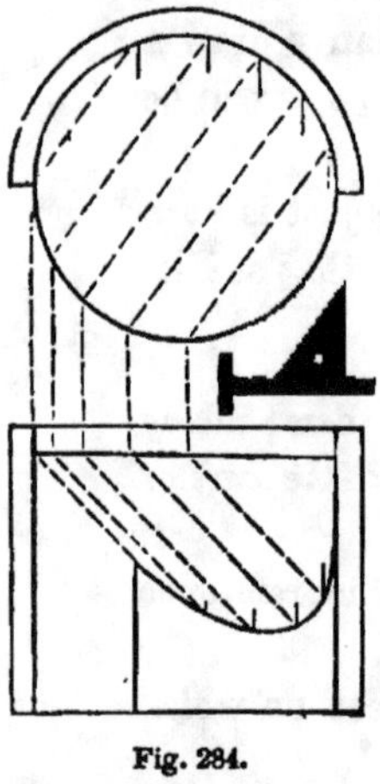

In projecting the shadow of the circumference of cover in a half cylinder, as at Fig. 284, the process is the same as at Fig. 283, just described.

Fig. 284.

To project the shadows in inclined half cylinders.

Let A, Fig. 285, be the section of a cylinder, having its cover *q r* in a line with the light, and B the section of a cylinder having its cover at right angles to the light; the covers of each cylinder being at right angles to its axis.

On *e* as a centre, in the line *q r*, on the centre line of cylinder *g f*, describe a semicircle *c g n*, representing a plan of half cylinder A. Draw the diagonal *c g*, from which it will be obvious that the shadow projected by the side of the

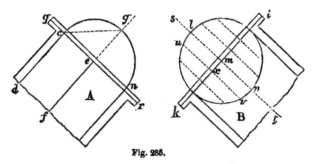

Fig. 285.

cylinder *c d* will fall on the centre line *g f*, and, as the line of cover *q r* is its own diagonal, there is no projection of shadow except at *e f*.

In cylinder B, on the intersectional point *m* as a centre, in the line *i k*, and centre line *s t*, describe a semicircle, to represent a plan of half cylinder B; draw the divisional lines at right angles to the line *i k*, as shown; make the length *m n* equal to the distance *m l*, and *n* will be a point in the projection of shadow. Also make *x v* equal to the distance *x u*, and *v* will be another point for the shadow. It will thus be quite obvious that the shadow will be a semicircle, similar to the plan of half cylinder B. There is no projection of shadow from the sides of cylinder B. The line *e f* in cylinder A, and semicircle in cylinder B, being the projections of shadows required.

To project the shadow of the end of a hollow cylinder which *is at right angles to its axis, on an inclined plane within the cylinder.**

Let A, Fig. 286, be the end view of cylinder, and B the inclined plane upon which the shadow is to be projected.

Draw a side view (or longitudinal section) c of the objects. From any point *d* in end view A draw the diagonal *d e*;

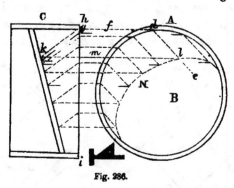

Fig. 286.

from *d* draw the horizontal line *f*, intersecting the line *h i* at *g*; from *g* draw the relative angle of light, intersecting the inclined plane at *k*; from the point *k* draw the horizontal line *m*, intersecting the diagonal *d e* at *l*, and *l* will be a point in the projection of the shadow. Find other points similarly, through which a curve line N passing will be the projection of shadow required.

To project the shadow of a horizontal straight object upon an inclined plane.

Let A, Fig. 287, be the plan of the inclined plane upon which the shadow of the horizontal object *c d* is to be projected. Draw a side view B of the objects, *h i* being the side view of straight object, and *h t* of the inclined plane. In plan A, from any point *e*, on the line *c d* (the farther to the right such point is chosen the greater the depth of the inclination, and the more correct the result is likely to be),

* This projection is similar to that produced by the open end of a steam pipe on a throttle valve.

draw the diagonal *e f*; from the point *e* draw a vertical line *e g*, intersecting the line *h i*, in side view B, at *g*; from *g* draw the relative angle of light *g p*, intersecting the plane *h t* at *p*; from *p* draw a vertical line, intersecting the diagonal *e f*

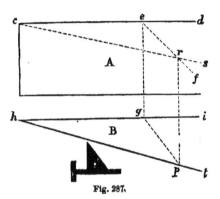

Fig. 287.

in plan A at *r*; from the point *c* in plan A, and through the point *r*, draw the line *c s*, which will be the projection of shadow required.

NOTE.—If the objects were vertical the projection of shadow would be found by the same process; the shadow being at the opposite side to that at Fig. 287.

To project the shadows of paddle floats on a plane adjacent and at right angles to their central axis.[*]

Let *a*, Fig. 288, be the end views of the floats, and D the plane on which the shadows are to be projected. From *a* draw the diagonals; set off the length *a b*, equal to the distance of lower end of float from the plane; set off the length *b c* equal to the length of float; draw *b f* and *c g* each parallel to *a e*. Proceed in the same manner with the others for the projection of shadows required.

* This and the following diagram, Fig. 289, in one sense belong to the first series of shadows, and the diagrams Figs. 290 and 291 to the second series. But as the four diagrams are different views of the same object it will be found more convenient to arrange them as her-

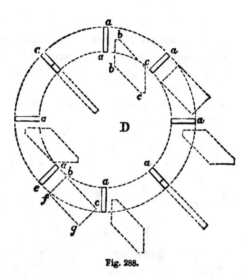

Fig. 288.

To project the shadow of a paddle ring on a horizontal plane (or float).

Let A, Fig. 289, be a plan of the float on which the shadow of the ring *x* is to be projected.

Draw a side view B of the objects. Divide the float *f* in view B into any number of parts, as at 1, 2, 3, &c.; from these points draw vertical lines, intersecting the inner and outer circumferences of ring; produce these lines to plan of ring in view A, intersecting it at 5, 6, 7, &c.; from the points on lower side of ring *d e* draw the diagonals; set off the length 5 *s* equal to the height 1 *a* in side view B, and *s* will be a point for the shadow of the outer circumference of ring. Proceed in a similar manner to find other points, through which a curve line *k* passing will be the projection of the shadow of the outer circumference of the ring.

From the points in the upper side of the ring *g h* in plan A, where the vertical lines intersect it, draw the diagonals; set off the length *m n* equal to the height 3 *c* in side view B, and *n* will be a point for the shadow of inner circumference of ring. Proceed in a similar manner to find other points, through which a curve line *p* passing will be the projection

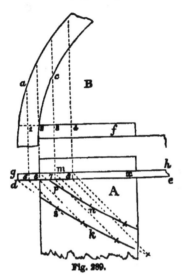

Fig. 289.

of shadow of inner circumference of ring, and which, with the curve for outer circumference *k*, will be the projection of shadow required.

To project the shadow of a paddle ring on an inclined plane (or float in an inclined position).

Let A, Fig. 290, be a plan of the float on which the shadow of the ring *x* is to be projected.

Draw a side view B of the objects. From any point *c* on the lower edge of ring *d e* in plan A, draw the diagonal; from *c* draw a vertical line *f*, intersecting the outer circumference of ring in side view B at *k*; from *k* draw the relative angle of light, intersecting the upper line of float at *l*; from *l* draw a vertical line, intersecting the diagonal drawn from *c* in plan A at *m*, and *m* will be a point for the shadow of the outer circumference of the ring. Proceed in a similar manner to find other points, through which a curve line *o*

passing will be the projection of shadow of outer circumference of ring.

From the point *t* in side view B, where the relative angle
of light intersects the inner circumference of the ring, draw a
vertical line *u*, intersecting the upper line of ring *g h* in plan A

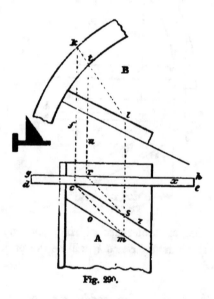

Fig. 290.

at *r*; from *r* draw the diagonal, intersecting the line
drawn from *l* at *s*, and *s* will be a point for the shadow
of inner circumference of ring. Proceed in a similar
manner to find other points, through which a curve line *z*
passing will be the projection of shadow of inner circumference of ring, and which with the curve for outer circumference
o, will be the projection of shadow required.

*To project the shadow of a paddle float on another adjacent,
both being inclined.*

Let A, Fig. 291, be a plan of the objects. It is required to project the shadow of upper float o on the lower float D.

Draw a side view B of the objects. From the point *e* in plan of float o draw the diagonal; from the point *k* in side view B, corresponding to *e* in plan, draw the relative angle of light, intersecting the upper line of lower float at *n*; from *n* draw a vertical line *n p*, intersecting the diagonal drawn from *e* at *o*; *o p* will be the projection of the shadow of edge *e g* of the upper float o.

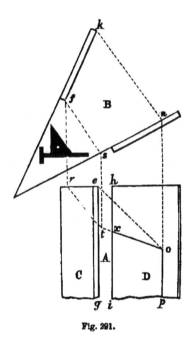

Fig. 291.

In upper float o in plan A, from the point *r* (which coincides with the point *f* in side view B) draw the diagonal; from the point *f*, in upper float in side view B, draw the relative angle of light, intersecting the upper line of the lower float at *s*; from *s* draw a vertical line, intersecting the diagonal drawn from *r* in plan A at *t*; join *t o*, intersecting the line of float *h i* at *x*; *x o* will be the projection of the shadow of the end of float *r e*, and, with *o p*, will be the projection of shadow required.

To project the shadow of a rectangular vertical object on a spherical body.

Let A, Fig. 292, be the front view of the sphere upon which the shadow of the rectangular object *e f* is to be projected.

Draw a plan B of the objects. Draw the centre line *i k* in both views A and B. Divide *e f* in front view into any number of parts, as at 1, 2, 8, from which points draw the diagonals *e x*, &c.; through the centre *c* of sphere A draw a line *l m* at right angles to the line *e x*. On the plan of sphere B draw the ellipses, or plans, *n, o,* &c., of the oblique sections *x* of sphere A,* in each of which the major axis will be on a vertical line drawn from the point of intersections of the line *l m* and the sectional line *x* in front view A. A part only of each ellipse is sufficient, as shown. From the point *h* in plan B, corresponding to *e* in front view A, draw the relative angle of light *h p*, intersecting the ellipses *n, o,* &c., in the points *y*; and from the points *y* draw the vertical lines *r, q,* &c., intersecting the corresponding diagonals from *e*, &c., in front view A, at *s, t, u,* &c. Through these points a curve line passing will be the projection of shadow required.

Another method is as follows:—Draw horizontal lines across the front view of sphere A; and from the centre of plan of sphere B draw circles of diameters corresponding to the lengths of the horizontal lines in front view A; from the points where the relative angle of the light *h p* intersects the circles in the plan B draw vertical lines intersecting the corresponding horizontal lines in front view A. A curve line drawn through the intersectional points will be the projection of shadow.

To project the shadow oj a vertical disc on a spherical body.

---

* The ellipses are found as described in Chapter XIII., Fig. 183.

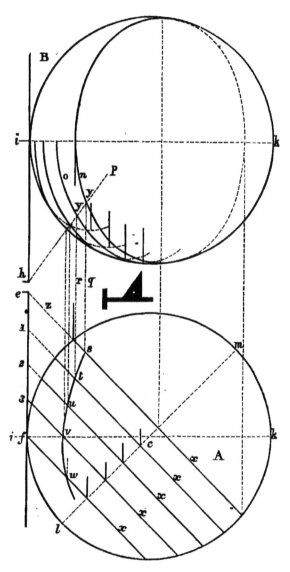

Fig. 293.

Let A, Fig. 293, be the front view of the sphere upon which the shadow of disc $f\,d$, is to be projected.

Draw a plan B of the objects. Draw the centre line $i\,k$ in

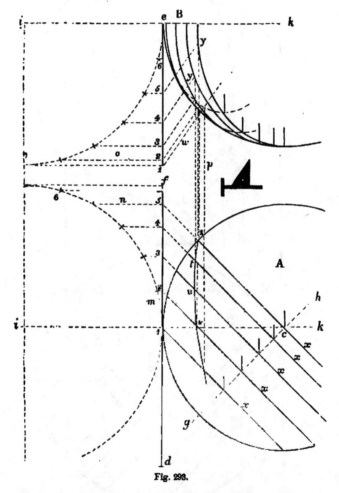

Fig. 293.

both views A and B. On each centre line $i\,k$, with half the diameter of disc as a radius, describe a part of a circle, representing as much of the circumference of disc as is necessary for projecting the required shadow, as the quadrants l and m in views A and B, l in plan B being in the relative position to m in front view B. Divide each quadrant into, say six equal parts; from the divisional points draw the horizontal lines o and n, &c., in each view A and B, intersecting the plan 1 e, and front view f d of disc, at 2, 8, 4, &c.; from these points on disc f d in front view A, where the horizontal lines intersect it, draw the diagonals 5 x, &c.; through the centre c of sphere A draw a line g h at right angles to the line 5 x. On the plan of sphere B draw the portions of ellipses, as shown, being plans of the oblique sections x in front view of sphere A, in each of which the major axis will be on a vertical line drawn from the points of intersections of the line g h and the sectional lines x in front view A. From the point 1 in plan B (corresponding to 1 in front view A) draw the relative angle of light w; from the points 2, 8, 4, &c., draw lines parallel to w, intersecting their corresponding ellipses in y; from the points y draw vertical lines p, intersecting their corresponding diagonals from 1, 2, 8, &c., in front view A at s, t, u, &c.; through which points a curve line passing will be the projection of shadow required.

To project the shadow of an elongated sphere on a plane parallel to its axis.

Let A, Fig. 294, be the front view of sphere, and M the plane on which the required shadow is to be projected.

Draw a plan B of the object, and a straight line c d to represent a plan of the plane M.

FIRSTLY, In plan B, from the centre e of the object, draw the relative angle of light e f.

SECONDLY, Through the centre e draw a centre line g h at right angles to the line e f, and upon it draw another view I of the object A. On this view it is required to find a sectional line which will divide the light from the dark side of the object, for which purpose it is necessary to project the rela-

tive angle of light *l n* * and *s t*, each tangentially to the
object, at *r* and *u* respectively.   Draw a straight line *r u*
between the tangential points, which will be the side view of
the section required.

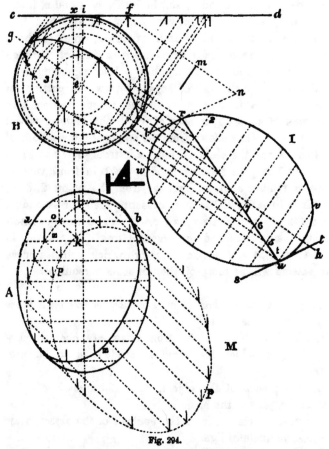

Fig. 294.

* *l n* represents the entire length of the line *e f*, which in view B is
observed (as in the other diagrams of this second series) in its oblique
position.

    The length of the line *l m* in view I is equal to the length of the
line *e f* as shown, and parallel to it; the distance *m n* is equal to *i f*
in plane *c d*. The angles *m l n* and *i e f* are therefore obviously dis-
similar in the views B and I.

THIRDLY, From the points *u* and *r* draw the lines *u v* and *r w*, each at right angles to the centre line *g h*, and divide the space between these lines by a number of parallels (equal parts on either side of the centre of the length of the object are more convenient in this instance, as, both ends of the object being similar, one series of corresponding circles in plan will prevent confusion).

FOURTHLY, Transfer these divisional lines from side view I to front view A.

FIFTHLY, On the plan B of object, from the centre *e*, with radii equal to the halves of the diameters of the transverse sections *a b*, &c., in front view A, draw the circles 3, 4, &c., and from the points 5, 6, 7, &c., in side view I, draw lines parallel to the centre line *g h*, intersecting their relative circles in plan B. A curve line drawn through the points of intersection will be a plan, in its oblique position, of sectional line *r u* in side view I. From the same points of intersections in plan B vertical lines to the respective transverse sections *a b*, &c., in front view A, will give intersectional points, through which a curve line z drawn will be the front view, in its oblique position, of the section *r u* in side view I.

SIXTHLY, On plan B, from the points in the circles intersected by the curve, draw the line *y x*, &c., parallel to *e f*, intersecting the plane *c d* in the point *x*.

SEVENTHLY, From the intersectional points of curve z with transverse sectional lines *a b*, &c., in front view A, draw the diagonals.

From the point *x*, in plan B, draw a vertical line, intersecting the diagonal drawn from the intersectional point *o*, in front view A; at *k*; *k* will be a point in the projection of the shadow. Having similarly found a sufficient number of points, a curve (P) passing through them will be the projection of shadow required.

NOTE.—The process just described is equally applicable in projecting the shadows of objects of a similar kind at any

moderate distance from the plane on which the shadow is to
be projected.

*To project the shadow of a ring of circular section on a plane
at right angles to it.*

Let A, Fig. 295, be the side view of the ring, and B the
plane on which the shadow is to be projected.

Draw a straight line *s t* to represent a plan of the plane B.
Draw a plan c of the ring at its distance from the plane *s t*.
On plan c draw the relative angle of light *e f*; and, from its
intersectional points *x* with outer and inner circumferences
of the ring, draw vertical lines *v*, which for each side of the
individual section will be the width or minor axis of elliptical
sections in side view A.

Describe the ellipses *g* and *h*.*

Draw the diagonals *i k* tangentially from *g* and *h*. From
the point *f* in the plane *s t* draw a vertical line, intersecting
the diagonals drawn from *h* at *o* and *n*; and from *g* at
m and *l* on the plane B respectively; *o, n,* and *m, l,* will each
be points in the projection of the shadow. Proceed in the
same manner for finding other points by drawing lines as at
p r, &c., parallel to *e f,* in plan c; curve lines passing
through the points found will be the projection of shadow
required.

NOTE.—In projecting such a shadow on a larger scale, a
good many sections would be required to ensure accuracy,
and these would produce much confusion from the multi-
plicity of the sectional lines and ovals. But this confusion
may be obviated. Having drawn the permanent side view,
as at A, Fig. 295, make as many side views with their plans,
of the same size, separately in pencil, as there are to be
sections, the sections obviously in all the views being dis-
similar. Having thus projected the points under each view
from its section, trace an outline of a side view; place it
above each of the other side views and trace the several pro-

* See Figs. 183 and 257.

jected points found on each, under the one side view on the tracing. The tracing can be placed on the permanent drawing, and the points on the tracing pricked through; or, by first marking the points with a soft pencil on under side of

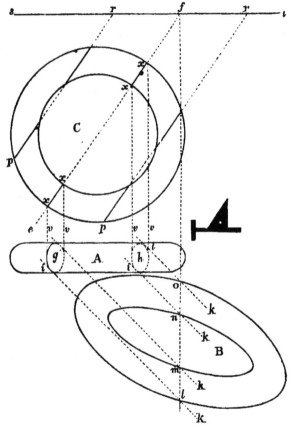

Fig. 296.

tracing paper, placing it in position and rubbing over the top side, there will be left a sufficient mark on the paper to enable the curve lines to be drawn in, giving projection of shadow required.

To project the shadow of a half ring (or elbow pipe) of circular section on a plane at right angles to it, either horizontal, as in last example, or vertical, as in subjoined diagram, Fig. 296.

The same process is followed exactly as described at Fig. 295—A, Fig. 296, being the front view of the ring, B the plane on which the shadow is to be projected, and C the face view of the object.

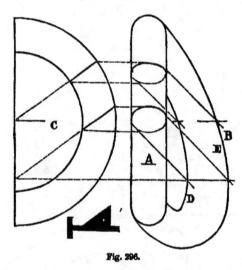

Fig. 296.

The curve lines D and E are the projection of shadow.

Projections of shadows of other objects might be given and multiplied almost indefinitely, but for all ordinary engineering purposes those given in this chapter will be found amply sufficient.

NOTE.—Before shading, the extraneous pencil lines for finding the several points in the projections of the shadows, and which should always be drawn very lightly, must be rubbed out carefully, so as to save the line of shadow only.

CHAPTER XVI.

SHADING AND COLOURING.

THE eye is naturally educated to recognise the form and distance of the objects which surround us from their lights and shades. The draughtsman's effort in shading is to deceive the eye by representing shadows as well as objects on the flat surface, thus making the latter appear to stand out in relief. The more perfect, therefore, the lights and shadows on the drawing, the more natural it will appear.

Any degree of taste and finish may be put into a shaded and coloured mechanical drawing, depending upon whether it is for working to, as a design, or for a picture, and whether such drawing is required quickly or not. It is hardly possible to make a first-rate, highly-finished shaded drawing quickly, though much depends, of course, on the ability of the manipulator, correctness being, in all cases, the first essential.

Summer is the worst part of the year for shading, the paper being so dry. Winter will be found always best for this operation, as under any circumstances the paper is damp.

Having a holder of the proper length (Chapter VI.), with proper sized brushes, one on each end, it is necessary to put a mark on the colour brush, which must be always used for the tint, the brush on opposite end being used for water only.

A small brush, unless for small objects, should never be used for anything larger than what it was intended for, as it will not lay on the tint equally; a brush of the proper size with a good point not only does the work better, but also quicker.

A brush, if laid down moist at any time, is apt either to soil or to get soiled, to obviate which, the little tumblers (referred to in Chapter VI.), having indentations round the rim, will be found handy for laying the brush across, besides containing the water for shading purposes. A very good brush-rest can also easily be made by cutting the edge of a little pasteboard box into notches like saw teeth.

Two kinds of palettes (Chapter VI.) are necessary, one having a sloping recess for rubbing down the Indian ink, and having three or more little cups in it for mixing up the tints; the other having three or four sloping recesses only, for rubbing down each colour separately, for using each by itself, or before mixing.

Tints should never be made by artificial light; if it is necessary to shade at night, they should be mixed up by daylight.

One colour should never be rubbed down among another, as in all likelihood it will be laid aside to dry with other colour on it. Colours should never be taken off the cake with the brush, as by repeatedly doing so hollows the cake, and renders it unfit to rub down when required; neither should they be dipped into the water for common use, for if good (as they should be) they soon crack and crumble to pieces; the proper way is, to rub them down on the palette, having put a very little water in it previously by the brush. A common card bent up half an inch at one end, upon which to place the Indian ink immediately after using, will be found useful; otherwise it is likely to soil everything with which it comes into contact.

The neutral tint for shading engineering drawings, and which generally gives satisfactory results, is composed of Indian ink, Prussian blue, and crimson lake, to which some draughtsmen add a little gamboge to give the tint a greyish hue. The tint should not be too dark, as by using light tints, and going frequently over the shadows, they can be better modified and corrected every time the process is repeated than by using dark tints.

To keep tints from evaporating over night, the little " cabinet nests " (Chapter VI.) are requisite, or (to descend to a common article) old pomatum pots, having a lid, are very good utensils for preserving the tint.

If one or two days are required to go all over an intricate drawing once, it is best to mix up fresh neutral tint for every coat, as even the best colours change in the course of a day or two though covered up from the light in a close pot; much of the blue disappears, leaving the tint similar to a mixture of lake and Indian ink alone. Should a tint evaporate a little in the course of a night, when it is wished to use it again the next day, there will generally be seen a mark round the dish; if water is added filling up to this mark, it will restore nearly the same degree of tint.

Tints left to dry completely upon the palette should never be moistened again for use, but should be washed clean out, and fresh tints made up for the occasion; Indian ink, especially, if dried up and moistened again for neutral tint, invariably leaves brush-marks in the shading.

In using one tint in a palette having other tints in the several recesses, it will be found safer to cover up those not being used at the moment with a card.

The proportions of the colours composing the tint throughout a drawing should never be altered. Every time the tint is used, it should be stirred up with the colour-brush. If an ordinary tumbler is used for the water, it should never be more than one-third full, otherwise every time the water-brush is put into it, it would wet the holder unnecessarily.

The palette, with the shading tints, and tumbler containing the water, should lie before the operator, placed upon the drawing on a sheet of thickish paper, so as to keep the drawing clean.

Fluid colours should never be passed across a drawing, but around it.

When shading, there should always be a sheet of clean white paper placed on the drawing under the hand, close to the part to be shaded, to preserve the drawing from any perspiration, which would prevent the paper taking the tint easily; this sheet of paper should also extend below the arm, to keep the drawing clean.

There is another method of keeping a drawing clean, which will be found in the latter part of Chapter IX.

Damping large surfaces by a large water-brush in warm weather, either for flat or round surfaces to be tinted, is quite necessary; otherwise the tint is apt to dry too quickly, and leave cloudy marks. The surface should not be too wet; clean blotting-paper being applied to take off the superfluous water, which if allowed to remain causes the dampest places to *buckle up*, and renders the tint difficult to put on equally, being apt to settle in the lower parts. It is easier, therefore, to do shading in the winter, the paper not being so dry; however, to put on a tint properly, the paper surface must be quite flat.

In shading a cylindrical object, it can be done with more facility when its position is horizontal, and with the light side next to the operator (the drawing being readily placed in any position by turning it); it being more difficult to wash from than towards you with the water-brush.

In the objects referred to, either in a vertical or horizontal position, the darkest place should be a quarter of the diameter from the edge on shade side, Fig. 297, and the lightest place about a quarter of the diameter from the opposite side; and when in position, either vertical, horizontal, or at right angles to the direction of the light, a little reflected light should be shown next the line

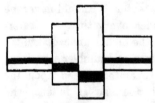

Fig. 297.

on the shade side, as in example, Fig. 298; it should also have a little shade close to the line on the light side, in contrast to the part that should be lightest of all.

When such object is inclined in the direction of the light, Fig. 299, the shade will be the same at each side, and narrower than in position, vertical or horizontal, lightest in the middle, and having no reflected light close to the line on either side. When such object is inclined at right angles

Fig. 298.   Fig. 2:9.

to the light, the shadow on the shade side should be broader than in a vertical or horizontal position.

Sections of cylinders lying at the angle of 45° should have the shadow graduated, as at *a b*, in diagram, Fig. 800, independently of the shadow of the side of the cylinder at section, and which should come over the graduated part.

 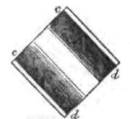

Fig. 300.

The sides of the cylinders at *c d* should have a shade close to the sectional line of cylinder, the part in the middle of the right-hand cylinder being the lightest.

The colour-brush, when about to apply the tint, ought not to have too much in it, or the tint will run in all directions when the water-brush is applied; and the water-brush must not have too much water for the same reason.

If at any time the tint should get beyond the line by accident, the best way is to push it hard within the line by the finger; in most cases it will come back and stop about the proper place; this will be found better than attempting to wash off the excess with the water-brush, which would only tend to increase the error.

In shading, the brush should be held in as vertical a position as possible ; it will be found much easier to keep any boundary line. Before every application of the water-brush to the shading it should be washed in the tumbler, and the superfluous water taken off, by either drawing it between the lips (for which reason the mouth should be rinsed out clean before shading, especially after meals, as the brush must be quite free from greasy matter), or the brush might be applied to blotting-paper.

In commencing to shade a cylindrical object—say, of two inches in diameter and six or seven inches long—begin at a quarter of the diameter from shade side, and put on the tint, about a quarter of an inch broad for the first coat, in short lengths at a time, washing off the side next the middle of cylinder first, as it is of more consequence than the edge of tint next the line. The water-brush should be drawn along as straight as the shadow is required to be, and a little in beyond the edge of the tint, taking care that the end of the tint does not get dry before the next little length is added to it.* In making the shadow with brush and tint, a part just done ought not to be gone over again until it is almost dry, otherwise it will run into clouds, though it is easier to go over it again before it is quite dry. As all shaded surfaces ought to have the same number of coats each, by the time the last part in an ordinary sized drawing is gone over, the first will generally be sufficiently dry for commencing on again. For such a length as six inches three lengths would be sufficient for the shade, though an adept at the work can take such lengths as six inches and more at a time. When this first coat is dry enough it should be gone over

* If any loose spec or hair appears during shading process it should be removed with the point of the penknife at once, for such little things suck up sufficient tint by capillary attraction as to leave a white mark when the tint dries. Brushes should always be laid aside as dry as possible to prevent the hairs rotting and coming out.

again broader, about an eighth of an inch more on each side of the last coat. It is better if this is done in two lengths, so as to hide any faults in the joinings of the first coat, taking care at every coat not to stop at a former joining of tint. The third time may reach to the line on shade side, over the reflected light, so that in other coats it will not be necessary to wash it off with the water-brush next to the line, the contrast between the darkest place and that next to the line being then sufficient; the tint may then start from the line of shade side, and when approaching nearly the centre of object a lighter tint must be used, by taking a little of the shading tint into another of the palette-cups and adding a little water to it.

Cylindrical objects, larger or less in diameter than that referred to, must have their breadths of tints in each coat in proportion. Round rods of such small diameter as one-eighth of an inch can hardly be shaded nicely with water so as to look effective; in these cases it is better to take a fine brush and light tint, beginning narrow and making it a little broader every new coat, without water.

For very large cylindrical objects, after being damped, it is better to have three or four gradations of tints and a brush belonging to each, beginning with the darkest, and the last pure water. By such a method the shading is less apt to get streaky, and it is better under such circumstances than dipping the tip of the colour-brush into the water every time such broad shade is gone along by way of graduating it more effectively.

Shadows should be darkest next the objects that project them, and graduated out to the extreme edge of the shadow, as the shading on any cylindrical object. A long narrow surface, to be graduated in the length, from dark at one end to light at the other, can be done with one dip of the brush of the proper size in the tint; the surface will get lighter going towards the light end as the tint recedes from the brush.

The shadow of one object should not cross the shadow of another adjacent to it, as will be sometimes observed in a room having two or more artificial lights.

Frequently in drawings, in many little details, sections, &c., shadows are put where they should not be.

If it is required to show a *sectional* plan *c d*, Fig. 301,

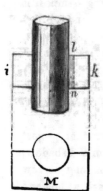

through the solid bush at *a b*, no shadow of the shaft *e* should appear at *f g*, being a *section*, and not in its natural state; but if it is a plan, as at *i k*, of the lower half bush ʍ, there ought to be a shadow of the shaft at *l n*, the half bush being complete in itself and in its natural state. A shadow should never be put on any sectional surface.

In any polished end of a shaft it gives a better effect to show the light radiated from the centre to the circumference, as at Fig. 302.

Fig. 302.   Fig. 303.

In putting in the shades of six-sided figures, such as nuts, the side 3, Fig. 303, should have two coats more than the side 2, of the same tint; 1 should not have any shading tint, the finishing colour coming over all.

If through inadvertence any part is made too dark, all the other parts must be darkened in proportion, making the

Fig. 301.

part alluded to appear lighter by comparison;* sponging

* The same applies to outline drawings within certain limits.

will then lighten it all equally. A shaded drawing should never be so dark as to render details almost invisible.

Flat Surfaces, &c.—All flat surfaces in a drawing should be darker or lighter, in proportion to their distances, the farthest being the darkest. In a front elevation these distances can be known from the plan, and in a plan from the elevation. The tint must be light, and of the same proportion of parts as the drawing is shaded with. Suppose, for example, that A, Fig. 304, is a plan of a series of steps, the side view of which is shown at B; 1, 2, and 8, are equidistant from each other, but 4 is twice as deep as any one of the others.

> In the plan 1 should have 1 coat of light tint.
>   ,, 2 ,, ,, 2 coats of do.
>   ,, 8 ,, ,, 8 ,,   do.
>   ,, 4 ,, ,, 5 ,,   do.

the fourth getting one more coat than the share it would have had, had it been equidistant from the others.

Were the object placed in the opposite direction to that shown at Fig. 304, the breadth of the shadows projected from each step would also show the comparative heights independently of the flat tints. Hence it is quite impossible to do a properly shaded view of an object having many parts in combination, unless their several distances are known. The

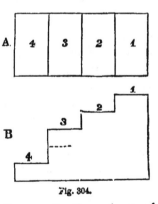

Fig. 304.

same rule holds good in elevations and other views of objects. The common way in any case is to put the tint on the furthest part first, and when it is dry, to go over it again, and take in the next nearest to the eye and so on. In going over such surfaces it is better not to begin at the same place with every new coat of tint, as the brush is very apt to leave more tint at the place begun at, so that to begin repeatedly at the same place would make it darker than the rest of the surface. The tints should come over any dark shadows that cross the flat surfaces equally with the other parts of the same surface where there are no such shadows.

If there are two views of the same object side by side, as at *b* and *a*, Fig. 305, *c* being a section, *b* being complete, and *a* having the little square part *d* removed to show structure, the corresponding parts of *a* and *b* should be exactly of the

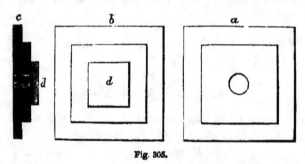

Fig. 305.

same depth of tint, as they are both supposed to be at the same distance from the eye, or in other words the same object with a part removed. The same rule applies to more intricate objects.

In putting a flat tint on a large broad surface, after being first damped, the board should be blocked up about two or three inches at one end, and the process begun with a good-sized brush at the raised end of the drawing, putting plenty of tint on and spreading it the whole breadth, keeping the front of tint as horizontal across as possible, and always taking care to stir up the tint mixture at every dip of the brush. The tint collecting in front, prevents the drying and clouding. When the surface has been gone over, and the last loose colour drawn into a corner by the colour-brush, having previously wiped any remaining colour out of it, the board should be laid down flat again to allow the tint to dry, otherwise it would run a good deal to the lower end of the board, making the surface darker at the lower than the upper end and clouding. As every flat surface, however light it is to be, is the better for having two or more coats, raise the opposite end of the board and repeat the process, beginning at opposite end of the surface, laying the board down flat immediately after each coat.

In any intricate surface to be flattened, such as framing with several diagonals, &c., where it would be impossible to keep all the different ends of the tint moving on alternately without drying, a convenient way is to have joinings at suitable places so as to allow each part to be finished separately, joining one place to another after the first is quite dry. In making such joint it is best not to have it straight across, which is more easily observed than a joint formed like saw teeth, but in angles more acute. When gone over several times and the joints thus made at different places for the several coats, and sponged when all the shading is ready for that process, if done properly, no joining can be detected.

Flat surfaces should have a little light on the top and left-hand edges (or those opposite the light) of all projecting parts. This is effected by leaving the required space when putting on the flattening tint at every operation, though the finishing colour should come to the line.

Where there are flush or level joinings as at *a* and *b*, Fig. 306, no light should be shown, as in such form it is the same as one solid. In sections, the part sectioned should have a slight tint.*

Fig. 306.

Cylindrical objects, such as columns, &c., at various distances from the eye, should have such light washes of tint all over them in proportion to their distances as will throw out those which are nearer the eye. Throwing back round

* Sectional work is also referred to further on in this chapter.

surfaces by a light tint over them is not generally adopted in mechanical drawings, though when it is done, the effect is admitted to be better.

All surfaces ought to be tinted and set back to their proper positions in distance before sponging, and should not be touched with the tint afterwards, unless for little repairs.

The accompanying shaded Tuscan order, Plate II., is given to show the ordinary depth of the darkest tints in a finished drawing, as also the depth of the flat tints relative to their degree of projection, the projections facing the observer being the same as the profile to the right.

If a drawing is to be sponged, no finishing colours or shade lines are put on before such process, and the latter only after all the tints and colours are put on. An experienced draughtsman is not supposed to use a sponge to his shadows, though the cases are rare in which the shadows are so perfect that sponging would not still farther soften them. The shaded drawings of those who are not accustomed to the process are always improved by the use of the sponge after having received five or six coats of thin tint. A beginner has difficulty in keeping to the line with his brush, and the excesses over the line are hardly ever in the same place, and as the tint is light, the sponge takes them off and softens down the legitimate shadows.

To sponge a drawing once after six or seven coats is sufficient. The surface of the paper, after the operation, generally takes the tints more easily, as it should receive two or three coats afterwards (the flat surfaces excepted). Some drawings are softened by going over them with a flat soft brush and water, before the finishing colour is put on; this requires some skill so as not to take off too much of the shading tint.

A drawing, when ready for sponging, should be quite dry, otherwise—parts thus sponged would be made much lighter. Neither should a drawing undergo the process immediately

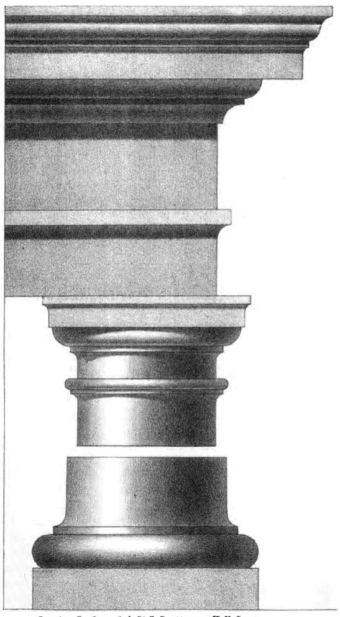

London; Lochwood & C.º 7 Stationers' Hall Court.

after being held to the fire to dry, or the first application of the sponge would, by the tint it always removes, leave a dark mark on the paper, which, drying quickly, no amount of sponging would ever take out again without injuring the surface of the paper. A drawing for the process must be dry and cold. A common tumbler is too small for the process for any sheet above eighteen inches square, a large bowl or basin, or two of either, being better, as a considerable quantity of dirty water has to be squeezed out of the sponge from the removal of tint from the drawing. Having taken the close grained 6-inch sponge and saturated it (not too fully), with water, all the *white* surface of the paper should be wetted well before going over the tinted part, so as to prevent the tint taken off by the sponge adhering to the dry white part of the sheet. The dirty water should be squeezed out, and with a fresh supply apply the sponge over all gently two or three times until scarcely any or no tint comes off, and keeping within an inch of the edge of the paper so as to preserve the gum joint. Large shadows are seldom so perfect but that they require in some places a touch of tint where they are lighter than they ought to be, and this before putting on a finishing colour over all. When the tint is put on in the way of repairing—it should be perfectly dry before being touched again, as when moist it looks always darker.

In such instances, when the paper takes a considerable time to dry—as in winter, a want of patience may prompt the draughtsman to apply a hot iron within a short distance of the drawing, a plan frequently resorted to in drawing-offices for drying a drawing quickly, when not intended to be highly finished; but neither that, nor the common prac-tice of holding a drawing over gas-light, in the absence of a fire, is to be recommended. A better way is to heat a sheet of drawing paper at either the fire or the gas and hold it sufficiently distant from the drawing so as to dry it without injuring it, though in all cases it is best, when circumstances will permit, to let a moist drawing dry naturally. Holding a drawing to the fire, if the paper has been properly stretched at first, is very apt to split it.

A stretched sheet of paper on a board having a drawing on it occupying a small part of the paper just damped with the shading, if held to the fire for the purpose of drying it quickly, is apt both to crease the sheet and split it.

For finishing colours or tints for malleable and cast iron, brass, copper, wood, &c., a great deal depends on the taste of the individual. In engines, and machinery, some prefer them washed all over with thin neutral tint, blue predominating in greater proportion. For malleable iron, the tint referred to is always used, but for cast iron there should be more lake in it, having more of the hue of writing ink. For any round or cylindrical object it is better to shade with the finishing tint once or twice over, it blends better with both shading and finishing tints when the drawing is finished. Green is sometimes used for cast iron, assimilating it to the paint on the machine it is intended to represent; a locomotive boiler, for instance, in a pictorial drawing is generally made the colour of the thing itself. In all such cases it should be a yellowish green, which, when put on above the neutral shading tint, having blue in it, makes the proper green. In all such cases the finishing colour must be well watered, even if necessary to go over it twice, which indeed in most cases is better, as it tends to equalize inequalities. Dirty green colour, on a ground shaded with pure Indian ink, as is sometimes the case, never looks well and ought to be avoided.

In iron work in a drawing intended to be a picture, such as the outside view of a boiler where the iron is generally painted red, the drawing should show that colour also. The finishing tint for red over all should be composed of lake, gamboge, and carmine. Blue as a finishing tint for such purposes is very well, in certain drawings only, for the representative colour of iron.

Light red, or as it is sometimes called Indian red, is used

more for mixing up with other colours such as for wood, brass, &c., than for use by itself.

Finishing Tints.—The finishing tint for *brass* is composed of gamboge, yellow ochre, and light red; for *wood*, of gamboge, yellow ochre, and a little burnt umber; for *copper*, of gamboge, yellow ochre, burnt umber, and lake (the latter predominating).

The finishing tint for *stone* seems to vary with the ideas of the individual, though a very good tint is composed of gamboge, light red, and burnt umber.

Finishing tints should never be mixed up at night, as by artificial light it is difficult to judge of them properly, especially yellows and greens. Such colours, if to be used at night, should be made ready in daylight.

Many coats of a chalky finishing tint over a shadow should be avoided, as it will lighten the shadow; and in any coloured drawing to be stretched on cloth for framing no chalky tints, such as indigo in iron plate sections, or shade lines, should be put on till after it is stretched, and if to be varnished, not until after the drawing is sized.

When wood work occurs, as it frequently does in engineering drawings, the best way for graining the side of fir or other soft wood is by using the colour for such a purpose (before referred to) and washing off the edge with water-brush as at A, Fig. 307; for oak with the drawing pen as at B.

Fig. 307.

The latter requires more practice to do it effectively than the former. In a drawing that is to be sponged the graining or any finishing colours or shade lines should never be put on previously. In end wood the ink compasses * are generally used for the circular work as shown at A, Fig. 308, with its colour (light red, called Indian red, or sienna).

Another effect is produced by doing these circles by hand with the brush, and shading one side off as at B, and showing a few radiated *shakes* from the centre; in either system both the side view of wood as well as the end views should have a coat of wood colour previously to graining. To distinguish a brass section from wood, of course the different yellow colour would so far assist, but in the former case the sectional lines should be straight and diagonal.

Fig. 308.

In some pictorial drawings for framing a very slight wash of thin gum or isinglass is put on the dark places, to bring out the effect; but this is very seldom resorted to; there ought to be effect enough without it.

Sections.—In cross sections not to be crossed with diagonal lines, light tint should be put on, and it should be the lightest part of any flat surface in the drawing; the light should be left at the edge, as explained for other projecting flat surfaces, the finishing colour coming over all. If to be crossed with diagonal lines they ought never to be so with Indian ink on a coloured drawing, but with bluish tint for iron, and yellowish for brass, and after all sponging, and before any shade lines. Even in a section to be crossed with diagonal lines, it is more effective to give a light wash all over first with blue for iron, and yellow for brass, but no other tint previously, as in the other instance. Crossing with diagonal lines is always difficult for a beginner; when not equidistant they destroy the look of the drawing. The other process, under such circumstances, is the better way.

* See remarks on spring bows, Chapter XIV., Fig. 217.

For drawings having sections of iron plates, if less than to a scale of ⅜-inch to a foot, the section of the plates or angle iron on a darkly shaded ground should be drawn in with indigo, or Prussian blue and flake white, after all the finishing colour is put on ; Indian ink never shows well, being of a glossy nature. In drawings to a larger scale the sections of iron plates are composed of two lines for the thickness, and should be filled up with light Prussian blue.

After all the colouring of a drawing is finished, if to be shade lined (which in most cases improves a drawing, the thick line taking off any little roughness left from the shading at lines at shade side, and on which side they always come), the circles, as in outline inking (Chapter XIV.), must be put in before the lines. (For border line, margin, and printing, see Chapter XVII.)

A shaded drawing should never be rubbed with India-rubber. Stale bread a day old is the best thing to rub the white part of the paper with, the crumbs of which, if not too dry, may be gently rubbed over the shaded part if it shows the least dirty.

If it is wished to give an uncoloured drawing the appearance of a shaded engraving, by fine lines (which can only be done after much practice), the flats should have a light tint of Indian ink, the rounds shaded also as in shaded drawings, but only with one coat of the thin tint referred to ; the shadows should then be ruled in by lines above the tint, with the drawing pen in the best possible condition. It will have a better effect than by simply being ruled without the tint.

In shading or colouring an outline engraving, unless it is printed on drawing paper, it must have a thin coating of size (isinglass) over it, otherwise the effect will be much the same as attempting to shade on ordinary blotting paper. The shading on paper prepared with size cannot be sponged. (For cutting off a finished drawing see Chapter XXIII.)

CHAPTER XVII.

PRINTING AND BORDER LINES.

THE plainer the printing appears on any drawing the better, and lettering such as A B C is admitted for common engineering purposes to be the best, as it is certainly of a form quickly made. The same form of lettering in outline looks well if properly done, but it is found that beginners generally manage the above better. In this work it is as well not to accustom one's self to the T-square and ink bows, as a stiffness results, which in print of the size in example given should be avoided; though for letters half an inch wide, either in outline or filled in with black or colour, the square and compasses are requisite. The style which can be done *most* quickly for drawings to be completed hastily, is somewhat similar to that first alluded to, but inclined thus

A B C Here, should any letter not be inclined exactly at the correct angle, the difference is not so easily detected as would be with the vertical letters. Set squares, as in subjoined diagram, may be used with advantage for the formation of the letters indicated on it for vertical print, having four angles on one side, as shown; any of which may also be used for ruling for inclined print. They cost about 1s. each, or 2s. 6d. for a set of three. The ordinary way of using them is by placing them against the T-square.

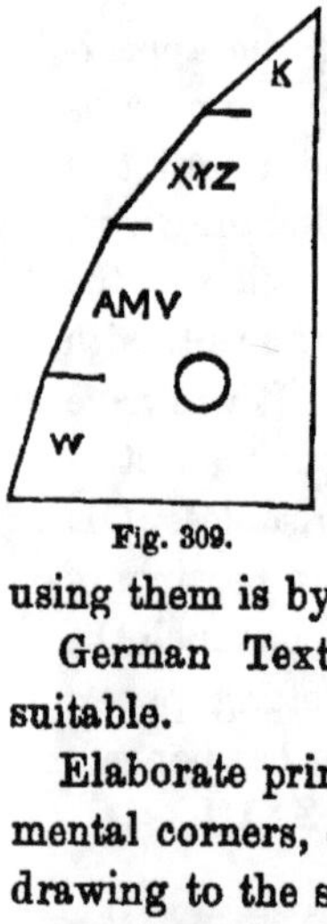

Fig. 309.

German Text or Old English, when done nicely, is suitable.

Elaborate printing and belaboured border lines with ornamental corners, divert the attention of the observer from the drawing to the surroundings; though it is admitted, at the same time, that indifferent print, or a thick black border line like a *mourning card*, on a good drawing, completely destroys the look of the drawing.

Where there are to be two or three lines of print under each other on a drawing, the easiest way of dividing off the lettering is to take a slip of writing-paper, draw a line at a distance from the edge equal to the size of the letters, then by hand—sketch in this space all the words that belong to one line ; take the half of the length of the lettering on the slip, and put a central mark on the edge.   Apply the edge of the slip with the sketched letters to the lower line for print on the drawing, having a centre line upon which to place the central mark of print on slip, and sketch in between the print lines every letter, opposite the corresponding letter on the slip, and so on with every fresh line of print.   This will be found a much better way than counting the letters in a line and dividing on each side of the centre line for the number of letters ; in this way there is always trouble with such letters as W's and I's not occupying the equal spaces.   Even with half-inch letters it is easier to print them on the edge of a slip of paper of their proper size, and finding the half of whole length, apply the centre of slip to centre line of printing on the drawing.

Each letter is drawn in correctly with the pencil previous to inking-in.   Where there is more than one line of print, the space between should not be less than between the lines containing the letters.

It is a question of taste and convenience where to place the printing on a drawing.   In a coloured picture of machinery to be framed, embracing several views—if each view is to have its special name of side elevation, &c.—the print should not be heavy looking ; though it is thought preferable only to state simply the sort of engine (if such) and its horse-power, under the lower border line, and between *it* and the edge of the frame line.

As a guide for printing letters of proper form, the following examples will always be found useful for reference :—

No. 1.

A B C D E F G H I J K L M N O P Q
R S T U V W X Y Z
1 2 3 4 5 6 7 8 9 0

*A B C D E F G H I J K L M N O P
Q R S T U V W X Y Z
1 2 3 4 5 6 7 8 9 0*

No. 2.

A B C D E F G H I J K L M N O P Q R
S T U V W X Y Z

A B C D E F G H I J K L M N
O P Q R S T U V W X Y Z

*a b c d e f g h i j k l m n o p q r
s t u v w x y z*

No. 3.

A B C D E F G H I J
K L M N O P Q R S
T U V W X Y Z

abcdefghijklmnopqrst
ubwxyz

No. 4.

ABCDEFGHIJKL
MNOPQRSTUVW
XYZ

abcdefghijklmnopqr
stuvwxyz

Stencilling the print on drawings with the thin copper-plate and hard brush is convenient when a drawing is required hastily; but, if not touched up afterwards, never looks equal to print carefully executed by hand.

The following is the price of stencil plates having letters similar to the examples given and correspondingly numbered 1, 2, 3. 4 :—

HEIGHT OF LETTERS	⅛ IN.	¼ IN.	⅜ IN.	½ IN.	⅝ IN.	¾ IN.
	s. d.	s. d.	s. d.	s. d.	s. d.	s. d.
No. 1 Alphabet, plain block..........	4 0	4 0	4 6	5 6	6 0	6 6
Do. Letters in words, per dozen	1 0	1 6	2 0	2 0	2 0	2 6
No. 2 Alphabet	4 6	4 6	5 0	6 0	6 0	7 0
Do. Letters in words, per dozen	2 0	2 0	2 0	2 0	2 0	2 6
No. 3 and 4 Alphabet, German Text or Old English...................		5 0	6 0	7 0		
Do. Letters in words, per dozen	2 6	2 6	3 0	3 0		

In regard to border lines for ordinary plain drawings, one single fine line, finished square, or rounded at the corners, and at such a distance from the edge of the paper as has been already elsewhere referred to, always looks well. Bor-

L 3

dering pens for drawing thick lines, if so required, will be found described in Chapter IV.

A drawing highly finished and coloured may have a border line composed of two fine lines one-sixteenth of an inch apart, with the upper corners rounded, either quadrant, or a parabolic curve, and the lower corners square, and these double lines filled in with gold size, or with light red, or burnt umber; either of which slightly mixed with Indian-ink has a good effect. Two or three coats should be put on thin, or the top and left-hand border lines (or those corresponding to the direction of the light for the shadows in the drawing) may be shaded with light Indian-ink, after which, going all over with the tints referred to will give the drawing that recessed appearance in which pictures are frequently mounted. When border lines, as those described, surround a drawing, the print looks better when of the same colour, and of a thickness corresponding to the border line; such print being first pencilled-in in outline and then filled in with the colour.

CHAPTER XVIII.

DELINEATION OF SCREW-PROPELLER SLIP AND PATH.

To delineate screw slip.

Having ascertained the speed of the vessel in miles per hour, or feet per minute, and the number of revolutions the

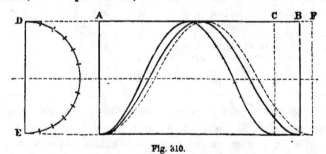

Fig. 310.

screw makes in the same time, it can then be easily deduced

how many feet the vessel passes
through during one revolution of
screw; which distance set off to a
convenient scale, at A C, Fig. 310,
making that a pitch in which to
draw the actual curve made by
the screw. Set off the distance
A B equal to the real pitch of the
screw; the difference between the
screw as working in a solid A B,
and compressed to the distance A C
by the friction of the vessel passing through the water, is the slip,
equal to C B or positive slip. Occasionally there are instances when
the given speed of ship and screw
show negative slip, as at A F. The
difference between the actual pitch
of screw and speed of vessel being
B F, and as also indicated by the
dotted curved line. The half diameter on D E is common to each
pitch—A C, A B, and A F; the curves
are drawn by the same process
as that described in Chapter XIII,
Fig. 204.

Figs. 311, 312, and 313, are
the delineations of the paths of
screws having two, three, and four
blades respectively.

The pitch, diameter, and speeds
shown, are the same for all the
diagrams, to delineate which requires only a little cardboard mould
having a curve equal to one-quarter
of revolution (as *a b c*, Fig. 311).
The curve is found by laying it off

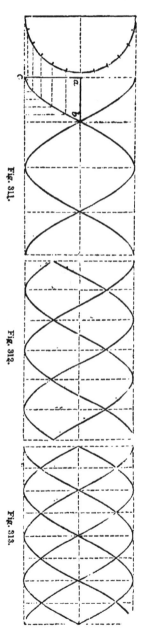

Fig. 311.

Fig. 312.

Fig. 313.

correctly in the first instance, as in Chapter XIII., Fig. 204. The respective centre lines are set off in position as indicated by the vertical dotted lines.

NOTE.—In finding the curves for these diagrams (Figs. 311, 312, and 313) it is better, so as to prevent confusion, to lay each path curve down separately, and then transfer each to the one diagram, where they are intended to be, by tracing.

CHAPTER XIX.

DELINEATION OF PADDLE-WHEEL SLIP AND PATH.

To delineate the cycloidal curve, or path of a paddle-wheel; the speed of the ship and rate of revolution of the paddle-wheel being given.

Let A B, Fig. 314, be the distance travelled by the ship in one revolution of the wheel, and A O the diameter, the wheel

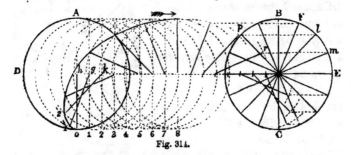

Fig. 314.

having sixteen arms or floats, which will be used in making the diagram—to render the process more easily understood. Divide A B into the same number of equal parts, in this instance, as there are arms in the wheel; and draw vertical lines, 1, 2, 3, 4, &c., through these points; on each of the points on the centre line D E, where the vertical lines intersect it, and with a radius equal to half diameter of wheel describe the dotted circles as shown. In each circle the one arm is drawn as advanced a sixteenth of a revolution upon its previous position. Suppose the float to start from its vertical position at the lowest point o ; take a sixteenth of the circumference of wheel (the distance between two floats B F), in the compasses, and on the circumference of the second circle from 1—set off to the left—the point 1', and join g 1', which will be the position of the arm when the paddle has advanced a sixteenth, or from h to g. Next, from vertical line at 2 set off the same distance twice on circumference to the left as from 2 to 2', and join k 2, which will be the position of the arm when the paddle has advanced two-sixteenths (or from h to k), and so on until the half, or 8, is reached ; a line passing through the points will give the curve of half a revolution of wheel, the other half of curve being similar. Another method of finding the points for the curve is shown for the half to the right. Draw the horizontal lines from the points l m, &c., where the several arms cut the circumference of the wheel to their respective radii p, r, &c., and the intersections are the points through which to draw the half of the curve. If a part of the curve is repeated at the lower part, as in Fig. 315, it shows the slip of the float during immersion.

In drawing the curve of a paddle having revolving floats, the process is somewhat similar. Having drawn the requisite number of circles, as in Fig. 314 (one for each float), with their centres at equal distances apart, the distance between the centres of the first and last

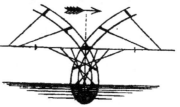

Fig. 315.

being equal to the distance the vessel travels during one revolution of wheel; also a temporary side view of the wheel, with its floats in position, each float is transferred to its own circle at the same angle and on the same level as its representative in the side view of the wheel.

The curve is drawn in with the moulds referred to in Chapter IV.

CHAPTER XX.

TRACING.

IF a drawing intended to be shaded is to be traced, the tracing should, if possible, be done first, as it is most difficult to see the lines on a shaded drawing through common tracing paper. However, shaded drawings have frequently to be traced, and for these the tracing-paper should have more than the ordinary proportion of oil in it, or engravers' tracing-paper should be used, though in such cases the oily tracing-paper is likely to make the original drawing oily, sometimes so much so as to alter its appearance. For a tracing simply to be outlined, the common way is to fasten the tracing-paper above the drawing round the edge with brass pins, the tracing-paper being large enough (especially if it is above a valuable drawing) to allow the pins to be clear of the original drawing. When a sheet of tracing-paper is not large enough to allow of this, and only an out-line tracing is required, then little strips of thin paper with one edge gummed on the tracing paper, and the other end on the board beyond the edge of the drawing, may be used, and placed about 6 inches apart. As weights on the corners come very much in the way of the square, the only other common way is to pin the tracing, and when it is removed the pin holes can be easily effaced from the drawing by turning it upside down and squeezing the projecting edge of the hole with the top of a pencil or ink-bows. Referring to such trifling matters may appear to be going too much into detail, but these little matters are of daily occurrence in most drawing offices.

In tracing at any time from another tracing both should be placed above a sheet of drawing-paper, the lines will then be better observed. In all the particulars of lining the same rules should be observed in regard to drawing circles before lines, &c., as is described in Chapter XIV.

As the breath affects unstretched tracing-paper while tracing, it is the more correct way to entirely finish both circles and lines within a small area at a time, as if all the circles were put in first (as in a drawing) many of them would be out of position before the lines could be drawn.

If a tracing is to be coloured it must be stretched, or it would never lie flat after being moistened; and if it is to undergo the colouring process after outlining before being removed from the original drawing underneath it—the tracing-paper must exceed the size of the drawing all round, sufficiently so, that when cut off it is cut clear of the drawing underneath it.

In an unstretched tracing to be coloured hastily, and for which process there is not sufficient time for stretching, weights placed close to and around any part immediately after the colouring is put on greatly lessens the buckling up as it becomes dry.

If a tracing is to be mounted it is unnecessary to stretch it before colouring, and even for colouring it can be done more easily after than before it is mounted.

In the stretching process, before gumming down, the sponge cannot be used, but if a clean sheet of any sort of white paper is laid over the tracing-paper and a sponge applied to the top side of the former, enough of moisture will be found to go through the upper paper in a few seconds to stretch the tracing-paper sufficiently. Sometimes merely to breathe on a small sheet of tracing-paper will be found equally effective.

In composition of tints, and shading, and colouring, the same rules as described at Chapter XVI. are applicable.

In colouring tracing-cloth it presents a more satisfactory looking front if the outline is turned upside down and the shading and colouring put on the back; the shaded side, at the best, is never very satisfactory, but there is produced a regular appearance on the right side. Tracing-cloth, although not damped, should be gummed to the board in the same

way as tracing-paper, and the tighter it is put down previously by brass pins the less liable it will be to buckle up
after being coloured upon.   The tints should be put on more
sparingly at a time than on drawing-paper.*

In joining sheets of tracing-paper the joint should not be
more than a quarter of an inch broad, and the gum should
be nearly as thin as water for this purpose.   Whenever the
joining is made the joined sheet should be rolled upon a
roller, and with the joining in a line with the roller; a strip
of drawing-paper should be placed on each side of the joint
until quite dry, when the joining will be found straight and
smooth.   Tracing-paper, or tracing-cloth, after being drawn
upon, is frequently mounted on thick calico when required
for constant reference; in which case it is better to first
mount the tracing on white paper and then paste the calico
on the back of the thicker paper.   Tracing-paper is first
stretched on a board by being damped and gummed down
at the edge all round; the white paper to which the tracing
is to be permanently attached having a thin coating of paste
is then turned over on the tracing (which should be perfectly
dry) and rubbed quickly all over the back; when completely
dry it is cut off as described in Chapter XXIII.

CHAPTER XXI.

DRAWINGS FOR ENGRAVINGS AND PHOTOGRAPHS.

A SHADED drawing to be engraved from should be traced,
when in outline only, with a fine-pointed pencil, not too
hard, and the tracing applied by the engraver to the copper
or steel plate upon which the engraving is to be made.   The
engraver prefers the tracing, if he cannot have the drawing
in outline before it is shaded.   Frequently the engraver pencils
the lines of shaded drawings over with a fine-pointed pencil,

---

* Some tracing-cloth will take the colour better if the part to be
coloured has a rub with hard chalk.

preferring that to tracing it himself; and such drawing when placed on the waxed surface of the metal plate, and well rubbed on the back to transfer the pencil lines to the wax surface, invariably soils it; but if traced—all the hard outlines of shadows should be dotted only by the pencil; and to preserve the shaded drawing it should be put on a board of the exact size, with a glass to fit, and pasted with paper all round the edge to keep it in its place. This, with the tracing, is all the engraver requires. The shaded drawing, as well as the tracing, is wanted to guide the engraver in copying the shadows generally. When only an outline engraving with shade lines is required the engraver need not have the drawing at all, if the pencil tracing has a mark on the lines that are to be shade lines. A dot in red ink on each of such lines is sufficient, as such mark is also transferred to the wax surface on the plate. Another way is to give the outline of a drawing (which is to have shadows on the finished engraving), with the required shadows dotted in; an engraved dry proof on drawing-paper of the plate in outline can then be given to the draughtsman to fill in with the shadows, and covered up by glass as before stated.

A scale should always be made with the engraving or lithograph, instead of saying (either on the plate or in any accompanying letterpress) that it is drawn to any particular scale. The reason is, that though the metal plate, or the stone, or the wood may have the correct size of the drawing on it, yet the paper just before receiving the impression is damped, and consequently expands. On a length of—say 2 feet the error will be $\frac{1}{4}$ or $\frac{3}{8}$th of an inch, a difference which means 2 or 3 feet in a drawing made to $\frac{1}{8}$th of an inch to a foot, and rendering it of no use. It is seldom any two engravings from the same plate are exactly of the same size, depending entirely on the degree of moisture in the paper at the time of printing from the plate; no engraving is ever of the same size as the original drawing unless printed on dry paper, a process at once unsatisfactory.

It is sometimes the practice when a drawing has to be reduced for engraving, or other purposes, to use photography; if the drawing is not too large this may be done satisfactorily enough, but beyond a certain size—to reduce it by hand is more correct. In reduced photographs of a large drawing the parallel lines of the latter converge in the former for the reason explained in perspective. Photography is also useful for enlarging within certain limits small intricate drawings. Drawings whose lines are in representative colours,* when photographed, never produce (for optical reasons) satisfactory results; blue colour, for instance, shows indistinctly, and yellow surfaces in shaded drawings come out very dark, to the disappointment of those inexperienced in the process. A drawing made for the purpose of being reduced by the process referred to should have all its lines (if an outline drawing) and shadows (if a shaded drawing) of indian-ink only.

CHAPTER XXII.

DRAWINGS FOR LECTURES.

In large illustrative drawings for lectures, too large to make on an ordinary drawing table, the best way is to tack the paper on the wall of a room, and use a line and plummet for the vertical lines and a straight-edge with spirit level for the horizontal lines. One good base line being made, the others can be made by measuring up from it at two points in the length, or a straight-edge may be nailed along the bottom of the paper and the flat stocked square, described at Fig. 14, Chapter III., used for the vertical lines. The lines on such drawings to be visible, ought to be at least $\frac{1}{16}$ of an inch thick, for which two pencil lines should be made and the space between filled up with the ink; and if a coloured illustration, should not be inked in till after the colouring, or after

* As in office drawings for reference (Chapter XIV.).

the sizing process before varnishing, otherwise the thick black lines would be apt to run. If for only an outline, common writing ink does as well as Indian ink for the purpose. If it is to be coloured it must be taken down and laid flat on a table, and if the table is not large enough to contain all the drawing, the drawing must be unrolled in such quantity at a time as will suit the size of board or table. Should the paper *buckle up* by the moisture in colouring (not being a stretched drawing) it is of very little consequence for the use it is to be put to. When large quantities of fluid colour are necessary, it will be found convenient, rather than continually rubbing down, to melt down a shilling cake or cakes of colour largely used, such as Prussian blue, or yellow, in a wide-necked phial containing eight cubic inches of water to the cake. The phial containing this diluted colour should be kept corked up when not in use, a little being taken out by the brush when required and diluted in water according to the depth of tint required.

Besides the ordinary way of shading these drawings (referred to in chapter on Shading), it is effective, for such as are to be viewed from a distance, to shade the rounds with lines of Indian ink as in an engraving, put on after the finishing colour, and if to be varnished, after the sizing process and before varnishing. Another way of shading the rounds is by using a neutral tint (as for iron work) without shading off with water as in ordinary drawings, putting on the tint broader every time, the central darkest place being put on first, and diluting the tint as it gets nearer the centre o the round object. A round when shaded thus, when observed closely, appears like a figure of many sides, but at a distance this is not observable.

Large illustrations can also be effectively done in oil colour, by sizing the paper, after the lining process by pencil or fine Indian ink lines. (For large sized brushes for these purposes, and their cost, see Chapter VI.)

CHAPTER XXIII.

CUTTING OFF A DRAWING.

BEFORE cutting off a stretched sheet care should be taken to observe that it is perfectly dry, for if cut off with parts of the surface a little damp it will never lie quite flat.

In cutting off a sheet which has been properly expanded before being gummed down at the edge, if the following rule is not observed, there is a risk of tearing out a piece from *one* corner of the sheet.

The opposite sides should never be cut first, for if so cut, upon nearly completing the cutting of the third side, the paper undergoes contraction, and the fourth side pulling against it, is apt to snap off the remaining inch or so, and generally in towards the sheet, seldom in the margin on the outside of the cutting off line. The sheet should be cut off all round, taking care, by applying the knife blade under the edge of the sheet, that it is free from the board before proceeding to cut off the side or end adjoining. When the knife is applied—it is better to cut by the line made at first for that purpose, without using the T-square or a wood straight-edge, the edges of either being apt to get cut from the process. A metallic straight-edge may, however, be used with advantage.

When the sheet is removed the strips of drawing paper which are left on the board should be simply sponged over two or three times, and they will peel off easily. It is better also to let the gum of the joint remain on the board to assist in the adhesion of the joint of the next sheet to be stretched, if of the same size as that cut off.

If, in a stretched sheet, it is found that only a portion is required for the drawing to be cut off, the remaining part of the paper being still required for another drawing, and requiring its tension ; rather than damp the remainder and fix the loose side, it is better to make a few incisions across, as at *c*, Fig. 316,

before the drawing, say on side at *b* is cut off, and having gummed and pinned down these at *c*, and let them dry, proceed to cut and gum the intermediate spaces *d* which will keep the remaining portion of paper *a* as tight as before while freeing the part *b* from the board.

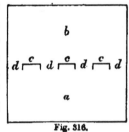

Fig. 316.

CHAPTER XXIV.

SUNDRY NOTES.

WHEN a drawing is cut off it is better to keep it flat in a drawer for the purpose, or in a portfolio, than rolled up, unless for exportation. Japanned tin cases are to be had for rolled drawings, and at the following prices: 80 inch 6s., 42 inch 7s. 6d., 54 inch 10s.

A common substitute for string for a rolled drawing, and one less likely to crease the drawing, is made as follows :— Take a strip of drawing paper from 1¼ to 2 inches broad and an inch longer than the circumference of the rolled drawing. About half an inch from each end, make incisions—at one end in the middle, and one-third of breadth across ; at the other end at the sides, each one-third across ; fold in the sides so that they may pass through the opening at the opposite end of the strip, and on being opened again after they have passed through, the whole will present a hoop, which, when slipped over the drawing, will keep it secure.

Should a fir drawing board get accidentally dented, within certain limits an application of water to the part will bring it up to its proper level.

Should a drawing get a grease spot, it can be very nearly removed (at least so far as to be hardly visible) by the application of a hot smoothing iron on clean blotting paper placed over the spot, but not sufficiently to be coloured over.

APPENDIX.

———

THE several matters contained in the following Appendix will be found useful for reference; they are so closely connected with the subject of the book as to render some mention of them necessary.

APPENDIX.

PART I.

ARCHITECTURAL ORDERS IN ENGINEERING.

THE following examples and description of the architectural orders, referred to in Chapter XIII., will be found useful, as giving the proportions of those most frequently adopted in engineering, namely, the Tuscan, Grecian, and Roman Doric orders. An example of each, Plates III., IV., and V., is given, drawn to a scale, with the proper proportions in the vertical spaces at the left hand side coinciding with the architectural scale of minutes on drawing (though an ordinary scale of feet and inches may be applied to these drawings, and the proportions will still be preserved). It may be as well to remark that the projections in front of the observer are the same as the projecting profile to the right, and the projections marked in figures are from the dotted line running through the centre of column, upwards. The shaft of a column is never cylindrical, that is, of equal diameter throughout, being always tapered to a certain extent towards the upper end. The degree of tapering is called the diminution of the shaft, and ranges between one-fourth and one-sixth of the diameter at the bottom of shaft.

TUSCAN ORDER.—The total height of the Tuscan order, Plate III., is divided into five equal parts; four of them are given to the column and the other part to the entablature. The column is seven diameters high, and is shorter in proportion to its diameter than any other of the orders. The capital is a semi-diameter high; the base with the lower cincture of the shaft is also half a diameter. The entablature, one-fourth

M

of the column, is one-and-three-quarters diameters high ; it is divided in the same proportion as the other Roman orders, two-fifths of its height being given to the cornice, and the other three-fifths divided equally between the architrave and frieze. The projection of the cornice over the vertical faces of the inferior members is equal to its height.

GRECIAN DORIC ORDER.—The following are the average proportions for the members of the order, Plate IV. Taking the diameter at the bottom of the shaft as the unit of measurement, the column is six diameters in height. The diameter at the upper end of the shaft is three-fourths of a diameter—that is, the shaft diminishes one-fourth of the diameter. The height of the capital is half a diameter. The height of the entablature is one-third of that of the column, or two diameters. The surface of the shaft is usually worked into twenty very flat flutes, meeting each other at an edge.

ROMAN DORIC ORDER.—Dividing the whole height of the order, Plate V., into five equal parts, one of these is given to the entablature, the height of which is therefore one-fourth of that of the column. The column tapers one-sixth throughout the shaft, and is eight diameters high, of which one diameter is distributed equally between the capital and the base. When fluted, the flutes are separated by fillets. The entablature is two diameters in height, and divided into eight equal parts; these are distributed among the cornice, the frieze, and the architrave according to the numbers 3, 3, and 2.

PART II.

VOLUTE.

To describe a Volute: given—the number of revolutions or quarters of which the spiral is to consist, the vertical height of the spiral, and the diameter of the eye.

Let A B, Plate VI., Fig. 1, be the height of the volute, and let

Base 27   Shut 6 hrans. 5 minutes.   Carriat

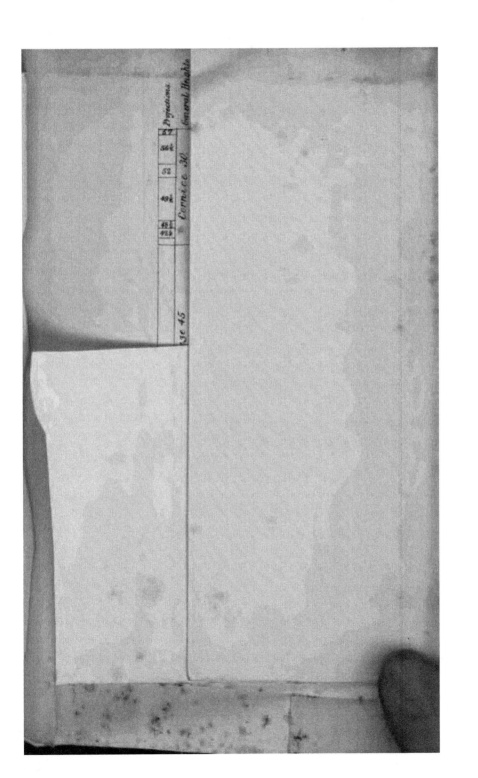

						Projections
17	56½	52	49½	48½ 43½		General Breadth

Cornice 30

Size 45

Projections. General Heights. Particular Hts.

Cornice 45.

Frieze 45.

Plate VI.

Fig. 2.

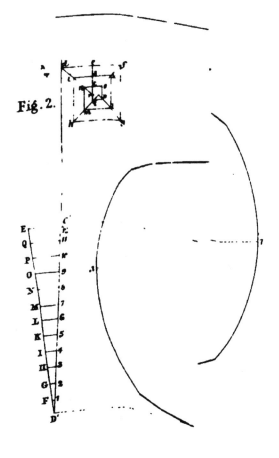

London

the spiral make three revolutions, consisting, therefore, of
twelve quarters; bisect A B at the point o, and from A B cut off
A D, equal to the given radius of the eye; divide D o into as
many equal parts as there are quarter revolutions in the spiral
to be drawn (which in this case are twelve in number) at the
points 1, 2, 3 .... 11, 12. To prevent confusion, this division is indicated upon a parallel line D′ o′; draw o′ E at any
angle with o′ D′, and make it equal to two of these parts;
join D′ E, and from the points 1, 2, 3 .... draw straight
lines 1 F, 2 G, 3 H .... parallel to o′ E; taking o d equal to
one part, draw d f perpendicular to A B, and equal to 12 E;
draw f g perpendicular to d f, and equal to 11 Q; draw again
g h perpendicular to f g, and equal to 10 P. Proceed in this
manner until all the sides are drawn; then, the points
d, f, g .... p, q, r, so found, are the centres from which the
quadrants which compose the spiral must be successively
described. For this purpose, produce d f to 1, f g to 2, g h
to 3, and so on; the quadrants, as they are described, will
be limited by these lines; from the centre d, with the radius
d B, describe the quadrant B 1; from the centre f, with the
radius f 1, describe the quadrant 1, 2; from g, with the
radius g 2, describe in like manner the quadrant 2, 3; proceed
in this way till the last arc, 11, 12, is described from the
centre q, with the radius q 11; then, finally, describe the
circle at the centre from the point r, and with the radius
r 12. If the operation be accurately performed, this radius
r 12 will be equal to A D, as required, and the spiral will be
completed.

But, as the process, as it is now described, is very liable
to inaccuracy, the method of finding the centres shown on a
larger scale at Fig. 2, is at once more expeditious and more
certain. Having drawn d f perpendicular to the vertical
line, bisect it at e; draw e r perpendicular to d f, equal to
d e or e f, and join d r and f r; divide e r into three equal
parts, e s, s t, t r, and draw i s k and n t o parallel to d f; draw
f g perpendicular to d f, and equal to 11 Q; draw g h and i h

respectively parallel and perpendicular to df, meeting at the point h; draw the diagonals gp and hq parallel to dr and fr, and draw the perpendiculars kl, op, rq, nm. In this way all the centres are determined, namely $d, f, g, h, \ldots$ o, p, q, r.

To describe a second spiral, which, with the first one, shall include the thickness of the hem, a similar process is applicable. Set off B R for the thickness of the hem at that part, and, supposing the hem to diminish in thickness equally for each half revolution, divide B R into six equal parts. As the spiral describes six half revolutions, it will diminish in thickness one-sixth of B R for each half revolution; set off, therefore, A s equal to five-sixths of B R, then R s is the heigh of the second spiral. Bisect B s at T, and set off s v equal to the radius of the eye; divide T v into twelve equal parts, and the method already described for finding the centres may be applied.

PART III.

EXPLANATION OF A SHIP DESIGN.

A SHIP's design, commonly called a ship's *lines*, is generally composed of three views, as shown in subjoined diagram, Fig. 817, namely:—

> The Profile, or sheer draught A.
> Half Breadth Plan B.
> And the Body Plan C.

These are always drawn together, and to the same scale, which is generally one-fourth or one-eighth inch to one foot;* and with the bow of the vessel invariably to the right-hand side, the half-breadth plan B always immediately below the profile, and the body plan C to the left of the profile.

As both sides of the drawing would be alike, one side, or one-half, is quite sufficient in both the half-breadth and the

* For the form of scale on ships designs, see Chapter V., Fig 21.

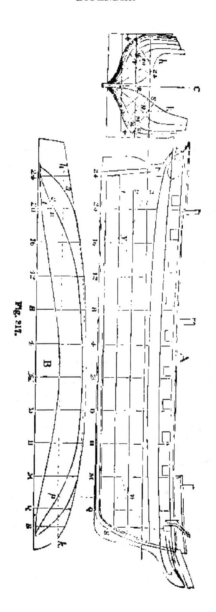

Fig. 217.

body plan ; the midship section being the same on each side
of the latter, one midship section is drawn, common to both
sides—the right-hand space containing the bow end view,
or fore-body, and the left the stern end view, or after-body,
each as seen from amidships. The profile A shows the general
contour of the vessel, in other words, the side elevation,
together with any carving, figure-head, ports, and other
openings in, and projections from, the ship's side, the stations of masts, &c. It is the part of the design which especially helps a person to realise what the ship's appearance
will be when built.

The vertical lines are sectional, and are generally placed
where the moulding edge of a frame or rib is to be, omitting
one or more between each vertical in the drawing. The one
at the broadest part of the vesel, or midship section, is distinguished by the conventional mark or sign $\oplus$ underneath
it, and to prevent confusion in the corresponding sections
(which will be presently explained) in body plan, these vertical sectional lines are usually marked alphabetically from
midships to the bow with capital letters, and, when these are
exhausted, by italics. The vertical lines towards the stern
from midships are usually distinguished by numerals ; but
sometimes numerals are used throughout the length, beginning at the bow. If a part of the vessel amidships is parallel
and has two or more frames or sections alike, these are
commonly distinguished by repeating the same letter or
numeral within parentheses. If the vertical section is where
every second frame is to be in the ship, the first vertical in
the drawing from midships aft would be marked 2, showing
that a 1 (frame) has to be placed between midships and 2,
in the construction of the ship. The same rule is observed
in proceeding forward from midships ; if every second frame
only is indicated by the verticals, the first letter from midships would be marked B, showing that between midships
and B another frame A is to be placed in the ship.

The longitudinal lines parallel to the lowest horizontal

line are called *water lines*, and named first, second, third, &c.,
placed two or three feet apart, the top line being the load-
water line ; it is frequently made stronger than the others.
When the lower line, or keel, is not parallel to the load-water
line, the intermediate lines, 1, 2, &c., would, in most cases,
be drawn parallel to that line ; if drawn parallel to the keel,
they are known as "level" lines. These water lines are
simply to indicate the position of the horizontal sections,
plans of which are given in the half-breadth plan B, below
the sheer draught A. The dotted curve line on side view (of
which there are generally more than one) forward of midships is named bow-line, and aft of midships buttock-line. It
represents the section of the ship made by the vertical
longitudinal plane of which *h k* shows the position in the half
breadth.

The half-breadth plan B shows the exterior plan of vessel
and the plan of the water lines, which are in this view
curves. The widths from the centre line to these correspond,
of course, to the positions of such sections, 1, 2, 3, &c., in side
view A, and body plan C. The longitudinal dotted line *h k*
gives, as has been said, the position of the bow and buttock-
lines, which, in the profile A, are represented by the curved
dotted line, and show the form of the longitudinal section at
the particular place indicated. Such lines are also a check on
the other lines in proving their fairness, inasmuch as all the
points in the intersection of the straight and curved lines
must coincide in each view : for instance, if from the point *n*
in profile A, where the curved bow line intersects the straight
side view of the second water line, a vertical line be drawn to
the half-breadth plan B, it should intersect the curved plan of
the second water line where the straight corresponding plan
of dotted bow line *h k* intersects it at *p*, and so with every
other point of intersection. The transverse lines which are
numbered and lettered correspond to the vertical lines in the
profile.

The body plan, or end elevation, C, shows the outline at

midships, and the curved form of frames corresponding to the positions of the lines of the vertical sections on profile and half-breadth plans, lettered and numbered to correspond. The water lines are straight, and correspond to the relative lines in the profile A. The bow and buttock-lines $h\,k$ are also straight, corresponding to the line $h\,k$ in half-breadth plan B. The breadth of the water lines, at any of the curved intersections of the frames, corresponds with the breadth at corresponding frame or section on half-breadth plan B. For instance, the breadth R G at the frame or section H, second water line, coincides with the breadth from H to the second water line, on half-breadth plan B. In after body O, the distance R V, frame 20, second water line, corresponds to the distance $20\,x$ on half-breadth plan B, and so on. The points also where the straight bow and buttock-lines in body plan O intersect the curved sections of frames, coincide with the relative intersections on profile A, where the sections at frames are straight lines, and the bow and buttock-lines are curves. For instance, the point y, where the buttock curve line on profile A intersects frame 16 between the first and second water lines, coincides with the point F in the body plan O, where the same buttock line intersects the frame 16. Frequently, as a further check, particularly for laying down the full size of the ship in the moulding loft, which often, for want of surface, has to be done in short lengths, diagonal lines are drawn, as shown on the body plan O, from the centre line to the side of body, which in the profile A and half-breadth plan B would be represented as curved lines, and all the other points of intersections of such additional lines and curves must agree in the three different views of the design.

The curves in profile A and half-breadth B are drawn by the baton held by weights, and the curves of the body plan O by parabolic and other moulds (page 78). The curves throughout a ship design always represent the form of vessel hout the planking.

Sail draughts are generally made to a scale of ½ or ¹⁄₁₆ inch to the foot, and ship details to ¼ inch to the foot. Some designs contain a scale of displacement, which may be explained as follows :—

A B, in Fig. 318, represents the ship's mean draught of water on a certain scale (usually ½ or ¼ inch = 1 foot); and C c, D d, &c., represent the several water-lines, A a being the load-water line. On A a (drawn perpendicular to A B) a length is set off, representing on a certain scale of tons per inch (say 100 tons = ¼ inch) the ship's load displacement; on C c a length representing her displacement at the draught B C,

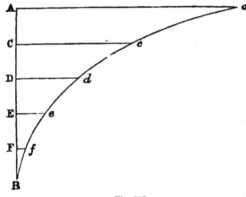

Fig. 318.

on D d a length representing her displacement at the draught B D, and so forth. Through the points thus obtained the curve a c d e f B is drawn, and from it the ship's displacement at any draught can be obtained by first measuring the draught upwards from B, and then measuring the length of the perpendicular meeting the curve. In calculating the tons weight of displacement from the cubic content, 35 cubic feet of salt water are taken as one ton avoirdupois.

NOTE.—The design shown at Fig. 317 is that of a sailing ship, and is selected in preference to the lines of a steamship, though the latter more immediately concerns the engineer; but the former, having a greater proportion of breadth to length, shows the several curves more distinctly.

PART IV.

DETAIL DRAWINGS OF STEAM-VESSELS.

DETAIL plans and sections have their outlines taken from a design similar to that described in Part III., and are filled in with the various fittings, machinery, boilers, coals, &c. If a plan is required of any section between any of the waterlines shown in the half-breadth plan of a design, a line of section at the required height is drawn on the body plan; and on this line measurements taken from the centre line to the intersectional points of the frames, and laid off from the centre line of the half-breadth plan at each corresponding transverse section, will be the points through which to draw the required sectional curve.

If a transverse (or cross) section is required between any of the curved sections or frames which are shown on the body plan of a design, a transverse line of section is drawn at the required position on the half-breadth plan in design, on which the several breadths are measured from the centre line to the intersections of the curved water lines, and laid off on the corresponding straight water lines in body plan from its centre line; a curve line passing through the several points will be the required cross section.

In mechanical details of matters connected with shipbuilding where an engineer would describe a circle a shipbuilder would draw a parabolic curve with the mould; the latter in most cases looks more " ship-shape ;" besides which, from a scientific point of view, it is allowed, to be more correct.

In making highly-finished coloured drawings of the exterior side view, deck, sections, and especially of a longitudinal section, there is scope for the exercise of much taste, as in

the representation of cabin fittings and general ornamental
work; and a little more skill—akin to art, than in shading and
colouring the engineering portion of such drawings.* The
projections of some of the shadows are also more intricate.†

The Exterior Broadside View.—In representing the lines
of plating, when they are to appear on a side view, they
should be first correctly drawn on the body plan; and the
measurements, taken vertically to the intersecting points on
the frames, should be laid off on vertical lines indicating the
positions of such frames on side view, and lines drawn through
the points with the baton and weights (Chapter IV.).

For a paddle steamer it is necessary to project the shadow
of the rings and floats on the side of the vessel. For the projection of the rings that described at Fig. 280, Chapter XV.,
is applicable. Having found the points for the shadow of
one set and its arms, the simplest way is to trace it, and
transfer each to its respective place corresponding to its
distance from the plane, and laid off from the centre of
the paddle, and at the same angle as indicated at Chapter
XV. For the projection of the shadow of the floats the method
described at Fig. 288, Chapter XV., is applicable. The projections of the sides of the floats on the rounded part of the vessel
at bilge are straight as in the upper floats, the ends of the lower
floats only being curved; the points being found as in projecting the shadow of a square flange on a horizontal cylinder.
The tints for shading are similar to those for engineering
drawing (Chapter XVI.).

In shading the outer and inner streaks of the iron plates a

* Additional colours to those given in Chapter VI. for engineering
drawings are requisite, comprising verdigris green, vermilion, and
cobalt blue. The two former cost 1s. each, small "half-cake" of
the latter, 5s.

† In projecting the shadows which follow, the same rule is observed
as for engineering drawings in Chapter XV. (or the process an
engineer would naturally follow in making finished coloured drawings
of a ship). In drawings by a shipbuilder both the shadows and shade
lines are generally on the opposite side to the engineer's (or on the
lower and left sides of projecting objects, the upper and right sides
being opposite the light). The angle of inclination of the shadow in
their drawings being the same as in engineering drawings.

little light should be left on the top edge of the former as in
shaded engineering details.   It costs much time and labour
to leave the light in the shading process, and to preserve
the general look of the shadow unbroken, doing it streak by
streak.   A better shade in every way is produced by going
over all the plates without leaving a light, one streak at a
time.   If the following method is observed time and trouble
will be saved.   Draw a line at the top of the plate with
flake-white by the drawing pen, colour over with washes of
tint, five or six coats, the sponge will then take off the flake-
white and leave a light line, which when coloured over with
more tint after being sponged and dry will present sufficient
contrast with the dark parts to give the effect required.   The
top sides after shading should be washed all over two or
three times with the ordinary neutral tint well watered,
after which a thin coating of burnt-umber.   The lower part
under the load-water line should have a yellowish tint, composed of yellow ochre, gamboge, and Indian red.   The red
colour for the paddle should be composed of gamboge, lake,
and a little carmine.

The masts, if to represent wood unpainted, should be
shaded first with the neutral tint, then with Indian red, and
washed all over with yellow ochre and Indian red combined,
then grained with Indian red not too thick.

If the water line is to be shown at the
ends in such drawing, or any other coloured
view, a thin wash of Prussian blue should
be laid on close to the line, washing off the
lower edge with water, and which, when
dry, should have graduated parallel lines
of verdigris green put on above it with
the drawing pen, the lower being broken
lines, as in adjacent diagram Fig. 319.

Fig. 319.

Longitudinal Section.—To project the shadow of the deck or
inner side in a longitudinal midship vertical section.

Let A, Fig. 320, be the longitudinal section, on which the shadow of the deck H is to be projected.

Transfer from working drawing of ship (as at Fig. 817, Part III.) a part K of body plan, having as many sections B, C, D, &c., as are contained in the length of the longitudinal part A.*

FIRSTLY.—*When the deck H is horizontal or without sheer.*—From the point *o* in end view K draw the relative angle of light *o r*; from the point where the line *o r* intersects the section or frame B, draw a horizontal line to the corresponding vertical section B in longitudinal view A, intersecting it at *i*, which will be a point for shadow. From the point where the line *o r* intersects the section or frame C, draw a hori-

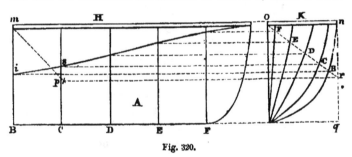

Fig. 320.

zontal line to the corresponding vertical section C in longitudinal view A, intersecting it at s, which will be a second point for the shadow. Proceed similarly for the other intersections. A curve line passing through the points thus found will be the projection of shadow required.

SECONDLY.—*When the deck has sheer.*—Let A, Fig. 321, be the longitudinal section upon which the shadow of the deck z is to be projected (the sheer is exaggerated so as to show the process more distinctly), and B the body plan, transferred from a working drawing, and having as many sections as are contained in the longitudinal part A. Draw the relative angle of light *d e* in body plan B. In this instance a part plan of

* To which add the thickness of side, if a wooden ship, to represent the inner surface on which to project the shadow.

form of ship's side between each of the vertical sections is necessary, such form being taken on the diagonal lines between each vertical section in body plan, each such diagonal being in the direction of the light. In plan c, from the points G, H, I (corresponding to the same sections in side view A), draw the relative angle of light G, m, &c. From the point e in body plan B, where the diagonal d e intersects the section G, draw a vertical line e l, intersecting the corresponding section G in plan c at l; and from the point f in body plan B, where the diagonal d e intersects the section H, draw a vertical line f k, intersecting the corresponding section H in plan c at k, and join l k, which will be the form of ship's side between the sections G and H in plan c. From the point n in plan c, where the angle of light G m intersects the line l k, draw the vertical line n o, intersecting the angle of light d e in body plan B at o. From the point o draw the

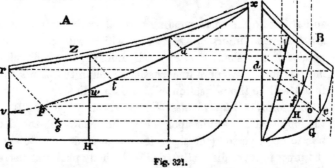

Fig. 321.

horizontal line o p, intersecting the ordinary diagonal line of light r s in side view A at p, which will be a point for required shadow. Repeat the same process with the remaining sections for the points t and u on the ordinary diagonals in side view A; a curve line passing through p, t, u, x, will be the projection of shadow required.

NOTE.—If the form of the ship between each of the cross sections on the line of relative angle of light in body plan B were straight, another method of finding points for the curve would be as follows:—Draw horizontal lines from the points e and f on sections G and H in body plan B, respectively, to the points v and w on the corresponding sections G and H in side view A, and draw the line v w, which will intersect the diagonal r s; the intersection would be a point for shadow; similarly from the other sections in body plan B would be found other intersectional points for shadow on their respective diagonals.

In a drawing intended to be a picture, such as the longitudinal or other sections of a ship, where the iron is painted red, the finishing tint should be composed of lake, gamboge, and carmine. The shade lines on the under sides of projecting plates, sides of frames, and rivets, should be lake only. The rivets, when to a scale of one-eighth of an inch to a foot, should not be *inked-in* previously. It is common in making such finished sections, to colour the inside of the hull blue, because it is iron. Blue is very well for the representative colour of the iron in certain drawings only. For drawings, if to a scale of less than three-eighths of an inch to a foot, the section of iron plates or angle iron on a darkly shaded ground should be drawn in with indigo, or Prussian blue mixed with flake white, after all the finishing colour is put on; Indian ink never shows well, being of a glossy nature. In drawings to a larger scale the sections of iron plates should be composed of two lines for the thickness filled up with light Prussian blue.*

---

* In sectional drawings, to be in outline only, to any scale under ⅜ths of an inch to a foot, where a thickness of iron plate is shown, it is better to make it a thick black line, a little thicker than any shade lines, if any, on the drawing; when to a scale above ⅜ths the thickness should be composed of two lines. The same remarks apply to angle iron.

Upper deck plan: After all the ordinary objects are drawn on this (or other deck plans) the deck lines should be drawn in. The best way to insure correctness is to set off the breadths from the centre line upwards on margin at each end, and from the centre line downwards; the lines being drawn with Indian ink not too thick along a straight-edge held by weights at each end at the divisions. (For projecting the shadows see Chapter XV., First Series. For projection of shadow of paddle box, if a paddle steamer, see Chapter XV., Fig. 247.)

The tint for the deck should be gamboge with a little yellow ochre, well watered; for coamings of hatchways and other dark wood-work, lake and burnt umber; for light wood-work, gamboge, yellow ochre, and Indian red combined. Glass of skylights, after being darkened a little by neutral tint, should have a coat of green, composed of Prussian blue and gamboge.

In cross sections, or longitudinal sectional plans of steamers, coals have frequently to be represented, to indicate their place. These, when done in Indian ink only, have always a brown appearance, and in some drawings (otherwise good and highly finished), are so *regularly* and ineffectively shown as to destroy the appearance of the drawing. Anything touching on fine art, and apart from plain lining and shading, the engineering draughtsman is generally apt to shrink from,[*] but a very good way of showing coals fit for coloured engineering drawings can be made in the following way:—

Though coals in themselves are always black, at a distance they are of a bluish colour. Therefore a little Prussian blue and Indian ink will be found the best tint with which to represent them. As they are of the most irregular forms, the difficulty is generally in making them so. To get such irregularities on the space allotted for them—put the tint named in patches here and there, as at *a*, Plate VII., and when the first lot are dry, come over them again anyhow, and in all directions, repeating the process many times until every

[*] Unless he has already some knowledge of the subject.

Plate VII.

a

a

b

c

d

London: Lockwood & C.º 7. Stationers' Hall Court.

white part of the paper in the space disappears. If then not dark enough, come over all the surface ; and making darker and lighter patches here and there to represent little hills and valleys, the patches being darkest next to any part that projects a shadow, such as would be caused by the side of the ship or bulkhead, &c., as shown at *b*. The space will now be filled with little irregular figures, some lighter and some darker. The lighter bits are supposed to be more opposite the light than the darker. Then with indigo and a fine brush surround each of these little irregular bits as at *c*, making the backs of the lighter ones with a broader line of indigo, as when inclined more opposite the light ; in such position more of the back of the piece will be seen. Then with a pricker scratch the fronts opposite the light of each individual piece as at *d*, but those down in a hollow more slightly. The front part of the shadow of projecting enclosure should be very irregular, and within that shadow the forms of the light and dark bits should have the indigo as in the others, but no light shown on front of them as in the parts exposed.

Note.—It is almost needless to add that if a drawing is to be sponged it must be done before such process as that just described, and before any thick lines or chalky colours are put on ; and if to be a varnished drawing, after being sized, but before being varnished.

A border line of a rope pattern looks appropriate when surrounding any highly finished drawing connected with naval architecture. The corners for this pattern should never be square.

PART V.

PERSPECTIVE DRAWING.

In the following example of perspective it will be seen that instead of the horizontal sides appearing parallel, when produced, they meet in a point. Perspective is simply a section, by a plane, cutting the rays from all the visible points of the object to the eye, giving the same proportion of the different parts of the object wherever that section is placed between such object and the eye.

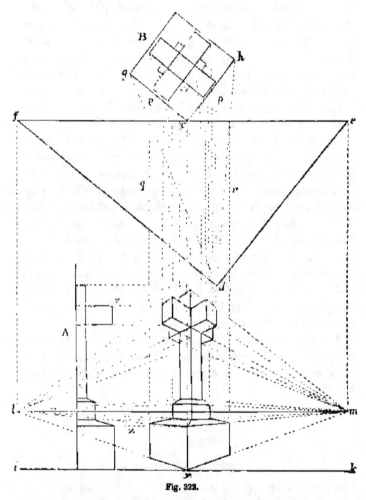

Fig. 322.

In the accompanying example, Fig. 322, A is the front eleva- tion and B the plan of an object, drawn to their proper proportions, or to a scale. The plan B being placed at such an angle to the horizontal line *f e* as is deemed suitable for the view required in perspective. The line *f e* is the plane of section of the rays from the several points to the eye of the observer at the point *d*, which point is placed in any suitable position; the lines *d e* and *d f* are drawn parallel to *c h* and *c g* respectively. The horizontal line *i k* represents the ground line on which the elevation A is erected. · The line *l m* is the height of the eye from the ground, and parallel to it. From the point *f*, on the line *f e*, a vertical line is drawn intersecting the line *l m* at *l*, which is the *vanishing point* for the lines to the left side of the perspective elevation; also, a vertical line is drawn from the point *e*, on the line *f e*, intersecting the line *l m* at *m*, which is the vanishing point for the lines to the right side of perspective elevation. The lines *p*, *p*, &c., are drawn from the points in the plan B towards the point of sight *d*, it being sufficient for the purpose to terminate them at the line of section *f e*. The vertical lines, as at *q, r*, are drawn from the points of intersection in the plane *f e*, which give the right and left *corners* of perspective pedestal; and from the point *x*, where the central line *c x* intersects the ground line *i k*, the line *x m* is drawn to the vanishing point *m*, which gives the base line of right side of pedestal, and the line *x l* is drawn to the vanishing point *l*, which gives the base line of left side of pedestal. Vertical lines are drawn from all the points in the plane *f e*, where the rays from the points in the plan of object intersect it. The horizontal lines z are drawn from the front elevation A to the vertical line *n o*, and from the points where they intersect it—lines are drawn to the vanishing point *m*. The perspective is completed from the points where the vertical lines intersect the vanishing lines on either side, and as explained by the dotted lines.*

* In a perspective drawing where the vanishing point is inconveniently distant, an instrument called a centrolinead will be found convenient. It is composed of three moveable bars, the price of which, 30 or 42 inches, in ebony, brass mounted. is 19*s.*; electrum mounted

PART VI.

ISOMETRICAL DRAWING.

ISOMETRICAL projection, though somewhat similar to real perspective, differs from it in this, that whereas the angles in the former, as a rule, are drawn at 80° with the horizon, and measurements of any part, as in common drawing, can be readily taken off; in the latter, parallel lines vanishing to a point (the objects getting less to the eye as they recede), the object cannot be measured readily enough for practical purposes.

An isometrical cube may be drawn by describing a circle, and with the radius dividing the circumference by it into six equal parts, as in Fig. 323, completing the hexagon by

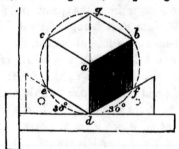

Fig. 323.

drawing the lines between the points thus found, and joining *a b*, *a c*, and *a d*, by straight lines to the centre *a* of the circle; the part between *c b* being the representation of the top, and that between *d c* and *d b* the two visible sides; the line *a d* being always drawn vertically from the centre of circle *a*, and thus parallel to the sides *c e* and *b f*.

Or the same results may be obtained by using the wood

25*s*., including studs to work against. A temporary instrument may be made by nailing two pieces of wood on the stock of the T-square, having first found the proper angle at which to set them, and having two nails on the margin of the board against which to bear it, taking care that the front edge of the blade of T-square is in a line with the centre of the circle which the square in its position would describe.

angle of 30° bearing on the edge of T-square set horizontally. Describe a circle, and through the centre *a*, Fig. 323, draw a vertical line *g d*, and from the point *d* where it intersects

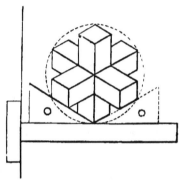

Fig. 324.

the circle, and with wood angle of 30° on the T-square draw the line *d f*, also the line *a b* from the centre *a* of the circle, and *c g* from the point *g*, where the vertical line *d g* intersects the circle ; also, by reversing the wood angle as at *d e*, and from the point *d*, *a*, and *g*, respectively—draw *d e*, *a c*, and *g b* ; join *c e*, *a d*, and *b f* by the vertical lines as shown, thus completing the isometrical cube, the lines of which are obviously all of equal length.

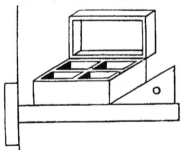

Fig. 325.

Almost any variety of such objects, all pleasing to the eye, can be projected, as at Figs. 324 and 325, with the T-square and little wood angle, hardly any measurements being necessary.

PART VII.

SIZING, VARNISHING, AND FRAMING.

In drawings to be varnished, thick lines, such as shade lines, and chalky colours should never be put on before sizing, as they blot under the process; and before sizing the drawing should be permanently stretched on cloth on a frame, as described in Chapter IX. The best size for drawings is isinglass. The little holes, if any, made by the compasses in drawing the shade circles, should have a little size put over them to prevent the varnish penetrating and making a brown mark.

The best varnish is Canada balsam, which, as in sizing— should be put on with a flat fine brush.

In a large drawing simply to be mounted on cloth for rollers, the cloth should be tacked as tightly as possible round the edge to a board or table, the tacks being driven only half in. The back of the drawing, or paper to be drawn on, should be damped before pasting,* and then laid on the stretched linen, or " brown holland," and pressed gently with a clean cloth. The size and varnish should be put on the drawing while laid horizontal, to prevent flowing to the lowest part of it. The varnish must be quite dry before detaching the drawing from its nailed position.

To Frame a Drawing.—In framing a drawing for hanging up, dust may be kept from it by pasting narrow strips of paper all round inside at the edge of glass and frame. If to be put in a plain frame having a gilt strip, it is a preservative from tarnishing to put *it* inside the glass. When the drawing on the stretcher is placed in the frame and paper stretched all over the back (being all slightly damped previously and pasted down at the edge) the dust will be entirely excluded from the drawing.

---

* The paste should be quite cold before using, for if put on hot the is apt to raise blisters on the paper.

A shaded drawing when hung up should be in such a position that the lights in the drawing coincide with the light through the window.

The same rule applies to an outline drawing having shade lines.

INDEX.

N

THE END.

VIRTUE AND CO., PRINTERS, CITY ROAD, LONDON.

A NEW LIST

OF

WEALE'S
RUDIMENTARY SCIENTIFIC, EDUCATIONAL, AND CLASSICAL SERIES.

These popular and cheap Series of Books, now comprising nearly Three Hundred distinct works in almost every department of Science, Art, and Education, are recommended to the notice of Engineers, Architects, Builders, Artisans, and Students generally, as well as to those interested in Workmen's Libraries, Free Libraries Literary and Scientific Institutions, Colleges, Schools, Science Classes, &c., &c.

N.B.—In ordering from this List it is recommended, as a means of facilitating business and obviating error, to quote the numbers affixed to the volumes, as well as the titles and prices.

** The books are bound in limp cloth, unless otherwise stated.

RUDIMENTARY SCIENTIFIC SERIES.

ARCHITECTURE, BUILDING, ETC.

No.

16. *ARCHITECTURE—ORDERS*—The Orders and their Æsthetic Principles. By W. H. LEEDS. Illustrated. 1s. 6d.

17. *ARCHITECTURE—STYLES*—The History and Description of the Styles of Architecture of Various Countries, from the Earliest to the Present Period. By T. TALBOT BURY, F.R.I.B.A., &c. Illustrated. 2s.
** ORDERS AND STYLES OF ARCHITECTURE, *in One Vol.*, 3s. 6d.

18. *ARCHITECTURE—DESIGN*—The Principles of Design in Architecture, as deducible from Nature and exemplified in the Works of the Greek and Gothic Architects. By E. L. GARBETT, Architect. Illustrated. 2s.
** The three preceding Works, in One handsome Vol., half bound, entitled "MODERN ARCHITECTURE," *Price 6s.*

22. *THE ART OF BUILDING*, Rudiments of. General Principles of Construction, Materials used in Building, Strength and Use of Materials, Working Drawings, Specifications, and Estimates. By EDWARD DOBSON, M.R.I.B.A., &c. Illustrated. 1s. 6d.

23. *BRICKS AND TILES*, Rudimentary Treatise on the Manufacture of; containing an Outline of the Principles of Brickmaking. By EDW. DOBSON, M.R.I.B.A. With Additions by C. TOMLINSON, F.R.S. Illustrated. 3s.

25. *MASONRY AND STONECUTTING*, Rudimentary Treatise on; in which the Principles of Masonic Projection and their application to the Construction of Curved Wing-Walls, Domes, Oblique Bridges, and Roman and Gothic Vaulting, are concisely explained. By EDWARD DOBSON, M.R.I.B.A., &c. Illustrated with Plates and Diagrams. 2s. 6d.

44. *FOUNDATIONS AND CONCRETE WORKS*, a Rudimentary Treatise on; containing a Synopsis of the principal cases of Foundation Works, with the usual Modes of Treatment, and Practical Remarks on Footings, Planking, Sand, Concrete, Béton, Pile-driving, Caissons, and Cofferdams. By E. DOBSON, M.R.I.B.A., &c. Third Edition, revised by GEORGE DODD, C.E. Illustrated. 1s. 6d.

Architecture, Building, etc., *continued.*

42. *COTTAGE BUILDING.* By C. BRUCE ALLEN, Architect. Eleventh Edition, revised and enlarged. Numerous Illustrations. 1s. 6d.

45. *LIMES, CEMENTS, MORTARS, CONCRETES, MASTICS,* PLASTERING, &c., Rudimentary Treatise on. By G. R. BURNELL, C.E. Ninth Edition, with Appendices. 1s. 6d.

57. *WARMING AND VENTILATION,* a Rudimentary Treatise on; being a concise Exposition of the General Principles of the Art of Warming and Ventilating Domestic and Public Buildings, Mines, Lighthouses, Ships, &c. By CHARLES TOMLINSON, F.R.S., &c. Illustrated. 3s.

83**. *CONSTRUCTION OF DOOR LOCKS.* Compiled from the Papers of A. C. HOBBS, Esq., of New York, and Edited by CHARLES TOMLINSON, F.R.S. To which is added, a Description of Fenby's Patent Locks, and a Note upon IRON SAFES by ROBERT MALLET, M.I.C.E. Illus. 2s. 6d.

111. *ARCHES, PIERS, BUTTRESSES, &c.:* Experimental Essays on the Principles of Construction in; made with a view to their being useful to the Practical Builder. By WILLIAM BLAND. Illustrated. 1s. 6d.

116. *THE ACOUSTICS OF PUBLIC BUILDINGS;* or, The Principles of the Science of Sound applied to the purposes of the Architect and Builder. By T. ROGER SMITH, M.R.I.B.A., Architect. Illustrated. 1s. 6d.

124. *CONSTRUCTION OF ROOFS,* Treatise on the, as regards Carpentry and Joinery. Deduced from the Works of ROBISON, PRICE, and TREDGOLD. Illustrated. 1s. 6d.

127. *ARCHITECTURAL MODELLING IN PAPER,* the Art of. By T. A. RICHARDSON, Architect. With Illustrations, designed by the Author, and engraved by O. JEWITT. 1s. 6d.

128. *VITRUVIUS—THE ARCHITECTURE OF MARCUS VITRUVIUS POLLO.* In Ten Books. Translated from the Latin by JOSEPH GWILT, F.S.A., F.R.A.S. With 23 Plates. 5s.

130. *GRECIAN ARCHITECTURE,* An Inquiry into the Principles of Beauty in; with an Historical View of the Rise and Progress of the Art in Greece. By the EARL OF ABERDEEN. 1s.

⁎ *The two Preceding Works in One handsome Vol., half bound, entitled* "ANCIENT ARCHITECTURE." *Price 6s.*

132. *DWELLING-HOUSES,* a Rudimentary Treatise on the Erection of. By S. H. BROOKS, Architect. New Edition, with plates. 2s. 6d.

156. *QUANTITIES AND MEASUREMENTS,* How to Calculate and Take them in Bricklayers', Masons', Plasterers', Plumbers', Painters', Paperhangers', Gilders', Smiths', Carpenters', and Joiners' Work. By A. C. BEATON, Architect and Surveyor. New and Enlarged Edition. Illus. 1s. 6d.

175. *LOCKWOOD & CO.'S BUILDER'S AND CONTRACTOR'S* PRICE BOOK, with which is incorporated ATCHLEY's and portions of the late G. R. BURNELL'S "BUILDER'S PRICE BOOKS," for 1875, published annually, containing the latest Prices of all kinds of Builders' Materials and Labour, and of all Trades connected with Building: with Memoranda and Tables required in making Estimates and taking out Quantities, &c. The whole Revised and Edited by FRANCIS T. W. MILLER, Architect and Surveyor. 3s. 6d.

182. *CARPENTRY AND JOINERY*—THE ELEMENTARY PRINCIPLES OF CARPENTRY. Chiefly composed from the Standard Work of THOMAS TREDGOLD, C.E. With Additions from the Works of the most Recent Authorities, and a TREATISE ON JOINERY by E. WYNDHAM TARN, M.A. Numerous Illustrations. 3s. 6d.

182*. *CARPENTRY AND JOINERY.* ATLAS of 35 Plates to accompany the foregoing book. With Descriptive Letterpress. 4to. 6s.

187. *HINTS TO YOUNG ARCHITECTS.* By GEORGE WIGHTWICK. New Edition, enlarged. By G. HUSKISSON GUILLAUME, Architect. With numerous Woodcuts. 3s. 6d.

189. *THE RUDIMENTS OF PRACTICAL BRICKLAYING.* In Six Sections. By ADAM HAMMOND. Illustrated with 68 Woodcuts. 1s. 6d.

CIVIL ENGINEERING, ETC.

13. *CIVIL ENGINEERING*, the Rudiments of; for the Use of Beginners, for Practical Engineers, and for the Army and Navy. By HENRY LAW, C.E. Including a Section on Hydraulic Engineering, by GEORGE R. BURNELL, C.E. 5th Edition, with Notes and Illustrations by ROBERT MALLET, A.M., F.R.S. Illustrated with Plates and Diagrams. 5s.

29. *THE DRAINAGE OF DISTRICTS AND LANDS.* By G. DRYSDALE DEMPSEY, C.E. New Edition, revised and enlarged. Illustrated. 1s. 6d.

30. *THE DRAINAGE OF TOWNS AND BUILDINGS.* By G. DRYSDALE DEMPSEY, C.E. New Edition. Illustrated. 2s. 6d.
  ‡ With "*Drainage of Districts and Lands,*" in One Vol., 3s. 6d.

31. *WELL-DIGGING, BORING, AND PUMP-WORK.* By JOHN GEORGE SWINDELL, Assoc. R.I.B.A. New Edition, revised by G. R. BURNELL, C.E. Illustrated. 1s.

35. *THE BLASTING AND QUARRYING OF STONE*, Rudimentary Treatise on; for Building and other Purposes, with the Constituents and Analyses of Granite, Slate, Limestone, and Sandstone : to which is added some Remarks on the Blowing up of Bridges. By Gen. Sir JOHN BURGOYNE, Bart., K.C.B. Illustrated. 1s. 6d.

43. *TUBULAR AND OTHER IRON GIRDER BRIDGES.* Particularly describing the BRITANNIA and CONWAY TUBULAR BRIDGES. With a Sketch of Iron Bridges, and Illustrations of the Application of Malleable Iron to the Art of Bridge Building. By G. D. DEMPSEY, C.E., Author of "The Practical Railway Engineer," &c., &c. New Edition, with Illustrations. 1s. 6d.

46. *CONSTRUCTING AND REPAIRING COMMON ROADS*, Papers on the Art of. Containing a Survey of the Metropolitan Roads, by S. HUGHES, C.E.; The Art of Constructing Common Roads, by HENRY LAW, C.E.; Remarks on the Maintenance of Macadamised Roads, by Field-Marshal Sir JOHN F. BURGOYNE, Bart., G.C.B., Royal Engineers, &c., &c. Illustrated. 1s. 6d.

62. *RAILWAY CONSTRUCTION*, Elementary and Practical Instruction on the Science of. By Sir MACDONALD STEPHENSON, C.E., Managing Director of the East India Railway Company. New Edition, revised and enlarged by EDWARD NUGENT, C.E. Plates and numerous Woodcuts. 3s.

62*. *RAILWAYS;* their Capital and Dividends. With Statistics of their Working in Great Britain, &c., &c. By E. D. CHATTAWAY. 1s.
  ‡ 62 and 62*, in One Vol., 3s. 6d.

80*. *EMBANKING LANDS FROM THE SEA*, the Practice of. Treated as a Means of Profitable Employment for Capital. With Examples and Particulars of actual Embankments, and also Practical Remarks on the Repair of old Sea Walls. By JOHN WIGGINS, F.G.S. New Edition, with Notes by ROBERT MALLET, F.R.S. 2s.

81. *WATER WORKS*, for the Supply of Cities and Towns. With a Description of the Principal Geological Formations of England as influencing Supplies of Water; and Details of Engines and Pumping Machinery for raising Water. By SAMUEL HUGHES, F.G.S., C.E. New Edition, revised and enlarged, with numerous Illustrations. 4s.

82**. *GAS WORKS*, and the Practice of Manufacturing and Distributing Coal Gas. By SAMUEL HUGHES, C.E. New Edition, revised by W. RICHARDS, C.E. Illustrated. 3s.

117. *SUBTERRANEOUS SURVEYING;* an Elementary and Practical Treatise on. By THOMAS FENWICK. Also the Method of Conducting Subterraneous Surveys without the Use of the Magnetic Needle, and other modern Improvements. By THOMAS BAKER, C.E. Illustrated. 2s. 6d.

118. *CIVIL ENGINEERING IN NORTH AMERICA*, a Sketch of. By DAVID STEVENSON, F.R.S.E., &c. Plates and Diagrams. 3s.

Civil Engineering, etc., *continued*.

120. *HYDRAULIC ENGINEERING*, the Rudiments of. By G.
R. BURNELL, C.E., F.G.S. Illustrated. 3s.

121. *RIVERS AND TORRENTS*. With the Method of Regulating
their Courses and Channels. By Professor PAUL FRISI, F.R.S., of Milan.
To which is added, AN ESSAY ON NAVIGABLE CANALS. Translated
by Major-General JOHN GARSTIN, of the Bengal Engineers. Plates. 2s. 6d.

MECHANICAL ENGINEERING, ETC.

33. *CRANES*, the Construction of, and other Machinery for Raising
Heavy Bodies for the Erection of Buildings, and for Hoisting Goods. By
JOSEPH GLYNN, F.R.S., &c. Illustrated. 1s. 6d.

34. *THE STEAM ENGINE*, a Rudimentary Treatise on. By Dr.
LARDNER. Illustrated. 1s.

59. *STEAM BOILERS*: Their Construction and Management. By
R. ARMSTRONG, C.E. Illustrated. 1s. 6d.

63. *AGRICULTURAL ENGINEERING*: Farm Buildings, Motive
Power, Field Machines, Machinery, and Implements. By G. H. ANDREWS,
C.E. Illustrated. 3s.

67. *CLOCKS, WATCHES, AND BELLS*, a Rudimentary Treatise
on. By Sir EDMUND BECKETT (late EDMUND BECKETT DENISON, LL.D., Q.C.)
*** *A New, Revised, and considerably Enlarged Edition of the above Standard
Treatise, with very numerous Illustrations, is now ready, price 4s. 6d.* :

77*. *THE ECONOMY OF FUEL*, particularly with Reference to
Reverbatory Furnaces for the Manufacture of Iron, and to Steam Boilers.
By T. SYMES PRIDEAUX. 1s. 6d.

82. *THE POWER OF WATER*, as applied to drive Flour Mills,
and to give motion to Turbines and other Hydrostatic Engines. By JOSEPH
GLYNN, F.R.S., &c. New Edition, Illustrated. 2s.

98. *PRACTICAL MECHANISM*, the Elements of; and Machine
Tools. By T. BAKER, C.E. With Remarks on Tools and Machinery, by
J. NASMYTH, C.E. Plates. 2s. 6d.

114. *MACHINERY*, Elementary Principles of, in its Construction and
Working. Illustrated by numerous Examples of Modern Machinery for
different Branches of Manufacture. By C. D. ABEL, C.E. 1s. 6d.

115. *ATLAS OF PLATES*. Illustrating the above Treatise. By
C. D. ABEL, C.E. 7s. 6d.

125. *THE COMBUSTION OF COAL AND THE PREVENTION*
OF SMOKE, Chemically and Practically Considered. With an Appendix.
By C. WYE WILLIAMS, A.I.C.E. Plates. 3s.

139. *THE STEAM ENGINE*, a Treatise on the Mathematical Theory
of, with Rules at length, and Examples for the Use of Practical Men. By
T. BAKER, C.E. Illustrated. 1s.

162. *THE BRASS FOUNDER'S MANUAL;* Instructions for
Modelling, Pattern-Making, Moulding, Turning, Filing, Burnishing,
Bronzing, &c. With copious Receipts, numerous Tables, and Notes on Prime
Costs and Estimates. By WALTER GRAHAM. Illustrated. 2s. 6d.

164. *MODERN WORKSHOP PRACTICE*, as applied to Marine,
Land, and Locomotive Engines, Floating Docks, Dredging Machines,
Bridges, Cranes, Ship-building, &c., &c. By J. G. WINTON. Illustrated. 3s.

165. *IRON AND HEAT*, exhibiting the Principles concerned in the
Construction of Iron Beams, Pillars, and Bridge Girders, and the Action of
Heat in the Smelting Furnace. By J. ARMOUR, C.E. Numerous Woodcuts.
2s. 6d.

LONDON : LOCKWOOD AND CO.,

Mechanical Engineering, etc., *continued.*

166. *POWER IN MOTION:* Horse-Power, Motion, Toothed-Wheel Gearing, Long and Short Driving Bands, Angular Forces. By JAMES ARMOUR, C.E. With 73 Diagrams. 2s. 6d.

167. *THE APPLICATION OF IRON TO THE CONSTRUCTION* OF BRIDGES, GIRDERS, ROOFS, AND OTHER WORKS. Showing the Principles upon which such Structures are designed, and their Practical Application. By FRANCIS CAMPIN, C.E. Numerous Woodcuts. 2s.

171. *THE WORKMAN'S MANUAL OF ENGINEERING* DRAWING. By JOHN MAXTON, Engineer, Instructor in Engineering Drawing, Royal School of Naval Architecture and Marine Engineering, South Kensington. Illustrated with 7 Plates and nearly 350 Woodcuts. 3s.6d.

SHIPBUILDING, NAVIGATION, MARINE ENGINEERING, ETC.

51. *NAVAL ARCHITECTURE,* the Rudiments of; or, an Exposition of the Elementary Principles of the Science, and their Practical Application to Naval Construction. Compiled for the Use of Beginners. By JAMES PEAKE, School of Naval Architecture, H.M. Dockyard, Portsmouth. Fourth Edition, corrected, with Plates and Diagrams. 3s. 6d.

53*. *SHIPS FOR OCEAN AND RIVER SERVICE,* Elementary and Practical Principles of the Construction of. By HAKON A. SOMMERFELDT, Surveyor of the Royal Norwegian Navy. With an Appendix. 1s.

53**. *AN ATLAS OF ENGRAVINGS* to Illustrate the above. Twelve large folding plates. Royal 4to, cloth. 7s. 6d.

54. *MASTING, MAST-MAKING, AND RIGGING OF SHIPS,* Rudimentary Treatise on. Also Tables of Spars, Rigging, Blocks; Chain, Wire, and Hemp Ropes, &c., relative to every class of vessels. Together with an Appendix of Dimensions of Masts and Yards of the Royal Navy of Great Britain and Ireland. By ROBERT KIPPING, N.A. Thirteenth Edition. Illustrated. 1s. 6d.

54*. *IRON SHIP-BUILDING.* With Practical Examples and Details for the Use of Ship Owners and Ship Builders. By JOHN GRANTHAM, Consulting Engineer and Naval Architect. Fifth Edition, with important Additions. 4s.

54**. *AN ATLAS OF FORTY PLATES* to Illustrate the above. Fifth Edition. Including the latest Examples, such as H.M. Steam Frigates "Warrior," "Hercules," "Bellerophon;" H.M. Troop Ship "Serapis," Iron Floating Dock, &c., &c. 4to, boards. 38s.

55. *THE SAILOR'S SEA BOOK:* A Rudimentary Treatise on Navigation. I. How to Keep the Log and Work it off. II. On Finding the Latitude and Longitude. By JAMES GREENWOOD, B.A., of Jesus College, Cambridge. To which are added, Directions for Great Circle Sailing; an Essay on the Law of Storms and Variable Winds; and Explanations of Terms used in Ship-building. Ninth Edition, with several Engravings and Coloured Illustrations of the Flags of Maritime Nations. 2s.

80. *MARINE ENGINES, AND STEAM VESSELS,* a Treatise on. Together with Practical Remarks on the Screw and Propelling Power, as used in the Royal and Merchant Navy. By ROBERT MURRAY, C.E., Engineer-Surveyor to the Board of Trade. With a Glossary of Technical Terms, and their Equivalents in French, German, and Spanish. Fifth Edition, revised and enlarged. Illustrated. 3s.

83bis. *THE FORMS OF SHIPS AND BOATS:* Hints, Experimentally Derived, on some of the Principles regulating Ship-building. By W. BLAND. Sixth Edition, revised, with numerous Illustrations and Models. 1s. 6d.

99. *NAVIGATION AND NAUTICAL ASTRONOMY,* in Theory and Practice. With Attempts to facilitate the Finding of the Time and the Longitude at Sea. By J. R. YOUNG, formerly Professor of Mathematics in Belfast College. Illustrated. 2s. 6d.

Shipbuilding, Navigation, etc., *continued.*

100*. *TABLES* intended to facilitate the Operations of Navigation and
Nautical Astronomy, as an Accompaniment to the above Book. By J. R.
YOUNG. 1s. 6d.

106. *SHIPS' ANCHORS*, a Treatise on. By GEORGE COTSELL,
N.A. Illustrated. 1s. 6d.

149. *SAILS AND SAIL-MAKING*, an Elementary Treatise on.
With Draughting, and the Centre of Effort of the Sails. Also, Weights
and Sizes of Ropes ; Masting, Rigging, and Sails of Steam Vessels, &c., &c.
Ninth Edition, enlarged, with an Appendix. By ROBERT KIPPING, N.A.,
Sailmaker, Quayside, Newcastle. Illustrated. 2s. 6d.

155. *THE ENGINEER'S GUIDE TO THE ROYAL AND*
MERCANTILE NAVIES. By a PRACTICAL ENGINEER. Revised by D.
F. M'CARTHY, late of the Ordnance Survey Office, Southampton. 3s.

PHYSICAL SCIENCE, NATURAL PHILO-SOPHY, ETC.

1. *CHEMISTRY*, for the Use of Beginners. By Professor GEORGE
FOWNES, F.R.S. With an Appendix, on the Application of Chemistry to
Agriculture. 1s.

2. *NATURAL PHILOSOPHY*, Introduction to the Study of; for
the Use of Beginners. By C. TOMLINSON, Lecturer on Natural Science in
King's College School, London. Woodcuts. 1s. 6d.

4. *MINERALOGY*, Rudiments of; a concise View of the Properties
of Minerals. By A. RAMSEY, Jun. Woodcuts and Steel Plates. 3s.

6. *MECHANICS*, Rudimentary Treatise on; Being a concise Exposition of the General Principles of Mechanical Science, and their Applications. By CHARLES TOMLINSON, Lecturer on Natural Science in King's
College School, London. Illustrated. 1s. 6d.

7. *ELECTRICITY;* showing the General Principles of Electrical
Science, and the purposes to which it has been applied. By Sir W. SNOW
HARRIS, F.R.S., &c. With considerable Additions by R. SABINE, C.E.,
F.S.A. Woodcuts. 1s. 6d.

7*. *GALVANISM*, Rudimentary Treatise on, and the General Prin-
ciples of Animal and Voltaic Electricity. By Sir W. SNOW HARRIS. New
Edition, revised, with considerable Additions, by ROBERT SABINE, C.E.,
F.S.A. Woodcuts. 1s. 6d.

8. *MAGNETISM;* being a concise Exposition of the General Prin-
ciples of Magnetical Science, and the Purposes to which it has been applied.
By Sir W. SNOW HARRIS. New Edition, revised and enlarged by H. M.
NOAD, Ph.D., Vice-President of the Chemical Society, Author of "A
Manual of Electricity," &c., &c. With 165 Wooocuts. 3s. 6d.

11. *THE ELECTRIC TELEGRAPH;* its History and Progress;
with Descriptions of some of the Apparatus. By R. SABINE, C.E., F.S.A., &c.
Woodcuts. 3s.

12. *PNEUMATICS*, for the Use of Beginners. By CHARLES
TOMLINSON. Illustrated. 1s. 6d.

72. *MANUAL OF THE MOLLUSCA;* a Treatise on Recent and
Fossil Shells. By Dr. S. P. WOODWARD, A.L.S. With Appendix by
RALPH TATE, A.L.S., F.G.S. With numerous Plates and 300 Woodcuts,
6s. 6d. Cloth boards, 7s. 6d.

79**. *PHOTOGRAPHY*, Popular Treatise on; with a Description of
the Stereoscope, &c. Translated from the French of D. VAN MONCKHOVEN,
by W. H. THORNTHWAITE, Ph.D. Woodcuts. 1s. 6d.

96. *ASTRONOMY*. By the Rev. R. MAIN, M.A., F.R.S., &c.
New and enlarged Edition, with an Appendix on "Spectrum Analysis."
Woodcuts. 1s. 6d.

LONDON : LOCKWOOD AND CO.,

Physical Science, Natural Philosophy, etc., *continued.*

97. *STATICS AND DYNAMICS*, the Principles and Practice of; embracing also a clear development of Hydrostatics, Hydrodynamics, and Central Forces. By T. BAKER, C.E. 1s. 6d.

138. *TELEGRAPH*, Handbook of the; a Manual of Telegraphy, Telegraph Clerks' Remembrancer, and Guide to Candidates for Employment in the Telegraph Service. By R. BOND. Fourth Edition, revised and enlarged: to which is appended, QUESTIONS on MAGNETISM, ELECTRICITY, and PRACTICAL TELEGRAPHY, for the Use of Students, by W. McGREGOR, First Assistant Superintendent, Indian Gov. Telegraphs. Woodcuts. 3s.

143. *EXPERIMENTAL ESSAYS.* By CHARLES TOMLINSON. I. On the Motions of Camphor on Water. II. On the Motion of Camphor towards the Light. III. History of the Modern Theory of Dew. Woodcuts. 1s.

173. *PHYSICAL GEOLOGY*, partly based on Major-General PORTLOCK's "Rudiments of Geology." By RALPH TATE, A.L.S., &c. Numerous Woodcuts. 2s.

174. *HISTORICAL GEOLOGY*, partly based on Major-General PORTLOCK's "Rudiments." By RALPH TATE, A.L.S., &c. Woodcuts. 2s. 6d.

173 *RUDIMENTARY TREATISE ON GEOLOGY*, Physical and
& Historical. Partly based on Major-General PORTLOCK's "Rudiments of
174. Geology." By RALPH TATE, A.L.S., F.G.S., &c., &c. Numerous Illustrations. In One Volume. 4s. 6d.

183. *ANIMAL PHYSICS*, Handbook of. By DIONYSIUS LARDNER,
& D.C.L., formerly Professor of Natural Philosophy and Astronomy in University College, London. With 520 Illustrations. In One Volume, cloth
184. boards. 7s. 6d.

, *Sold also in Two Parts, as follows :—*

183. ANIMAL PHYSICS. By Dr. LARDNER. Part I., Chapter I—VII. 4s.
184. ANIMAL PHYSICS. By Dr. LARDNER. Part II. Chapter VIII—XVIII. 3s.

MINING, METALLURGY, ETC.

117. *SUBTERRANEOUS SURVEYING*, Elementary and Practical Treatise on, with and without the Magnetic Needle. By THOMAS FENWICK, Surveyor of Mines, and THOMAS BAKER, C.E. Illustrated. 2s. 6d.

133. *METALLURGY OF COPPER ;* an Introduction to the Methods of Seeking, Mining, and Assaying Copper, and Manufacturing its Alloys. By ROBERT H. LAMBORN, Ph.D. Woodcuts. 2s.

134. *METALLURGY OF SILVER AND LEAD.* A Description of the Ores; their Assay and Treatment, and valuable Constituents. By Dr. R. H. LAMBORN. Woodcuts. 2s.

135. *ELECTRO-METALLURGY;* Practically Treated. By ALEXANDER WATT, F.R.S.S.A. New Edition. Woodcuts. 2s.

172. *MINING TOOLS*, Manual of. For the Use of Mine Managers, Agents, Students, &c. Comprising Observations on the Materials from, and Processes by which, they are manufactured ; their Special Uses, Applications, Qualities, and Efficiency. By WILLIAM MORGANS, Lecturer on Mining at the Bristol School of Mines. 2s. 6d.

172*. *MINING TOOLS, ATLAS* of Engravings to Illustrate the above, containing 235 Illustrations of Mining Tools, drawn to Scale. 4to. 4s. 6d.

176. *METALLURGY OF IRON*, a Treatise on the. Containing Outlines of the History of Iron Manufacture, Methods of Assay, and Analyses of Iron Ores, Processes of Manufacture of Iron and Steel, &c. By H. BAUERMAN, F.G.S., Associate of the Royal School of Mines. Fourth Edition, revised and enlarged, with numerous Illustrations. 4s. 6d.

Mining, Metallurgy, etc., *continued.*

180. *COAL AND COAL MINING:* A Rudimentary Treatise on.
By WARINGTON W. SMYTH, M.A., F.R.S., &c., Chief Inspector of the
Mines of the Crown and of the Duchy of Cornwall. Second Edition, revised
and corrected. With numerous Illustrations. 3s. 6d.

EMIGRATION.

154. *GENERAL HINTS TO EMIGRANTS.* Containing Notices
of the various Fields for Emigration. With Hints on Preparation for
Emigrating, Outfits, &c., &c. With Directions and Recipes useful to the
Emigrant. With a Map of the World. 2s.

157. *THE EMIGRANT'S GUIDE TO NATAL.* By ROBERT
JAMES MANN, F.R.A.S., F.M.S. Second Edition, carefully corrected to
the present Date. Map. 2s.

159. *THE EMIGRANT'S GUIDE TO AUSTRALIA, New South
Wales, Western Australia, South Australia, Victoria, and Queensland.* By
the Rev. JAMES BAIRD, B.A. Map. 2s. 6d.

160. *THE EMIGRANT'S GUIDE TO TASMANIA and NEW
ZEALAND.* By the Rev. JAMES BAIRD, B.A. With a Map. 2s.

159 & *THE EMIGRANT'S GUIDE TO AUSTRALASIA.* By the
160. Rev. J. BAIRD, B.A. Comprising the above two volumes, 12mo, cloth boards.
With Maps of Australia and New Zealand. 5s.

AGRICULTURE.

29. *THE DRAINAGE OF DISTRICTS AND LANDS.* By
G. DRYSDALE DEMPSEY, C.E. Illustrated. 1s. 6d.
  ₊ With "*Drainage of Towns and Buildings,*" in One Vol., 3s.

63. *AGRICULTURAL ENGINEERING:* Farm Buildings, Motive
Powers and Machinery of the Steading, Field Machines, and Implements.
By G. H. ANDREWS, C.E. Illustrated. 3s.

66. *CLAY LANDS AND LOAMY SOILS.* By Professor
DONALDSON. 1s.

131. *MILLER'S, MERCHANT'S, AND FARMER'S READY
RECKONER,* for ascertaining at sight the value of any quantity of Corn,
from One Bushel to One Hundred Quarters, at any given price, from £1 to
£5 per quarter. Together with the approximate values of Millstones and
Millwork, &c. 1s.

140. *SOILS, MANURES, AND CROPS* (Vol. 1. OUTLINES OF
MODERN FARMING.) By R. SCOTT BURN. Woodcuts. 2s.

141. *FARMING AND FARMING ECONOMY,* Notes, Historical
and Practical on. (Vol. 2. OUTLINES OF MODERN FARMING.) By R. SCOTT
BURN. Woodcuts. 3s.

142. *STOCK; CATTLE, SHEEP, AND HORSES.* (Vol. 3.
OUTLINES OF MODERN FARMING.) By R. SCOTT BURN. Woodcuts. 2s. 6d.

145. *DAIRY, PIGS, AND POULTRY,* Management of the. By
R. SCOTT BURN. With Notes on the Diseases of Stock. (Vol. 4. OUTLINES
OF MODERN FARMING.) Woodcuts. 2s.

146. *UTILIZATION OF SEWAGE, IRRIGATION, AND
RECLAMATION OF WASTE LAND.* (Vol. 5. OUTLINES OF MODERN
FARMING.) By R. SCOTT BURN. Woodcuts. 2s. 6d.

  ₊ Nos. 140-1-2-5-6, in One Vol., handsomely half-bound, entitled "OUTLINES OF
MODERN FARMING." By ROBERT SCOTT BURN. Price 12s.

177. *FRUIT TREES;* The Scientific and Profitable Culture of. From
the French of DU BREUIL, Revised by GEO. GLENNY. 187 Woodcuts. 3s. 6d.

LONDON: LOCKWOOD AND CO.,

FINE ARTS.

20. *PERSPECTIVE FOR BEGINNERS.* Adapted to Young Students and Amateurs in Architecture, Painting, &c. By GEORGE PYNE, Artist. Woodcuts. 2s.

27. *A GRAMMAR OF COLOURING*, applicable to House Painting, Decorative Architecture, and the Arts, for the Use of Practical Painters and Decorators. By GEORGE FIELD, Author of "Chromatics; or, The Analogy, Harmony, and Philosophy of Colours," &c. Enlarged by ELLIS A. DAVIDSON. Coloured Illustrations. 2s. 6d.

40. *GLASS STAINING;* or, Painting on Glass, The Art of. Comprising Directions for Preparing the Pigments and Fluxes, laying them upon the Glass, and Firing or Burning in the Colours. From the German of Dr. GESSERT. To which is added, an Appendix on THE ART OF ENAMELLING, &c. 1s.

41. *PAINTING ON GLASS*, The Art of. From the German of EMANUEL OTTO FROMBERG. 1s.

69. *MUSIC*, A Rudimentary and Practical Treatise on. With numerous Examples. By CHARLES CHILD SPENCER. 2s.

71. *PIANOFORTE*, The Art of Playing the. With numerous Exercises and Lessons. Written and Selected from the Best Masters, by CHARLES CHILD SPENCER. 1s. 6d.

181. *PAINTING POPULARLY EXPLAINED*, including Fresco, Oil, Mosaic, Water Colour, Water-Glass, Tempera, Encaustic, Miniature, Painting on Ivory, Vellum, Pottery, Enamel, Glass, &c. With Historical Sketches of the Progress of the Art by THOMAS JOHN GULLICK, assisted by JOHN TIMBS, F.S.A. Third Edition, revised and enlarged, with Frontispiece and Vignette. 5s.

ARITHMETIC, GEOMETRY, MATHEMATICS, ETC.

32. *MATHEMATICAL INSTRUMENTS*, a Treatise on; in which their Construction, and the Methods of Testing, Adjusting, and Using them are concisely Explained. By J. F. HEATHER, M.A., of the Royal Military Academy, Woolwich. Original Edition, in 1 vol., Illustrated. 1s. 6d.

₊ *In ordering the above, be careful to say, "Original Edition," or give the number in the Series (32) to distinguish it from the Enlarged Edition in 3 vols.* (Nos. 168-9-70).

60. *LAND AND ENGINEERING SURVEYING*, a Treatise on; with all the Modern Improvements. Arranged for the Use of Schools and Private Students; also for Practical Land Surveyors and Engineers. By T. BAKER, C.E. New Edition, revised by EDWARD NUGENT, C.E. Illustrated with Plates and Diagrams. 2s.

61*. *READY RECKONER FOR THE ADMEASUREMENT OF LAND.* By ABRAHAM ARMAN, Schoolmaster, Thurleigh, Beds. To which is added a Table, showing the Price of Work, from 2s. 6d. to £1 per acre, and Tables for the Valuation of Land, from 1s. to £1,000 per acre, and from one pole to two thousand acres in extent, &c., &c. 1s. 6d.

76. *DESCRIPTIVE GEOMETRY*, an Elementary Treatise on; with a Theory of Shadows and of Perspective, extracted from the French of G. MONGE. To which is added, a description of the Principles and Practice of Isometrical Projection; the whole being intended as an introduction to the Application of Descriptive Geometry to various branches of the Arts. By J. F. HEATHER, M.A. Illustrated with 14 Plates. 2s.

178. *PRACTICAL PLANE GEOMETRY:* giving the Simplest Modes of Constructing Figures contained in one Plane and Geometrical Construction of the Ground. By J. F. HEATHER, M.A. With 215 Woodcuts. 2s.

179. *PROJECTION:* Orthographic, Topographic, and Perspective: giving the various Modes of Delineating Solid Forms by Constructions on a Single Plane Surface. By J. F. HEATHER, M.A. [*In preparation.*

₊ *The above three volumes will form a COMPLETE ELEMENTARY COURSE OF MATHEMATICAL DRAWING.*

Arithmetic, Geometry, Mathematics, etc., *continued.*

83. *COMMERCIAL BOOK-KEEPING.* With Commercial Phrases and Forms in English, French, Italian, and German. By JAMES HADDON, M.A., Arithmetical Master of King's College School, London. 1s.

84. *ARITHMETIC,* a Rudimentary Treatise on: with full Explanations of its Theoretical Principles, and numerous Examples for Practice. For the Use of Schools and for Self-Instruction. By J. R. Young, late Professor of Mathematics in Belfast College. New Edition, with Index. 1s. 6d.

8½.* A KEY to the above, containing Solutions in full to the Exercises, together with Comments, Explanations, and Improved Processes, for the Use of Teachers and Unassisted Learners. By J. R. YOUNG. 1s. 6d.

85. *EQUATIONAL ARITHMETIC,* applied to Questions of Interest,
85.*. Annuities, Life Assurance, and General Commerce; with various Tables by which all Calculations may be greatly facilitated. By W. HIPSLEY. In Two Parts, 1s. each; or in One Vol. 2s.

86. *ALGEBRA,* the Elements of. By JAMES HADDON, M.A., Second Mathematical Master of King's College School. With Appendix, containing miscellaneous Investigations, and a Collection of Problems in various parts of Algebra. 2s.

86* A KEY AND COMPANION to the above Book, forming an extensive repository of Solved Examples and Problems in Illustration of the various Expedients necessary in Algebraical Operations. Especially adapted for Self-Instruction. By J. R. YOUNG. 1s. 6d.

88. *EUCLID,* THE ELEMENTS OF: with many additional Propositions
89. and Explanatory Notes: to which is prefixed, an Introductory Essay on Logic. By HENRY LAW, C.E. 2s. 6d.

。 *Sold also separately, viz. :—*

88. EUCLID, The First Three Books. By HENRY LAW, C.E. 1s.
89. EUCLID, Books 4, 5, 6, 11, 12. By HENRY LAW, C.E. 1s. 6d.

90. *ANALYTICAL GEOMETRY AND CONICAL SECTIONS,* a Rudimentary Treatise on. By JAMES HANN, late Mathematical Master of King's College School, London. A New Edition, re-written and enlarged by J. R. YOUNG, formerly Professor of Mathematics at Belfast College. 2s.

91. *PLANE TRIGONOMETRY,* the Elements of. By JAMES HANN, formerly Mathematical Master of King's College, London. 1s.

92. *SPHERICAL TRIGONOMETRY,* the Elements of. By JAMES HANN. Revised by CHARLES H. DOWLING, C.E. 1s.
。 *Or with " The Elements of Plane Trigonometry," in One Volume, 2s.*

93. *MENSURATION AND MEASURING,* for Students and Practical Use. With the Mensuration and Levelling of Land for the Purposes of Modern Engineering. By T. BAKER, C.E. New Edition, with Corrections and Additions by E. NUGENT, C.E. Illustrated. 1s. 6d.

94. *LOGARITHMS,* a Treatise on; with Mathematical Tables for facilitating Astronomical, Nautical, Trigonometrical, and Logarithmic Calculations; Tables of Natural Sines and Tangents and Natural Cosines. By HENRY LAW, C.E. Illustrated. 2s. 6d.

101*. *MEASURES, WEIGHTS, AND MONEYS OF ALL NATIONS,* and an Analysis of the Christian, Hebrew, and Mahometan Calendars. By W. S. B. WOOLHOUSE, F.R.A.S., &c. 1s. 6d.

102. *INTEGRAL CALCULUS,* Rudimentary Treatise on the. By HOMERSHAM COX, B.A. Illustrated. 1s.

103. *INTEGRAL CALCULUS,* Examples on the. By JAMES HANN, late of King's College, London. Illustrated. 1s.

101. *DIFFERENTIAL CALCULUS,* Examples of the. By W. S. B. WOOLHOUSE, F.R.A.S., &c. 1s. 6d.

104. *DIFFERENTIAL CALCULUS,* Examples and Solutions of the. By JAMES HADDON, M.A. 1s.

Arithmetic, Geometry, Mathematics, etc., *continued.*

105. *MNEMONICAL LESSONS.* — GEOMETRY, ALGEBRA, AND TRIGONOMETRY, in Easy Mnemonical Lessons. By the Rev. THOMAS PENYNGTON KIRKMAN, M.A. 1s. 6d.

136. *ARITHMETIC,* Rudimentary, for the Use of Schools and Self-Instruction. By JAMES HADDON, M.A. Revised by ABRAHAM ARMAN. 1s. 6d.

137. A KEY TO HADDON'S RUDIMENTARY ARITHMETIC. By A. ARMAN. 1s. 6d.

147. *ARITHMETIC,* STEPPING-STONE TO; Being a Complete Course of Exercises in the First Four Rules (Simple and Compound), on an entirely new principle. For the Use of Elementary Schools of every Grade. Intended as an Introduction to the more extended works on Arithmetic. By ABRAHAM ARMAN. 1s.

148. A KEY TO STEPPING-STONE TO ARITHMETIC. By A. ARMAN. 1s.

158. *THE SLIDE RULE, AND HOW TO USE IT;* Containing full, easy, and simple Instructions to perform all Business Calculations with unexampled rapidity and accuracy. By CHARLES HOARE, C.E. With a Slide Rule in tuck of cover. 3s.

168. *DRAWING AND MEASURING INSTRUMENTS.* Including—I. Instruments employed in Geometrical and Mechanical Drawing, and in the Construction, Copying, and Measurement of Maps and Plans. II. Instruments Used for the purposes of Accurate Measurement, and for Arithmetical Computations. By J. F. HEATHER, M.A., late of the Royal Military Academy, Woolwich, Author of "Descriptive Geometry," &c., &c. Illustrated. 1s. 6d.

169. *OPTICAL INSTRUMENTS.* Including (more especially) Telescopes, Microscopes, and Apparatus for producing copies of Maps and Plans by Photography. By J. F. HEATHER, M.A. Illustrated. 1s. 6d.

170. *SURVEYING AND ASTRONOMICAL INSTRUMENTS.* Including—I. Instruments Used for Determining the Geometrical Features of a portion of Ground. II. Instruments Employed in Astronomical Observations. By J. F. HEATHER, M.A. Illustrated. 1s. 6d.

⁎ *The above three volumes form an enlargement of the Author's original work,* "*Mathematical Instruments: their Construction, Adjustment, Testing, and Use,*" *the Eleventh Edition of which is on sale, price* 1s. 6d. *(See No.* 32 *in the Series.)*

168.⎫ *MATHEMATICAL INSTRUMENTS.* By J. F. HEATHER,
169.⎬ M.A. Enlarged Edition, for the most part entirely re-written. The 3 Parts as
170.⎭ above, in One thick Volume. With numerous Illustrations. Cloth boards. 5s.

LEGAL TREATISES.

50. *THE LAW OF CONTRACTS FOR WORKS AND SERVICES.* By DAVID GIBBONS. Third Edition, Enlarged. 3s.

107. *COUNTY COURT GUIDE,* Plain Guide for Suitors in the County Court. By a BARRISTER. 1s. 6d.

108. *THE METROPOLIS LOCAL MANAGEMENT ACT,* 18th and 19th Vict., c. 120; 19th and 20th Vict., c. 112; 21st and 22nd Vict., c. 104; 24th and 25th Vict., c. 61; also, the last Pauper Removal Act., and the Parochial Assessment Act. 1s. 6d.

108⁎. *THE METROPOLIS LOCAL MANAGEMENT AMENDMENT ACT,* 1862, 25th and 26th Vict., c. 120. Notes and an Index. 1s.
⁎ *With the Local Management Act, in One Volume,* 2s. 6d. ⎬

151. *A HANDY BOOK ON THE LAW OF FRIENDLY, INDUSTRIAL & PROVIDENT BUILDING & LOAN SOCIETIES.* With copious Notes. By NATHANIEL WHITE, of H.M. Civil Service. 1s.

163. *THE LAW OF PATENTS FOR INVENTIONS;* and on the Protection of Designs and Trade Marks. By F. W. CAMPIN, Barrister-at-Law. 2s.

MISCELLANEOUS VOLUMES.

36. *A DICTIONARY OF TERMS used in ARCHITECTURE, BUILDING, ENGINEERING, MINING, METALLURGY, ARCHÆ-OLOGY, the FINE ARTS, &c.* With Explanatory Observations on various Subjects connected with Applied Science and Art. By JOHN WEALE. Fourth Edition, with numerous Additions. Edited by ROBERT HUNT, F.R.S., Keeper of Mining Records, Editor of Ure's " Dictionary of Arts, Manufactures, and Mines." Numerous Illustrations. 5s.

112. *MANUAL OF DOMESTIC MEDICINE.* Describing the Symptoms, Causes, and Treatment of the most common Medical and Surgical Affections. By R. GOODING, B.A., M.B.. The whole intended as a Family Guide in all Cases of Accident and Emergency. 2s.

112*. *MANAGEMENT OF HEALTH.* A Manual of Home and Personal Hygiene. Being Practical Hints on Air, Light, and Ventilation; Exercise, Diet, and Clothing; Rest, Sleep, and Mental Discipline; Bathing and Therapeutics. By the Rev. JAMES BAIRD, B.A. 1s.

113. *FIELD ARTILLERY ON SERVICE,* on the Use of. With especial Reference to that of an Army Corps. For Officers of all Arms. By TAUBERT, Captain, Prussian Artillery. Translated from the German by Lieut.-Col. HENRY HAMILTON MAXWELL, Bengal Artillery. 1s. 6d.

113*. *SWORDS, AND OTHER ARMS* used for Cutting and Thrusting, Memoir on. By Colonel MARRY. Translated from the French by Colonel H. H. MAXWELL. With Notes and Plates. 1s.

150. *LOGIC,* Pure and Applied. By S. H. EMMENS. Third Edition. 1s. 6d.

152. *PRACTICAL HINTS FOR INVESTING MONEY.* With an Explanation of the Mode of Transacting Business on the Stock Exchange. By FRANCIS PLAYFORD, Sworn Broker. 1s.

153. *SELECTIONS FROM LOCKE'S ESSAYS ON THE HUMAN UNDERSTANDING.* With Notes by S. H. EMMENS. 2s.

EDUCATIONAL AND CLASSICAL SERIES.

HISTORY.

1. **England, Outlines of the History of;** more especially with reference to the Origin and Progress of the English Constitution. A Text Book for Schools and Colleges. By WILLIAM DOUGLAS HAMILTON, F.S.A., of Her Majesty's Public Record Office. Fourth Edition, revised and brought down to 1872. Maps and Woodcuts. 5s.; cloth boards, 6s. Also in Five Parts, 1s. each.

5. **Greece, Outlines of the History of;** in connection with the Rise of the Arts and Civilization in Europe. By W. DOUGLAS HAMILTON, of University College, London, and EDWARD LEVIEN, M.A., of Balliol College, Oxford. 2s. 6d.; cloth boards, 3s. 6d.

7. **Rome, Outlines of the History of:** From the Earliest Period to the Christian Era and the Commencement of the Decline of the Empire. By EDWARD LEVIEN, of Balliol College, Oxford. Map, 2s. 6d.; cl. bds. 3s. 6d.

9. **Chronology of History, Art, Literature, and Progress,** from the Creation of the World to the Conclusion of the Franco-German War. The Continuation by W. D. HAMILTON, F.S.A., of Her Majesty's Record Office. 3s.; cloth boards, 3s. 6d.

50. **Dates and Events in English History,** for the use of Candidates in Public and Private Examinations. By the Rev. EDGAR RAND, B.A. 1s.

LONDON : LOCKWOOD AND CO.,

ENGLISH LANGUAGE AND MISCEL-LANEOUS.

11. **Grammar of the English Tongue,** Spoken and Written. With an Introduction to the Study of Comparative Philology. By HYDE CLARKE, D.C.L. Third Edition. 1s.

11*. **Philology:** Handbook of the Comparative Philology of English, Anglo-Saxon, Frisian, Flemish or Dutch, Low or Platt Dutch, High Dutch or German, Danish, Swedish, Icelandic, Latin, Italian, French, Spanish, and Portuguese Tongues. By HYDE CLARKE, D.C.L. 1s.

12. **Dictionary of the English Language,** as Spoken and Written. Containing above 100,000 Words. By HYDE CLARKE, D.C.L. 3s. 6d.; cloth boards, 4s. 6d.; complete with the GRAMMAR, cloth bds., 5s. 6d.

48. **Composition and Punctuation,** familiarly Explained for those who have neglected the Study of Grammar. By AUSTIN BRENAN. 16th Edition. 1s.

49. **Derivative Spelling-Book:** Giving the Origin of Every Word from the Greek, Latin, Saxon, German, Teutonic, Dutch, French, Spanish, and other Languages; with their present Acceptation and Pronunciation. By J. ROWBOTHAM, F.R.A.S. Improved Edition. 1s. 6d.

51. **The Art of Extempore Speaking:** Hints for the Pulpit, the Senate, and the Bar. By M. BAUTAIN, Vicar-General and Professor at the Sorbonne. Translated from the French. Fifth Edition, carefully corrected. 2s. 6d.

52. **Mining and Quarrying,** with the Sciences connected therewith. First Book of, for Schools. By J. H. COLLINS, F.G.S., Lecturer to the Miners' Association of Cornwall and Devon. 1s. 6d.

53. **Places and Facts in Political and Physical Geography,** for Candidates in Public and Private Examinations. By the Rev. EDGAR RAND, B.A. 1s.

54. **Analytical Chemistry,** Qualitative and Quantitative, a Course of. To which is prefixed, a Brief Treatise upon Modern Chemical Nomenclature and Notation. By WM. W. PINK, Practical Chemist, &c., and GEORGE E. WEBSTER, Lecturer on Metallurgy and the Applied Sciences, Nottingham. 2s.

THE SCHOOL MANAGERS' SERIES OF READING BOOKS,

Adapted to the Requirements of the New Code. Edited by the Rev. A. R. GRANT, Rector of Hitcham, and Honorary Canon of Ely; formerly H.M. Inspector of Schools.

	s.	d.		s.	d.
INTRODUCTORY PRIMER	0	3	THIRD STANDARD	1	0
FIRST STANDARD	0	6	FOURTH ,,	1	2
SECOND ,,	0	10	FIFTH ,,	1	6

*** *A Sixth Standard in Preparation.*

LESSONS FROM THE BIBLE. Part I. Old Testament. 1s.
LESSONS FROM THE BIBLE. Part II. New Testament, to which is added THE GEOGRAPHY OF THE BIBLE, for very young Children. By Rev. C. THORNTON FORSTER. 1s. 2d. *** Or the Two Parts in One Volume. 2s.

FRENCH.

24. **French Grammar.** With Complete and Concise Rules on the Genders of French Nouns. By G. L. STRAUSS, Ph.D. 1s.

25. **French-English Dictionary.** Comprising a large number of New Terms used in Engineering, Mining, on Railways, &c. By ALFRED ELWES. 1s. 6d.

French, *continued.*

26. English-French Dictionary. By ALFRED ELWES. 2s.
25,26. French Dictionary (as above). Complete, in One Vol., 3s.;
cloth boards, 3s. 6d. *₊* Or with the GRAMMAR, cloth boards, 4s. 6d.
47. French and English Phrase Book : Containing Intro-
ductory Lessons, with Translations, for the convenience of Students; several
Vocabularies of Words, a Collection of suitable Phrases, and Easy Familiar
Dialogues. 1s.

GERMAN.

39. German Grammar. Adapted for English Students, from
Heyse's Theoretical and Practical Grammar, by Dr. G. L. STRAUSS. 1s.
40. German Reader : A Series of Extracts, carefully culled from the
most approved Authors of Germany; with Notes, Philological and Explanatory. By G. L. STRAUSS, Ph.D. 1s.
41. German Triglot Dictionary. By NICHOLAS ESTERHAZY,
S. A. HAMILTON. Part I. English-German-French. 1s.
42. German Triglot Dictionary. Part II. German-French-
English. 1s.
43. German Triglot Dictionary. Part III. French-German-
English. 1s.
41-43. German Triglot Dictionary (as above), in One Vol., 3s.;
cloth boards, 4s. *₊* Or with the GERMAN GRAMMAR, cloth boards, 5s.

ITALIAN.

27. Italian Grammar, arranged in Twenty Lessons, with a Course
of Exercises. By ALFRED ELWES. 1s.
28. Italian Triglot Dictionary, wherein the Genders of all the
Italian and French Nouns are carefully noted down. By ALFRED ELWES.
Vol. 1. Italian-English-French. 2s.
30. Italian Triglot Dictionary. By A. ELWES. Vol. 2.
English-French-Italian. 2s.
32. Italian Triglot Dictionary. By ALFRED ELWES. Vol. 3.
French-Italian-English. 2s.
28,30, Italian Triglot Dictionary (as above). In One Vol., 6s.;
32. cloth boards, 7s. 6d. *₊* Or with the ITALIAN GRAMMAR, cloth bds., 8s. 6d.

SPANISH.

34. Spanish Grammar, in a Simple and Practical Form. With
a Course of Exercises. By ALFRED ELWES. 1s.
35. Spanish-English and English-Spanish Dictionary.
Including a large number of Technical Terms used in Mining, Engineering, &c.,
with the proper Accents and the Gender of every Noun. By ALFRED ELWES.
4s.; cloth boards, 5s. *₊* Or with the GRAMMAR, cloth boards, 6s.

HEBREW.

46*. Hebrew Grammar. By Dr. BRESSLAU. 1s.
44. Hebrew and English Dictionary, Biblical and Rabbinical;
containing the Hebrew and Chaldee Roots of the Old Testament Post-
Rabbinical Writings. By Dr. BRESSLAU. 6s. *₊* Or with the GRAMMAR, 7s.
46. English and Hebrew Dictionary. By Dr. BRESSLAU. 3s.
44,46. Hebrew Dictionary (as above), in Two Vols., complete, with
46*. the GRAMMAR, cloth boards, 12s.

LATIN.

19. **Latin Grammar.** Containing the Inflections and Elementary Principles of Translation and Construction. By the Rev. THOMAS GOODWIN, M.A., Head Master of the Greenwich Proprietary School. 1s.

20. **Latin-English Dictionary.** Compiled from the best Authorities. By the Rev. THOMAS GOODWIN, M.A. 2s.

22. **English-Latin Dictionary;** together with an Appendix of French and Italian Words which have their origin from the Latin. By the Rev. THOMAS GOODWIN, M.A. 1s. 6d.

20, 22. **Latin Dictionary** (as above). Complete in One Vol., 3s. 6d.; cloth boards, 4s. 6d. •¸• Or with the GRAMMAR, cloth boards, 5s. 6d.

LATIN CLASSICS. With Explanatory Notes in English.

1. **Latin Delectus.** Containing Extracts from Classical Authors, with Genealogical Vocabularies and Explanatory Notes, by HENRY YOUNG, lately Second Master of the Royal Grammar School, Guildford. 1s.

2. **Cæsaris Commentarii de Bello Gallico.** Notes, and a Geographical Register for the Use of Schools, by H. YOUNG. 2s.

12. **Ciceronis Oratio pro Sexto Roscio Amerino.** Edited, with an Introduction, Analysis, and Notes Explanatory and Critical, by the Rev. JAMES DAVIES, M.A. 1s.

14. **Ciceronis Cato Major, Lælius, Brutus, sive de Senectute, de Amicitia, de Claris Oratoribus Dialogi.** With Notes by W. BROWNRIGG SMITH, M.A., F.R.G.S. 2s

3. **Cornelius Nepos.** With Notes. Intended for the Use of Schools. By H. YOUNG. 1s.

6. **Horace; Odes, Epode, and Carmen Sæculare.** Notes by H. YOUNG. 1s. 6d.

7. **Horace; Satires, Epistles, and Ars Poetica.** Notes by W. BROWNRIGG SMITH, M.A., F.R.G.S. 1s. 6d.

21. **Juvenalis Satiræ.** With Prolegomena and Notes by T. H. S. ESCOTT, B.A., Lecturer on Logic at King's College, London. 1s. 6d.

16. **Livy: History of Rome.** Notes by H. YOUNG and W. B. SMITH, M.A. Part 1. Books i., ii., 1s. 6d.

16*. ———— Part 2. Books iii., iv., v., 1s. 6d.

17. ———— Part 3. Books xxi. xxii., 1s. 6d.

8. **Sallustii Crispi Catalina et Bellum Jugurthinum.** Notes Critical and Explanatory, by W. M. DONNE, B.A., Trinity College, Cambridge. 1s. 6d.

10. **Terentii Adelphi Hecyra, Phormio.** Edited, with Notes, Critical and Explanatory, by the Rev. JAMES DAVIES, M.A. 2s.

9. **Terentii Andria et Heautontimorumenos.** With Notes, Critical and Explanatory, by the Rev. JAMES DAVIES, M.A. 1s. 6d.

11. **Terentii Eunuchus, Comœdia.** Edited, with Notes, by the Rev. JAMES DAVIES, M.A. 1s. 6d. Or the Adelphi, Andria, and Eunuchus, 3 vols. in 1, cloth boards, 6s.

4. **Virgilii Maronis Bucolica et Georgica.** With Notes on the Bucolics by W. RUSHTON, M.A., and on the Georgics by H. YOUNG. 1s. 6d.

5. **Virgilii Maronis Æneis.** Notes, Critical and Explanatory, by H. YOUNG. 2s.

19. **Latin Verse Selections,** from Catullus, Tibullus, Propertius, and Ovid. Notes by W. B. DONNE, M.A., Trinity College, Cambridge. 2s.

20. **Latin Prose Selections,** from Varro, Columella, Vitruvius, Seneca, Quintilian, Florus, Velleius Paterculus, Valerius Maximus Suetonius, Apuleius, &c. Notes by W. B. DONNE, M.A. 2s.

Humber's Modern Engineering. First Series.

A RECORD of the PROGRESS of MODERN ENGINEER-
ING, 1863. Comprising Civil, Mechanical, Marine, Hydraulic,
Railway, Bridge, and other Engineering Works, &c. By WILLIAM
HUMBER, Assoc. Inst. C.E., &c.   Imp. 4to, with 36 Double
Plates, drawn to a large scale, and Photographic Portrait of John
Hawkshaw, C.E., F.R.S., &c.   Price 3*l*. 3*s*. half morocco.

List of the Plates.

NAME AND DESCRIPTION.	PLATES.	NAME OF ENGINEER.
Victoria Station and Roof—L. B.& S. C. Rail.	1 to 8	Mr. R. Jacomb Hood, C.E.
Southport Pier	9 and 10	Mr. James Brunlees, C.E.
Victoria Station and Roof—L. C. & D. & G.W. Railways	11 to 15A	Mr. John Fowler, C.E.
Roof of Cremorne Music Hall	16	Mr. William Humber, C.E.
Bridge over G. N. Railway	17	Mr. Joseph Cubitt, C.E.
Roof of Station—Dutch Rhenish Railway	18 and 19	Mr. Euschedi, C.E.
Bridge over the Thames—West London Extension Railway	20 to 24	Mr. William Baker, C.E.
Armour Plates	25	Mr. James Chalmers, C.E.
Suspension Bridge, Thames	26 to 29	Mr. Peter W. Barlow, C.E.
The Allen Engine	30	Mr. G. T. Porter, M.E.
Suspension Bridge, Avon	31 to 33	Mr. John Hawkshaw, C.E. and W. H. Barlow, C.E.
Underground Railway	34 to 36	Mr. John Fowler, C.E.

With copious Descriptive Letterpress, Specifications, &c.

" Handsomely lithographed and printed. It will find favour with many who desire
to preserve in a permanent form copies of the plans and specifications prepared for the
guidance of the contractors for many important engineering works."—*Engineer*.

Humber's Modern Engineering. Second Series.

A RECORD of the PROGRESS of MODERN ENGINEER-
ING, 1864 ; with Photographic Portrait of Robert Stephenson,
C.E., M.P., F.R.S., &c.   Price 3*l*. 3*s*. half morocco.

List of the Plates.

NAME AND DESCRIPTION.	PLATES.	NAME OF ENGINEER.
Birkenhead Docks, Low Water Basin	1 to 15	Mr. G. F. Lyster, C.E.
Charing Cross Station Roof—C. C. Railway.	16 to 18	Mr. Hawkshaw, C.E.
Digswell Viaduct—Great Northern Railway.	19	Mr. J. Cubitt, C.E.
Robbery Wood Viaduct—Great N. Railway.	20	Mr. J. Cubitt, C.E.
Iron Permanent Way	20A	
Clydach Viaduct —Merthyr, Tredegar, and Abergavenny Railway	21	Mr. Gardner, C.E.
Ebbw Viaduct ditto ditto ditto	22	Mr. Gardner, C.E.
College Wood Viaduct—Cornwall Railway	23	Mr. Brunel.
Dublin Winter Palace Roof	24 to 26	Messrs. Ordish & Le Feuvre.
Bridge over the Thames—L. C. & D. Railw.	27 to 32	Mr. J. Cubitt, C.E.
Albert Harbour, Greenock	33 to 36	Messrs. Bell & Miller.

With copious Descriptive Letterpress, Specifications, &c.

" A *resumé* of all the more interesting and important works lately completed in Great
Britain ; and containing, as it does, carefully executed drawings, with full working
details, it will be found a valuable accessory to the profession at large."—*Engineer*.

" Mr. Humber has done the profession good and true service, by the fine collection
of examples he has here brought before the profession and the public."—*Practical
Mechanics' Journal*.

Humber's Modern Engineering. Third Series.

A RECORD of the PROGRESS of MODERN ENGINEER-
ING, 1865. Imp. 4to, with 40 Double Plates, drawn to a large
scale, and Photographic Portrait of J. R. M'Clean, Esq., late President of the Institution of Civil Engineers.   Price 3*l*. 3*s*. half
morocco.

List of Plates and Diagrams.

MAIN DRAINAGE, METROPOLIS.

North Side.

Map showing Interception of Sewers.
Middle Level Sewer. Sewer under Re-
gent's Canal.
Middle Level Sewer. Junction with Fleet
Ditch.
Outfall Sewer. Bridge over River Lea.
Elevation.
Outfall Sewer. Bridge over River Lea.
Details.
Outfall Sewer. Bridge over River Lea.
Details.
Outfall Sewer. Bridge over Marsh Lane,
North Woolwich Railway, and Bow and
Barking Railway Junction.
Outfall Sewer. Bridge over Bow and
Barking Railway. Elevation.
Outfall Sewer. Bridge over Bow and
Barking Railway. Details.
Outfall Sewer. Bridge over Bow and
Barking Railway. Details.
Outfall Sewer. Bridge over East London
Waterworks' Feeder. Elevation.
Outfall Sewer. Bridge over East London
Waterworks' Feeder. Details.
Outfall Sewer. Reservoir. Plan.
Outfall Sewer. Reservoir. Section.
Outfall Sewer. Tumbling Bay and Outlet.
Outfall Sewer. Penstocks.

South Side.

Outfall Sewer. Bermondsey Branch.
Outfall Sewer. Bermondsey Branch.
Outfall Sewer. Reservoir and Outlet.
Plan.

MAIN DRAINAGE, METROPOLIS,
continued—

Outfall Sewer. Reservoir and Outlet.
Details.
Outfall Sewer. Reservoir and Outlet.
Details.
Outfall Sewer. Reservoir and Outlet.
Details.
Outfall Sewer. Filth Hoist.
Sections of Sewers (North and South
Sides).

THAMES EMBANKMENT.

Section of River Wall.
Steam-boat Pier, Westminster. Elevation.
Steam-boat Pier, Westminster. Details.
Landing Stairs between Charing Cross
and Waterloo Bridges.
York Gate. Front Elevation.
York Gate. Side Elevation and Details.
Overflow and Outlet at Savoy Street Sewer.
Details.
Overflow and Outlet at Savoy Street Sewer.
Penstock.
Overflow and Outlet at Savoy Street Sewer.
Penstock.
Steam-boat Pier, Waterloo Bridge. Eleva-
tion.
Steam-boat Pier, Waterloo Bridge. De-
tails.
Steam-boat Pier, Waterloo Bridge. De-
tails.
Junction of Sewers. Plans and Sections.
Gullies. Plans and Sections.
Rolling Stock.
Granite and Iron Forts.

With copious Descriptive Letterpress, Specifications, &c.

Opinions of the Press.

"Mr. Humber's works—especially his annual 'Record,' with which so many of our
readers are now familiar—fill a void occupied by no other branch of literature. . . . .
The drawings have a constantly increasing value, and whoever desires to possess clear
representations of the two great works carried out by our Metropolitan Board will
obtain Mr. Humber's last volume."—*Engineering.*

"No engineer, architect, or contractor should fail to preserve these records of works
which, for magnitude, have not their parallel in the present day, no student in the
profession but should carefully study the details of these great works, which he may be
one day called upon to imitate."—*Mechanics' Magazine.*

"A work highly creditable to the industry of its author. . . . . The volume is quite
an encyclopædia for the study of the student who desires to master the subject of
municipal drainage on its scale of greatest development."—*Practical Mechanics
Journal.*

Humber's Modern Engineering. Fourth Series.

A RECORD of the PROGRESS of MODERN ENGINEER-ING, 1866. Imp. 4to, with 36 Double Plates, drawn to a large scale, and Photographic Portrait of John Fowler, Esq., President of the Institution of Civil Engineers. Price 3*l.* 3*s.* half-morocco.

List of the Plates and Diagrams.

NAME AND DESCRIPTION.	PLATES.	NAME OF ENGINEER.
Abbey Mills Pumping Station, Main Drainage, Metropolis.	1 to 4	Mr. Bazalgette, C.E.
Barrow Docks	5 to 9	Messrs. M'Clean & Stillman, [C.E.
Manquis Viaduct, Santiago and Valparaiso Railway	10, 11	Mr. W. Loyd, C.E.
Adams' Locomotive, St. Helen's Canal Railw.	12, 13	Mr. H. Cross, C.E.
Cannon Street Station Roof, Charing Cross Railway	14 to 16	Mr. J. Hawkshaw, C.E.
Read Bridge over the River Moka	17, 18	Mr. H. Wakefield, C.E.
Telegraphic Apparatus for Mesopotamia	19	Mr. Siemens, C.E.
Viaduct over the River Wye, Midland Railw.	20 to 22	Mr. W. H. Barlow, C.E.
St. Germans Viaduct, Cornwall Railway	23, 24	Mr. Brunel, C.E.
Wrought-Iron Cylinder for Diving Bell	25	Mr. J. Coode, C.E.
Millwall Docks	26 to 31	Messrs. J. Fowler, C.E., and William Wilson, C.E.
Milroy's Patent Excavator	32	Mr. Milroy, C.E.
Metropolitan District Railway	33 to 38	Mr. J. Fowler, Engineer-in-Chief, and Mr. T. M. Johnson, C.E.
Harbours, Ports, and Breakwaters	A to C	—

The Letterpress comprises—

A concluding article on Harbours, Ports, and Breakwaters, with Illustrations and detailed descriptions of the Breakwater at Cherbourg, and other important modern works; an article on the Telegraph Lines of Mesopotamia; a full description of the Wrought-iron Diving Cylinder for Ceylon, the circumstances under which it was used, and the means of working it; full description of the Millwall Docks; &c., &c., &c.

Opinions of the Press.

"Mr. Humber's 'Record of Modern Engineering' is a work of peculiar value, as well to those who design as to those who study the art of engineering construction. It embodies a vast amount of practical information in the form of full descriptions and working drawings of all the most recent and noteworthy engineering works. The plates are excellently lithographed, and the present volume of the 'Record' is not a whit behind its predecessors."—*Mechanics' Magazine.*

"We gladly welcome another year's issue of this valuable publication from the able pen of Mr. Humber. The accuracy and general excellence of this work are well known, while its usefulness in giving the measurements and details of some of the latest examples of engineering, as carried out by the most eminent men in the profession, cannot be too highly prized."—*Artisan.*

"The volume forms a valuable companion to those which have preceded it, and cannot fail to prove a most important addition to every engineering library."—*Mining Journal.*

"No one of Mr. Humber's volumes was bad; all were worth their cost, from the mass of plates from well-executed drawings which they contained. In this respect, perhaps, this last volume is the most valuable that the author has produced."—*Practical Mechanics' Journal.*

Humber's Great Work on Bridge Construction.

A COMPLETE and PRACTICAL TREATISE on CAST and WROUGHT-IRON BRIDGE CONSTRUCTION, including Iron Foundations. In Three Parts—Theoretical, Practical, and Descriptive. By WILLIAM HUMBER, Assoc. Inst. C. E., and M. Inst. M.E. Third Edition, revised and much improved, with 115 Double Plates (20 of which now first appear in this edition), and numerous additions to the Text. In 2 vols. imp. 4to., price 6*l.* 16*s.* 6*d.* half-bound in morocco.

"A very valuable contribution to the standard literature of civil engineering. In addition to elevations, plans, and sections, large scale details are given, which very much enhance the instructive worth of these illustrations. No engineer would willingly be without so valuable a fund of information."—*Civil Engineer and Architect's Journal.*

"Mr. Humber's stately volumes lately issued—in which the most important bridges erected during the last five years, under the direction of the late Mr. Brunel, Sir W. Cubitt, Mr. Hawkshaw, Mr. Page, Mr. Fowler, Mr. Hemans, and others among our most eminent engineers, are drawn and specified in great detail."—*Engineer.*

Weale's Engineers' Pocket-Book.

THE ENGINEERS', ARCHITECTS', and CONTRACTORS' POCKET-BOOK (LOCKWOOD & Co.'s; formerly WEALE'S). Published Annually. In roan tuck, gilt edges, with 10 Copper-Plates and numerous Woodcuts. Price 6*s.*

" A vast amount of really valuable matter condensed into the small dimensions of a book which is, in reality, what it professes to be—a pocket-book. . . . . We cordially recommend the book to the notice of the managers of coal and other mines; to them it will prove a handy book of reference on a variety of subjects more or less intimately connected with their profession."—*Colliery Guardian.*

" Every branch of engineering is treated of, and facts, figures, and data of every kind abound."—*Mechanics' Mag.*

" It contains a large amount of information peculiarly valuable to those for whose use it is compiled. We cordially commend it to the engineering and architectural professions generally."—*Mining Journal.*

Iron Bridges, Girders, Roofs, &c.

A TREATISE on the APPLICATION of IRON to the CONSTRUCTION of BRIDGES, GIRDERS, ROOFS, and OTHER WORKS ; showing the Principles upon which such Structures are Designed, and their Practical Application. Especially arranged for the use of Students and Practical Mechanics, all Mathematical Formulæ and Symbols being excluded. By FRANCIS CAMPIN, C.E. With numerous Diagrams. 12mo., cloth boards, 3*s.*

" For numbers of young engineers the book is just the cheap, handy, first guide they want."—*Middlesborough Weekly News.*

" Invaluable to those who have not been educated in mathematics."—*Colliery Guardian.*

" Remarkably accurate and well written."—*Artisan.*

Iron and Steel.

'IRON AND STEEL': a Work for the Forge, Foundry, Factory, and Office. Containing Ready, Useful, and Trustworthy Information for Ironmasters and their Stocktakers; Managers of Bar, Rail, Plate, and Sheet Rolling Mills; Iron and Metal Founders; Iron Ship and Bridge Builders; Mechanical, Mining, and Consulting Engineers; Architects, Contractors, Builders, an' Professional Draughtsmen. By CHARLES HOARE, Author 'The Slide Rule,' &c. Oblong, 18mo, 5*s.* cloth.

Barlow on the Strength of Materials, enlarged.

A TREATISE ON THE STRENGTH OF MATERIALS, with Rules for application in Architecture, the Construction of Suspension Bridges, Railways, &c. ; and an Appendix on the Power of Locomotive Engines, and the effect of Inclined Planes and Gradients. By PETER BARLOW, F.R.S. A New Edition, revised by his Sons, P. W. BARLOW, F.R.S., and W. H. BARLOW, F.R.S., to which are added Experiments by HODGKINSON, FAIRBAIRN, and KIRKALDY ; an Essay (with Illustrations) on the effect produced by passing Weights over Elastic Bars, by the Rev. ROBERT WILLIS, M.A., F.R.S. And Formulæ for Calculating Girders, &c. The whole arranged and edited by W. HUMBER, Assoc. Inst. C.E., Author of " A Complete and Practical Treatise on Cast and Wrought-Iron Bridge Construction," &c. &c. Demy 8vo, 400 pp., with 19 large Plates, and numerous woodcuts, price 18*s*. cloth.

" The book is undoubtedly worthy of the highest commendation."—*Mining Journal.*

" The best book on the subject which has yet appeared.   . . . .   We know of no work that so completely fulfils its mission."—*English Mechanic.*

" The standard treatise upon this particular subject."—*Engineer.*

Strains, Formulæ & Diagrams for Calculation of.

A HANDY BOOK for the CALCULATION of STRAINS in GIRDERS and SIMILAR STRUCTURES, and their STRENGTH ; consisting of Formulæ and Corresponding Diagrams, with numerous Details for Practical Application, &c. By WILLIAM HUMBER, Assoc. Inst. C.E., &c. Fcap. 8vo, with nearly 100 Woodcuts and 3 Plates, price 7*s. 6d.* cloth.

" The arrangement of the matter in this little volume is as convenient as it well could be. . . . . The system of employing diagrams as a substitute for complex computations is one justly coming into great favour, and in that respect Mr. Humber's volume is fully up to the times."—*Engineering.*

" The formulæ are neatly expressed, and the diagrams good."—*Athenæum.*

" We heartily commend this really *handy* book to our engineer and architect readers."—*English Mechanic.*

Mechanical Engineering.

A PRACTICAL TREATISE ON MECHANICAL ENGINEERING : comprising Metallurgy, Moulding, Casting, Forging, Tools, Workshop Machinery, Mechanical Manipulation, Manufacture of the Steam Engine, &c. &c. With an Appendix on the Analysis of Iron and Iron Ore, and Glossary of Terms. By FRANCIS CAMPIN, C.E. Illustrated with 91 Woodcuts and 28 Plates of Slotting, Shaping, Drilling, Punching, Shearing, and Riveting Machines—Blast, Refining, and Reverberatory Furnaces—Steam Engines, Governors, Boilers, Locomotives, &c. 8vo, cloth, 12*s.*

Steam Engine.

STEAM AND THE STEAM ENGINE, Stationary and Portable, an Elementary Treatise on. Being an Extension of Mr. John Sewell's Treatise on Steam. By D. KINNEAR CLARK, C.E., M.I.C.E., Author of 'Railway Machinery,' 'Railway Locomotives,' &c., &c. With numerous Illustrations. 12mo, cloth ͖ards, 4*s.*

ᷭ essential part of the subject is treated of competently, and in a popular ᷭ*n.*

Strains.

THE STRAINS ON STRUCTURES OF IRONWORK; with Practical Remarks on Iron Construction. By F. W. SHIELDS, M. Inst. C. E. Second Edition, with 5 plates. Royal 8vo, 5s. cloth.
CONTENTS.—Introductory Remarks ; Beams Loaded at Centre ; Beams Loaded at unequal distances between supports ; Beams uniformly Loaded ; Girders with triangular bracing Loaded at centre ; Ditto, Loaded at unequal distances between supports ; Ditto, uniformly Loaded ; Calculation of the Strains on Girders with triangular Bracings ; Cantilevers ; Continuous Girders ; Lattice Girders ; Girders with Vertical Struts and Diagonal Ties ; Calculation of the Strains on Ditto ; Bow and String Girders ; Girders of a form not belonging to any regular figure ; Plate Girders ; Apportionments of Material to Strain ; Comparison of different Girders ; Proportion of Length to Depth of Girders ; Character of the Work ; Iron Roofs.

Construction of Iron Beams, Pillars, &c.

IRON AND HEAT, Exhibiting the Principles concerned in the Construction of Iron Beams, Pillars, and Bridge Girders, and the Action of Heat in the Smelting Furnace. By JAMES ARMOUR, C. E. Woodcuts, 12mo, cloth boards, 3s. 6d. ; cloth limp, 2s. 6d.

"A very useful and thoroughly practical little volume, in every way deserving of circulation amongst working men."—*Mining Journal.*
"No ironworker who wishes to acquaint himself with the principles of his own trade can afford to be without it."—*South Durham Mercury.*

Power in Motion.

POWER IN MOTION : Horse Power, Motion, Toothed Wheel Gearing, Long and Short Driving Bands, Angular Forces, &c. By JAMES ARMOUR, C.E. With 73 Diagrams. 12mo, cloth boards, 3s. 6d. [*Recently published.*
"Numerous illustrations enable the author to convey his meaning as explicitly as it is perhaps possible to be conveyed. The value of the theoretic and practical knowledge imparted cannot well be over estimated."—*Newcastle Weekly Chronicle.*

Metallurgy of Iron.

A TREATISE ON THE METALLURGY OF IRON : containing Outlines of the History of Iron Manufacture, Methods of Assay, and Analyses of Iron Ores, Processes of Manufacture of Iron and Steel, &c. By H. BAUERMAN, F.G.S., Associate of the Royal School of Mines. With numerous Illustrations. Fourth Edition, revised and much enlarged. 12mo., cloth boards, 5s. 6d. [*Just published.*
"Carefully written, it has the merit of brevity and conciseness, as to less important points, while all material matters are very fully and thoroughly entered into."—*Standard.*

Trigonometrical Surveying.

AN OUTLINE OF THE METHOD OF CONDUCTING A TRIGONOMETRICAL SURVEY, for the Formation of Geographical and Topographical Maps and Plans, Military Reconnaissance, Levelling, &c., with the most useful Problems in Geodesy and Practical Astronomy, and Formulæ and Tables for Facilitating their Calculation. By LIEUT-GENERAL FROME, R.E., late Inspector-General of Fortifications, &c. Fourth Edition, Enlarged, thoroughly Revised, and partly Re-written. By CAPTAIN CHARLES WARREN, R.E., F.G.S. With 19 Plates and 115 Woodcuts, royal 8vo, price 16s. cloth.

Hydraulics.

HYDRAULIC TABLES, CO-EFFICIENTS, and FORMULÆ for finding the Discharge of Water from Orifices, Notches, Weirs, Pipes, and Rivers. With New Formulæ, Tables, and General Information on Rain-fall, Catchment-Basins, Drainage, Sewerage, Water Supply for Towns and Mill Power. By JOHN NEVILLE, Civil Engineer, M.R.I.A. Third Edition, carefully revised, with considerable Additions. Numerous Illustrations. Crown 8vo, 14s. cloth. [*Now ready.*

Drawing for Engineers, &c.

THE WORKMAN'S MANUAL OF ENGINEERING DRAWING. By JOHN MAXTON, Instructor in Engineering Drawing, South Kensington. Second Edition, carefully revised. With upwards of 300 Plates and Diagrams. 12mo, cloth, strongly bound, 4s. 6d.

" Even accomplished draughtsmen will find in it much that will be of use to them. A copy of it should be kept for reference in every drawing office."—*Engineering*.

"An indispensable book for teachers of engineering drawing." — *Mechanics' Magazine*.

Levelling.

A TREATISE on the PRINCIPLES and PRACTICE of LEVELLING; showing its Application to Purposes of Railway and Civil Engineering, in the Construction of Roads; with Mr. TELFORD'S Rules for the same. By FREDERICK W. SIMMS, F.G.S., M. Inst. C.E. Sixth Edition, very carefully revised, with the addition of Mr. LAW'S Practical Examples for Setting out Railway Curves, and Mr. TRAUTWINE'S Field Practice of Laying out Circular Curves. With 7 Plates and numerous Woodcuts. 8vo, 8s. 6d. cloth.   *⁎* TRAUTWINE on Curves, separate, price 5s.

"One of the most important text-books for the general surveyor, and there is scarcely a question connected with levelling for which a solution would be sought but that would be satisfactorily answered by consulting the volume."—*Mining Journal*.

"The text-book on levelling in most of our engineering schools and colleges."—*Engineer*.

"The publishers have rendered a substantial service to the profession, especially to the younger members, by bringing out the present edition of Mr. Simms's useful work."—*Engineering*.

Earthwork.

EARTHWORK TABLES, showing the Contents in Cubic Yards of Embankments, Cuttings, &c., of Heights or Depths up to an average of 80 feet. By JOSEPH BROADBENT, C.E., and FRANCIS CAMPIN, C.E. Cr. 8vo. oblong, 5s. cloth.

"Creditable to both the authors and the publishers. . . . The way in which accuracy is attained, by a simple division of each cross section into three elements, two of which are constant and one variable, is ingenious."—*Athenæum*.

" Likely to be of considerable service to engineers."—*Building News*.

" Contractors, builders, and engineers should not be without it."—*Builders' Weekly Reporter*.

" Cannot fail to come into general use."—*Mining Journal*.

Tunnelling.

PRACTICAL TUNNELLING. By F. W. SIMMS. An entirely new edition, revised and greatly enlarged by D. KINNEAR CLARK, C.E. Imp. 8vo.   [*In the Press.*

Strength of Cast Iron, &c.

A PRACTICAL ESSAY on the STRENGTH of CAST IRON and OTHER METALS. By the late THOMAS TREDGOLD, Mem. Inst. C.E., Author of " Elementary Principles of Carpentry," &c. Fifth Edition, Edited by EATON HODGKINSON, F.R.S. ; to which are added EXPERIMENTAL RESEARCHES on the STRENGTH and OTHER PROPERTIES of CAST IRON. By the EDITOR. The whole Illustrated with 9 Engravings and numerous Woodcuts. 8vo, 12s. cloth.

*** HODGKINSON'S EXPERIMENTAL RESEARCHES ON THE STRENGTH AND OTHER PROPERTIES OF CAST IRON may be had separately. With Engravings and Woodcuts. 8vo, price 6s. cloth.

The High-Pressure Steam Engine.

THE HIGH-PRESSURE STEAM ENGINE ; an Exposition of its Comparative Merits, and an Essay towards an Improved System of Construction, adapted especially to secure Safety and Economy. By Dr. ERNST ALBAN, Practical Machine Maker, Plau, Mecklenberg. Translated from the German, with Notes, by Dr. POLE, F.R.S., M. Inst. C.E., &c. &c. With 28 fine Plates, 8vo, 16s. 6d. cloth.

" A work like this, which goes thoroughly into the examination of the high-pressure engine, the boiler, and its appendages, &c., is exceedingly useful, and deserves a place in every scientific library."—*Steam Shipping Chronicle.*

Steam Boilers.

A TREATISE ON STEAM BOILERS : their Strength, Construction, and Economical Working. By ROBERT WILSON, late Inspector for the Manchester Steam Users' Association for the Prevention of Steam Boiler Explosions, and for the Attainment of Economy in the Application of Steam. Third Edition. 12mo, cloth boards, 328 pages, price 6s.

Tables of Curves.

TABLES OF TANGENTIAL ANGLES and MULTIPLES for setting out Curves from 5 to 200 Radius. By ALEXANDER BEAZELEY, M. Inst. C.E. Printed on 48 Cards, and sold in a cloth box, waistcoat-pocket size, price 3s. 6d.

" Each table is printed on a small card, which, being placed on the theodolite, leaves the hands free to manipulate the instrument—no small advantage as regards the rapidity of work. They are clearly printed, and compactly fitted into a small case for the pocket—an arrangement that will recommend them to all practical men."—*Engineer.*

" Very handy : a man may know that all his day's work must fall on two of these cards, which he puts into his own card-case, and leaves the rest behind."—*Athenæum.*

Laying Out Curves.

THE FIELD PRACTICE of LAYING OUT CIRCULAR CURVES for RAILROADS. By JOHN C. TRAUTWINE, C.E. (Extracted from SIMMS's Work on Levelling). 8vo, 5s. sewed.

Estimate and Price Book.

THE CIVIL ENGINEER'S AND CONTRACTOR'S ESTI-
MATE AND PRICE BOOK for Home or Foreign Service :
in reference to Roads, Railways, Tramways, Docks, Harbours,
Forts, Fortifications, Bridges, Aqueducts, Tunnels, Sewers, Water-
works, Gasworks, Stations, Barracks, Warehouses, &c. &c. &c.
With Specifications for Permanent Way, Telegraph Materials,
Plant, Maintenance, and Working of a Railway ; and a Priced List
of Machinery, Plant, Tools, &c. By W. D. HASKOLL, C.E.
Plates and Woodcuts. Published annually. 8vo, cloth, 6s.

"As furnishing a variety of data on every conceivable want to civil engineers and
contractors, this book has ever stood perhaps unrivalled."—*Architect.*

Surveying (Land and Marine).

LAND AND MARINE SURVEYING, in Reference to the
Preparation of Plans for Roads and Railways, Canals, Rivers,
Towns' Water Supplies, Docks and Harbours ; with Description
and Use of Surveying Instruments. By W. DAVIS HASKOLL, C.E.,
Author of "The Engineer's Field Book," "Examples of Bridge
and Viaduct Construction," &c.   Demy 8vo, price 12s. 6d. cloth,
with 14 folding Plates, and numerous Woodcuts.

"A most useful and well arranged book for the aid of a student. . . . . We
can strongly recommend it as a carefully-written and valuable text-book."—*Builder.*

"Mr. Haskoll has knowledge and experience, and can so give expression to it as
to make any matter on which he writes, clear to the youngest pupil in a surveyor's
office."—*Colliery Guardian.*

"A volume which cannot fail to prove of the utmost practical utility. . . . . It
is one which may be safely recommended to all students who aspire to become clean
and expert surveyors."—*Mining Journal.*

Engineering Fieldwork.

THE PRACTICE OF ENGINEERING FIELDWORK,
applied to Land and Hydraulic, Hydrographic, and Submarine
Surveying and Levelling.   Second Edition, revised, with considerable additions, and a Supplementary Volume on WATER-
WORKS, SEWERS, SEWAGE, and IRRIGATION. By W.
DAVIS HASKOLL, C.E.   Numerous folding Plates. Demy 8vo, 2
vols. in one, cloth boards, 1l. 1s. (published at 2l. 4s.)

Mining, Surveying and Valuing.

THE MINERAL SURVEYOR AND VALUER'S COM-
PLETE GUIDE, comprising a Treatise on Improved Mining
Surveying, with new Traverse Tables ; and Descriptions of Im-
proved Instruments ; also an Exposition of the Correct Principles
of Laying out and Valuing Home and Foreign Iron and Coal
Mineral Properties: to which is appended M. THOMAN'S (of
the Crédit Mobilier, Paris) TREATISE on COMPOUND IN-
TEREST and ANNUITIES, with LOGARITHMIC TABLES.
By WILLIAM LINTERN, Mining and Civil Engineer.   12mo,
strongly bound in cloth boards, with four Plates of Diagrams,
Plans, &c., price 10s. 6d.

"Contains much valuable information given in a small compass, and which, as far
as we have tested it, is thoroughly trustworthy."—*Iron and Coal Trades' Review.*

"The matter, arrangement, and illustration of this work are all excellent, and make
it one of the best of its kind."—*Standard.*

Fire Engineering.

FIRES, FIRE-ENGINES, AND FIRE BRIGADES. With a History of Fire-Engines, their Construction, Use, and Management; Remarks on Fire-Proof Buildings, and the Preservation of Life from Fire; Statistics of the Fire Appliances in English Towns; Foreign Fire Systems; Hints on Fire Brigades, &c., &c. By CHARLES F. T. YOUNG, C.E. With numerous Illustrations, handsomely printed, 544 pp., demy 8vo, price 1l. 4s. cloth.

"We can most heartily commend this book. . . . . It is really the only English work we now have upon the subject."—*Engineering*.

'We strongly recommend the book to the notice of all who are in any way interested in fires, fire-engines, or fire-brigades."—*Mechanics' Magazine*.

Manual of Mining Tools.

MINING TOOLS. For the use of Mine Managers, Agents, Mining Students, &c. By WILLIAM MORGANS, Lecturer on Practical Mining at the Bristol School of Mines. Volume of Text. 12mo. With an Atlas of Plates, containing 235 Illustrations. 4to. Together, price 9s. cloth boards. [*Recently published.*

"Students in the Science of Mining, and not only they, but subordinate officials in mines, and even Overmen, Captains, Managers, and Viewers may gain practical knowledge and useful hints by the study of Mr. Morgans's Manual."—*Colliery Guardian*.

"A very valuable work, which will tend materially to improve our mining literature."—*Mining Journal*.

Gas and Gasworks.

A TREATISE on GASWORKS and the PRACTICE of MANUFACTURING and DISTRIBUTING COAL GAS. By SAMUEL HUGHES, C.E. Fourth Edition, revised by W. RICHARDS, C.E. With 68 Woodcuts, bound in cloth boards, 12mo, price 4s.

Waterworks for Cities and Towns.

WATERWORKS for the SUPPLY of CITIES and TOWNS, with a Description of the Principal Geological Formations of England as influencing Supplies of Water. By SAMUEL HUGHES, F.G.S., Civil Engineer. New and enlarged edition, 12mo, cloth boards, with numerous Illustrations, price 5s.

"One of the most convenient, and at the same time reliable works on a subject, the vital importance of which cannot be over-estimated."—*Bradford Observer*.

Coal and Coal Mining.

COAL AND COAL MINING: a Rudimentary Treatise on. By WARINGTON W. SMYTH, M.A., F.R.S., &c., Chief Inspector of the Mines of the Crown and of the Duchy of Cornwall. New edition, revised and corrected. 12mo., cloth boards, with numerous Illustrations, price 4s. 6d.

"Every portion of the volume appears to have been prepared with much care, and as an outline is given of every known coal-field in this and other countries, as well as of the two principal methods of working, the book will doubtless interest a very large number of readers."—*Mining Journal*.

"Certainly experimental skill and rule-of-thumb practice would be greatly enriched by the addition of the theoretical knowledge and scientific information which Mr. Warington Smyth communicates in combination with the results of his own experience and personal research."—*Colliery Guardian*.

Field-Book for Engineers.

THE ENGINEER'S, MINING SURVEYOR'S, and CONTRACTOR'S FIELD-BOOK. By W. DAVIS HASKOLL, Civil Engineer. Third Edition, much enlarged, consisting of a Series of Tables, with Rules, Explanations of Systems, and Use of Theodolite for Traverse Surveying and Plotting the Work with minute accuracy by means of Straight Edge and Set Square only; Levelling with the Theodolite, Casting out and Reducing Levels to Datum, and Plotting Sections in the ordinary manner; Setting out Curves with the Theodolite by Tangential Angles and Multiples with Right and Left-hand Readings of the Instrument; Setting out Curves without Theodolite on the System of Tangential Angles by Sets of Tangents and Offsets; and Earthwork Tables to 80 feet deep, calculated for every 6 inches in depth. With numerous wood-cuts, 12mo, price 12s. cloth.

"A very useful work for the practical engineer and surveyor. Every person engaged in engineering field operations will estimate the importance of such a work and the amount of valuable time which will be saved by reference to a set of reliable tables prepared with the accuracy and fulness of those given in this volume."—*Railway News.*

"The book is very handy, and the author might have added that the separate tables of sines and tangents to every minute will make it useful for many other purposes, the genuine traverse tables existing all the same."—*Athenæum.*

"The work forms a handsome pocket volume, and cannot fail, from its portability and utility, to be extensively patronised by the engineering profession."—*Mining Journal.*

"We strongly recommend this second edition of Mr. Haskoll's 'Field Book' to all classes of surveyors."—*Colliery Guardian.*

Earthwork, Measurement and Calculation of.

A MANUAL on EARTHWORK. By ALEX. J. S. GRAHAM, C.E., Resident Engineer, Forest of Dean Central Railway. With numerous Diagrams. 18mo, 2s. 6d. cloth.

"As a really handy book for reference, we know of no work equal to it; and the railway engineers and others employed in the measurement and calculation of earth work will find a great amount of practical information very admirably arranged, and available for general or rough estimates, as well as for the more exact calculations required in the engineers' contractor's offices."—*Artizan.*

Harbours.

THE DESIGN and CONSTRUCTION of HARBOURS: A Treatise on Maritime Engineering. By THOMAS STEVENSON, F.R.S.E., F.G.S., M.I.C.E. Second Edition, containing many additional subjects, and otherwise generally extended and revised. With 20 Plates and numerous Cuts. Small 4to, 15s. cloth.

Mathematical and Drawing Instruments.

A TREATISE ON THE PRINCIPAL MATHEMATICAL AND DRAWING INSTRUMENTS employed by the Engineer, Architect, and Surveyor. By FREDERICK W. SIMMS, M. Inst. C.E., Author of "Practical Tunnelling," &c. Third Edition, with numerous Cuts. 12mo, price 3s. 6d. cloth.

Bridge Construction in Masonry, Timber, & Iron.

EXAMPLES OF BRIDGE AND VIADUCT CONSTRUC-
TION OF MASONRY, TIMBER, AND IRON ; consisting of
46 Plates from the Contract Drawings or Admeasurement of select
Works. By W. DAVIS HASKOLL, C.E. Second Edition, with
the addition of 554 Estimates, and the Practice of Setting out Works,
illustrated with 6 pages of Diagrams. Imp. 4to, price 2*l.* 12*s.* 6*d.*
half-morocco.

"One of the very few works extant descending to the level of ordinary routine, and
treating on the common every-day practice of the railway engineer. . . . A work of
the present nature by a man of Mr. Haskoll's experience, must prove invaluable to
hundreds. The tables of estimates appended to this edition will considerably enhance
its value."—*Engineering.*

Mathematical Instruments, their Construction, &c.

MATHEMATICAL INSTRUMENTS : THEIR CONSTRUC-
TION, ADJUSTMENT, TESTING, AND USE; comprising
Drawing, Measuring, Optical, Surveying, and Astronomical Instruments. By J. F. HEATHER, M.A., Author of "Practical Plane
Geometry," "Descriptive Geometry," &c. Enlarged Edition, for
the most part entirely rewritten. With numerous Wood-cuts.
12mo, cloth boards, price 5*s.*

Oblique Arches.

A PRACTICAL TREATISE ON THE CONSTRUCTION of
OBLIQUE ARCHES. By JOHN HART. Third Edition, with
Plates. Imperial 8vo, price 8*s.* cloth.

Oblique Bridges.

A PRACTICAL and THEORETICAL ESSAY on OBLIQUE
BRIDGES, with 13 large folding Plates. By GEO. WATSON
BUCK, M. Inst. C.E. Second Edition, corrected by W. H.
BARLOW, M. Inst. C.E. Imperial 8vo, 12*s.* cloth.

"The standard text-book for all engineers regarding skew arches, is Mr. Buck's
treatise, and it would be impossible to consult a better."—*Engineer.*

Pocket-Book for Marine Engineers.

A POCKET BOOK FOR MARINE ENGINEERS. Con-
taining useful Rules and Formulæ in a compact form. By FRANK
PROCTOR, A.I.N.A. Second Edition, revised and enlarged.
Royal 32mo, leather, gilt edges, with strap, price 4*s.*

"We recommend it to our readers as going far to supply a long-felt want."—
Naval Science.
"A most useful companion to all marine engineers."—*United Service Gazette.*
"Scarcely anything required by a naval engineer appears to have been for-
gotten.—*Iron.*
"A very valuable publication . . . a means of saving much time and labour."—
New York Monthly Record.

Weale's Dictionary of Terms.

A DICTIONARY of TERMS used in ARCHITECTURE,
BUILDING, ENGINEERING, MINING, METALLURGY,
ARCHÆOLOGY, the FINE ARTS, &c. By JOHN WEALE.
Fourth Edition, enlarged and revised by ROBERT HUNT, F.R.S.,
Keeper of Mining Records, Editor of "Ure's Dictionary of Arts,"
&c. 12mo, cloth boards, price 6*s.*

Grantham's Iron Ship-Building, enlarged.

ON IRON SHIP-BUILDING; with Practical Examples and Details. Fifth Edition. Imp. 4to, boards, enlarged from 24 to 40 Plates (21 quite new), including the latest Examples. Together with separate Text, 12mo, cloth limp, also considerably enlarged. By JOHN GRANTHAM, M. Inst. C.E., &c.   Price 2l. 2s. complete.

Description of Plates.

1. Hollow and Bar Keels, Stem and Stern Posts.   [Pieces.
2. Side Frames, Floorings, and Bilge
3. Floorings continued—Keelsons, Deck Beams, Gunwales, and Stringers.
4. Gunwales continued—Lower Decks, and Orlop Beams.
4a. Gunwales and Deck Beam Iron.
5. Angle-Iron, T Iron, Z Iron, Bulb Iron, as Rolled for Building.
6. Rivets, shown in section, natural size; Flush and Lapped Joints, with Single and Double Riveting.
7. Plating, three plans; Bulkheads and Modes of Securing them.
8. Iron Masts, with Longitudinal and Transverse Sections.
9. Sliding Keel, Water Ballast, Moulding the Frames in Iron Ship Building, Levelling Plates.
10. Longitudinal Section, and Half-breadth Deck Plan of Large Vessels on a reduced Scale.
11. Midship Sections of Three Vessels.
12. Large Vessel, showing Details—Fore End in Section, and End View, with Stern Post, Crutches, &c.
13. Large Vessel, showing Details—After End in Section, with End View, Stern Frame for Screw, and Rudder.
14. Large Vessel, showing Details—Midship Section, half breadth.
15. Machines for Punching and Shearing Plates and Angle-Iron, and for Bending Plates ; Rivet Hearth.
15a. Beam-Bending Machine, Independent Shearing, Punching and Angle-Iron Machine.
15b. Double Lever Punching and Shearing Machine, arranged for cutting Angle and T Iron, with Dividing Table and Engine.
16. Machines.—Garforth's Riveting Machine, Drilling and Counter-Sinking Machine.
16a. Plate Planing Machine.
17. Air Furnace for Heating Plates and Angle-Iron : Various Tools used in Riveting and Plating.
18. Gunwale ; Keel and Flooring ; Plan for Sheathing with Copper.
18a. Grantham's Improved Plan of Sheathing Iron Ships with Copper.
19. Illustrations of the Magnetic Condition of various Iron Ships.
20. Gray's Floating Compass and Binnacle, with Adjusting Magnets, &c.
21. Corroded Iron Bolt in Frame of Wooden Ship ; Jointing Plates.
22-4. Great Eastern—Longitudinal Sections and Half-breadth Plans—Midship Section, with Details—Section in Engine Room, and Paddle Boxes.
25-6. Paddle Steam Vessel of Steel.
27. Scarbrough—Paddle Vessel of Steel.
28-9. Proposed Passenger Steamer.
30. Persian—Iron Screw Steamer.
31. Midship Section of H.M. Steam Frigate, Warrior.
32. Midship Section of H.M. Steam Frigate, Hercules.
33. Stem, Stern, and Rudder of H.M. Steam Frigate, Bellerophon.
34. Midship Section of H.M. Troop Ship, Serapis.
35. Iron Floating Dock.

"A thoroughly practical work, and every question of the many in relation to iron shipping which admit of diversity of opinion, or have various and conflicting personal interests attached to them, is treated with sober and impartial wisdom and good sense. . . . . As good a volume for the instruction of the pupil or student of iron naval architecture as can be found in any language."—Practical Mechanics' Journal.

"A very elaborate work. . . . It forms a most valuable addition to the history of iron shipbuilding, while its having been prepared by one who has made the subject his study for many years, and whose qualifications have been repeatedly recognised, will recommend it as one of practical utility to all interested in shipbuilding."—Army and Navy Gazette.

Steam.

THE SAFE USE OF STEAM : containing Rules for Unprofessional Steam Users. By an ENGINEER. Second Edition. 12mo. Sewed, 6d.

N. B.—This little work should be in the hands of every person having to deal with a Steam Engine of any kind.

"If steam-users would but learn this little book by heart, and then hand it to their stokers to do the same, and see that the latter do it, boiler explosions would become sensations by their rarity."—English Mechanic.

ARCHITECTURE, &c.

Construction.

THE SCIENCE of BUILDING: An Elementary Treatise on the Principles of Construction. By E. WYNDHAM TARN, M.A., Architect. Illustrated with 47 Wood Engravings. Demy 8vo, price 8s. 6d. cloth. [*Recently published.*

" A very valuable book, which we strongly recommend to all students."—*Builder.*
" The treatise does credit alike to the author and the publisher."—*Engineer.*
" No architectural student should be without this hand-book."—*Architect.*
"The book is very far from being a mere compilation ; it is an able digest of information which is only to be found scattered through various works, and contains more really original writing than many putting forth far stronger claims to originality."
—*Engineering.*

Beaton's Pocket Estimator.

THE POCKET ESTIMATOR FOR THE BUILDING TRADES, being an easy method of estimating the various parts of a Building collectively, more especially applied to Carpenters' and Joiners' work, priced according to the present value of material and labour. By A. C. BEATON, Author of ' Quantities and Measurements.' 33 Woodcuts. Leather. Waistcoat-pocket size. 2s.

Beaton's Builders' and Surveyors' Technical Guide.

THE POCKET TECHNICAL GUIDE AND MEASURER FOR BUILDERS AND SURVEYORS: containing a Complete Explanation of the Terms used in Building Construction, Memoranda for Reference, Technical Directions for Measuring Work in all the Building Trades, with a Treatise on the Measurement of Timbers, and Complete Specifications for Houses, Roads, and Drains. By A. C. BEATON, Author of ' Quantities and Measurements.' With 19 Woodcuts. Leather. Waistcoat-pocket size. 2s.

Villa Architecture.

A HANDY BOOK of VILLA ARCHITECTURE ; being a Series of Designs for Villa Residences in various Styles. With Detailed Specifications and Estimates. By C. WICKES, Architect, Author of " The Spires and Towers of the Mediæval Churches of England," &c. First Series, consisting of 30 Plates ; Second Series, 31 Plates. Complete in 1 vol. 4to, price 2l. 10s. half morocco. Either Series separate, price 1l. 7s. each, half morocco.

" The whole of the designs bear evidence of their being the work of an artistic architect, and they will prove very valuable and suggestive to architects, students, and amateurs."—*Building News.*

House Painting.

HOUSE PAINTING, GRAINING, MARBLING, AND SIGN WRITING : a Practical Manual of, containing full information on the Processes of House Painting in Oil and Distemper, the Formation of Letters and Practice of Sign Writing, the Principles of Decorative Art, a Course of Elementary Drawing for House Painters, Writers, &c., and a Collection of Useful Receipts. With 9 Coloured Plates of Woods and Marbles, and nearly 150 Wood Engravings. By ELLIS A. DAVIDSON, Author of 'Building Construction,' 'Drawing for Carpenters,' &c. 12mo, 6s. cloth boards.

Architecture, Ancient and Modern.

RUDIMENTARY ARCHITECTURE, Ancient and Modern. Consisting of VITRUVIUS, translated by JOSEPH GWILT, F.S.A., &c., with 23 fine copper plates; GRECIAN Architecture, by the EARL of ABERDEEN; the ORDERS of Architecture, by W. H. LEEDS, Esq.; The STYLES of Architecture of Various Countries, by T. TALBOT BURY; The PRINCIPLES of DESIGN in Architecture, by E. L. GARBETT. In one handsome volume, half-bound (pp. 1,100), copiously illustrated, price 12s.

** *Sold separately, in two vols., as follows, price 6s. each, hf.-bd.*
ANCIENT ARCHITECTURE. Containing Gwilt's Vitruvius and Aberdeen's Grecian Architecture.

N.B.—*This is the only edition of VITRUVIUS procurable at a moderate price.*
MODERN ARCHITECTURE. Containing the Orders, by Leeds; The Styles, by Bury; and Principles of Design, by Garbett.

The Young Architect's Book.

HINTS TO YOUNG ARCHITECTS. By GEORGE WIGHTWICK, Architect, Author of "The Palace of Architecture," &c. &c. New Edition, revised and enlarged. By G. HUSKISSON GUILLAUME, Architect. With numerous illustrations. 12mo. cloth boards, 4s.

Drawing for Builders and Students.

PRACTICAL RULES ON DRAWING for the OPERATIVE BUILDER and YOUNG STUDENT in ARCHITECTURE. By GEORGE PYNE, Author of a "Rudimentary Treatise on Perspective for Beginners." With 14 Plates, 4to, 7s. 6d., boards.
CONTENTS.—I. Practical Rules on Drawing—Outlines. II. Ditto—the Grecian and Roman Orders. III. Practical Rules on Drawing—Perspective. IV. Practical Rules on Light and Shade. V. Practical Rules on Colour, &c. &c.

Cottages, Villas, and Country Houses.

DESIGNS and EXAMPLES of COTTAGES, VILLAS, and COUNTRY HOUSES; being the Studies of several eminent Architects and Builders; consisting of Plans, Elevations, and Perspective Views; with approximate Estimates of the Cost of each. In 4to, with 67 plates, price 1l. 1s., cloth.

Builder's Price Book.

LOCKWOOD & CO.'S BUILDER'S AND CONTRACTOR'S PRICE BOOK—with which is incorporated ATCHLEY'S, and portions of the late G. R. BURNELL'S Builders' Price Books—for 1875, containing the latest prices of all kinds of Builders' Materials and Labour, and of all Trades connected with Building; with many useful and important Memoranda and Tables; Lists of the Members of the Metropolitan Board of Works, of Districts, District Officers, and District Surveyors, and the Metropolitan Bye-laws. The whole revised and edited by FRANCIS T. W. MILLER, Architect and Surveyor. Fcap. 8vo, strongly half-bound, price 4s.

Handbook of Specifications.

THE HANDBOOK OF SPECIFICATIONS; or, Practical Guide to the Architect, Engineer, Surveyor, and Builder, in drawing up Specifications and Contracts for Works and Constructions. Illustrated by Precedents of Buildings actually executed by eminent Architects and Engineers. Preceded by a Preliminary Essay, and Skeletons of Specifications and Contracts, &c., &c., and explained by numerous Lithograph Plates and Woodcuts. By Professor THOMAS L. DONALDSON, President of the Royal Institute of British Architects, Professor of Architecture and Construction, University College, London, M.I.B.A., Member of the various European Academies of the Fine Arts. With A REVIEW OF THE LAW OF CONTRACTS, and of the Responsibilities of Architects, Engineers, and Builders. By W. CUNNINGHAM GLEN, Barrister-at-Law, of the Middle Temple. 2 vols., 8vo, with upwards of 1100 pp. of text, and 33 Lithographic Plates, cloth, 2l. 2s. (Published at 4l.)

"In these two volumes of 1,100 pages (together), forty-four specifications of executed works are given, including the specifications for parts of the new Houses of Parliament, by Sir Charles Barry, and for the new Royal Exchange, by Mr. Tite, M.P.

"Amongst the other known buildings, the specifications of which are given, are the Wiltshire Lunatic Asylum (Wyatt and Brandon) ; Tothill Fields Prison (R. Abraham) ; the City Prison, Holloway (Bunning) ; the High School, Edinburgh (Hamilton); Clothworkers' Hall, London (Angel) ; Wellington College, Sandhurst (J. Shaw) ; Houses in Grosvenor Square, and elsewhere ; St. George's Church, Doncaster (Scott) ; several works of smaller size by the Author, including Messrs. Shaw's Warehouse in Fetter Lane, a very successful elevation ; the Newcastle-upon-Tyne Railway Station (J. Dobson) ; new Westminster Bridge (Page) ; the High Level Bridge, Newcastle (R. Stephenson) ; various works on the Great Northern Railway (Brydone) ; and one French specification for Houses in the Rue de Rivoli, Paris (MM. Armand, Hittorff, Pellechet, and Rohault de Fleury, architects). The majority of the specifications have illustrations in the shape of elevations and plans.

"About 140 pages of the second volume are appropriated to an exposition of the law in relation to the legal liabilities of engineers, architects, contractors, and builders, by Mr. W. Cunningham Glen, Barrister-at-law. Donaldson's Handbook of Specifications must be bought by all architects."—*Builder*.

Specifications for Practical Architecture.

SPECIFICATIONS FOR PRACTICAL ARCHITECTURE: A Guide to the Architect, Engineer, Surveyor, and Builder ; with an Essay on the Structure and Science of Modern Buildings. By FREDERICK ROGERS, Architect. With numerous Illustrations. Demy 8vo, price 15s., cloth. (Published at 1l. 10s.)

*** A volume of specifications of a practical character being greatly required, and the old standard work of Alfred Bartholomew being out of print, the author, on the basis of that work, has produced the above. Some of the specifications he has so altered as to bring in the now universal use of concrete, the improvements in drainage, the use of iron, glass, asphalte, and other material. He has also inserted specifications of works that have been erected in his own practice.

The House-Owner's Estimator.

THE HOUSE-OWNER'S ESTIMATOR; or, What will it Cost to Build, Alter, or Repair? A Price-Book adapted to the Use of Unprofessional People as well as for the Architectural Surveyor and Builder. By the late JAMES D. SIMON, A.R.I.B.A. Edited and Revised by FRANCIS T. W. MILLER, Surveyor. With numerous Illustrations. Second Edition, with the prices carefully revised to 1875. Crown 8vo, cloth, price 3s. 6d.

CARPENTRY, TIMBER, &c.

Tredgold's Carpentry, new, enlarged, and cheaper Edition.

THE ELEMENTARY PRINCIPLES OF CARPENTRY :
a Treatise on the Pressure and Equilibrium of Timber Framing, the
Resistance of Timber, and the Construction of Floors, Arches,
Bridges, Roofs, Uniting Iron and Stone with Timber, &c. To which
is added an Essay on the Nature and Properties of Timber, &c.,
with Descriptions of the Kinds of Wood used in Building ; also
numerous Tables of the Scantlings of Timber for different purposes,
the Specific Gravities of Materials, &c. By THOMAS TREDGOLD,
C.E. Edited by PETER BARLOW, F.R.S. Fifth Edition, corrected and enlarged. With 64 Plates (11 of which now first appear
in this edition), Portrait of the Author, and several Woodcuts. In
1 vol., 4to, published at 2*l*. 2*s*., reduced to 1*l*. 5*s*., cloth.

" 'Tredgold's Carpentry' ought to be in every architect's and every builder's
library, and those who do not already possess it ought to avail themselves of the new
issue."—*Builder*.

"A work whose monumental excellence must commend it wherever skilful carpentry is concerned. The Author's principles are rather confirmed than impaired by
time, and, as now presented, combine the surest base with the most interesting display
of progressive science. The additional plates are of great intrinsic value."—*Building
News*.

Grandy's Timber Tables.

THE TIMBER IMPORTER'S, TIMBER MERCHANT'S,
and BUILDER'S STANDARD GUIDE. By RICHARD E.
GRANDY. Comprising :—An Analysis of Deal Standards, Home
and Foreign, with comparative Values and Tabular Arrangements
for Fixing Nett Landed Cost on Baltic and North American Deals,
including all intermediate Expenses, Freight, Insurance, &c., &c. ;
together with Copious Information for the Retailer and Builder.
Second Edition. Carefully revised and corrected. 12mo, price
3*s*. 6*d*. cloth.

"Everything it pretends to be : built up gradually, it leads one from a forest to a
treenail, and throws in, as a makeweight, a host of material concerning bricks, columns,
cisterns, &c.—all that the class to whom it appeals requires."—*English Mechanic*.

"The only difficulty we have is as to what is NOT in its pages. What we have tested
of the contents, taken at random, is invariably correct."—*Illustrated Builder's Journal*.

Tables for Packing-Case Makers.

PACKING-CASE TABLES ; showing the number of Superficial
Feet in Boxes or Packing-Cases, from six inches square and
upwards. Compiled by WILLIAM RICHARDSON, Accountant.
Oblong 4to, cloth, price 3*s*. 6*d*.

"Will save much labour and calculation to packing-case makers and those who use
packing-cases."—*Grocer*.   "Invaluable labour-saving tables."—*Ironmonger*.

Nicholson's Carpenter's Guide.

THE CARPENTER'S NEW GUIDE ; or, BOOK of LINES
for CARPENTERS : comprising all the Elementary Principles
essential for acquiring a knowledge of Carpentry. Founded on the
late PETER NICHOLSON's standard work. A new Edition, revised
by ARTHUR ASHPITEL, F.S.A., together with Practical Rules on
Drawing, by GEORGE PYNE. With 74 Plates, 4to, 1*l*. 1*s*. cloth.

Dowsing's Timber Merchant's Companion.

THE TIMBER MERCHANT'S AND BUILDER'S COM-
PANION; containing New and Copious Tables of the Reduced
Weight and Measurement of Deals and Battens, of all sizes, from
One to a Thousand Pieces, and the relative Price that each size
bears per Lineal Foot to any given Price per Petersburgh Standard
Hundred; the Price per Cube Foot of Square Timber to any given
Price per Load of 50 Feet; the proportionate Value of Deals and
Battens by the Standard, to Square Timber by the Load of 50 Feet;
the readiest mode of ascertaining the Price of Scantling per Lineal
Foot of any size, to any given Figure per Cube Foot. Also a
variety of other valuable information. By WILLIAM DOWSING,
Timber Merchant. Second Edition. Crown 8vo, 3s. cloth.
"Everything is as concise and clear as it can possibly be made. There can be no
doubt that every timber merchant and builder ought to possess it."—*Hull Advertiser.*

Timber Freight Book.

THE TIMBER IMPORTERS' AND SHIPOWNERS'
FREIGHT BOOK : Being a Comprehensive Series of Tables for
the Use of Timber Importers, Captains of Ships, Shipbrokers,
Builders, and all Dealers in Wood whatsoever. By WILLIAM
RICHARDSON, Timber Broker, author of "Packing Case Tables,"
&c. Crown 8vo, cloth, price 6s.

MECHANICS, &c.

Horton's Measurer.

THE COMPLETE MEASURER; setting forth the Measurement of Boards, Glass, &c., &c.; Unequal-sided, Square-sided,
Octagonal-sided, Round Timber and Stone, and Standing Timber.
With just allowances for the bark in the respective species of
trees, and proper deductions for the waste in hewing the trees,
&c.; also a Table showing the solidity of hewn or eight-sided
timber, or of any octagonal-sided column. Compiled for the
accommodation of Timber-growers, Merchants, and Surveyors,
Stonemasons, Architects, and others. By RICHARD HORTON.
Second edition, with considerable and valuable additions, 12mo,
strongly bound in leather, 5s.
"The office of the architect, engineer, building surveyor, or land agent that is
without this excellent and useful work cannot truly be considered perfect in its
furnishing."—*Irish Builder.*
"We have used the improved and other tables in this volume, and have not
observed any unfairness or inaccuracy."—*Builder.*
"The tables we have tested are accurate. . . . . To the builder and estate
agents this work will be most acceptable."—*British Architect.*
"Not only are the best methods of measurement shown, and in some instances
illustrated by means of woodcuts, but the erroneous systems pursued by dishonest
dealers are fully exposed. . . . . The work must be considered to be a valuable addition to every gardener's library.—*Garden.*

Superficial Measurement.

THE TRADESMAN'S GUIDE TO SUPERFICIAL MEA-
SUREMENT. Tables calculated from 1 to 200 inches in length,
by 1 to 108 inches in breadth. For the use of Architects, Surveyors,
Engineers, Timber Merchants, Builders, &c. By JAMES HAW-
KINGS. Fcp. 3s. 6d. cloth.

Mechanic's Workshop Companion.

THE OPERATIVE MECHANIC'S WORKSHOP COM-PANION, and THE SCIENTIFIC GENTLEMAN'S PRAC-TICAL ASSISTANT ; comprising a great variety of the most useful Rules in Mechanical Science; with numerous Tables of Practical Data and Calculated Results. By W. TEMPLETON, Author of "The Engineer's, Millwright's, and Machinist's Practical Assistant." Eleventh Edition, with Mechanical Tables for Operative Smiths, Millwrights, Engineers, &c.; together with several Useful and Practical Rules in Hydraulics and Hydrodynamics, a variety of Experimental Results, and an Extensive Table of Powers and Roots. 11 Plates. 12mo, 5s. bound.

"As a text-book of reference, in which mechanical and commercial demands are judiciously met, TEMPLETON'S COMPANION stands unrivalled."—*Mechanics' Magazine.*

"Admirably adapted to the wants of a very large class. It has met with great success in the engineering workshop, as we can testify ; and there are a great many men who, in a great measure, owe their rise in life to this little work."—*Building News.*

Engineer's Assistant.

THE ENGINEER'S, MILLWRIGHT'S, and MACHINIST'S PRACTICAL ASSISTANT ; comprising a Collection of Useful Tables, Rules, and Data. Compiled and Arranged, with Original Matter, by W. TEMPLETON. 5th Edition. 18mo, 2s. 6d. cloth.

"So much varied information compressed into so small a space, and published at a price which places it within the reach of the humblest mechanic, cannot fail to command the sale which it deserves. With the utmost confidence we commend this book to the attention of our readers.—*Mechanics' Magazine.*

"Every mechanic should become the possessor of the volume, and a more suitable present to an apprentice to any of the mechanical trades could not possibly be made."—*Building News.*

Designing, Measuring, and Valuing.

THE STUDENT'S GUIDE to the PRACTICE of MEA-SURING, and VALUING ARTIFICERS' WORKS; containing Directions for taking Dimensions, Abstracting the same, and bringing the Quantities into Bill, with Tables of Constants, and copious Memoranda for the Valuation of Labour and Materials in the respective Trades of Bricklayer and Slater, Carpenter and Joiner, Painter and Glazier, Paperhanger, &c. With 43 Plates and Woodcuts. Originally edited by EDWARD DOBSON, Architect. New Edition, re-written, with Additions on Mensuration and Construction, and useful Tables for facilitating Calculations and Measurements. By E. WYNDHAM TARN, M.A., 8vo, 10s. 6d. cloth.

"This useful book should be in every architect's and builder's office. It contains a vast amount of information absolutely necessary to be known."—*The Irish Builder.*

"We have failed to discover anything connected with the building trade, from excavating foundations to bell-hanging, that is not fully treated upon in this valuable work."—*The Artizan.*

"Mr. Tarn has well performed the task imposed upon him, and has made many further and valuable additions, embodying a large amount of information relating to the technicalities and modes of construction employed in the several branches of the building trade."—*Colliery Guardian.*

"Altogether the book is one which well fulfils the promise of its title-page, and we can thoroughly recommend it to the class for whose use it has been compiled. Mr. Tarn's additions and revisions have much increased the usefulness of the work, and have especially augmented its value to students."—*Engineering.*

MATHEMATICS, &c.

Gregory's Practical Mathematics.

MATHEMATICS for PRACTICAL MEN ; being a Common-place Book of Pure and Mixed Mathematics. Designed chiefly for the Use of Civil Engineers, Architects, and Surveyors. Part I. PURE MATHEMATICS—comprising Arithmetic, Algebra, Geometry, Mensuration, Trigonometry, Conic Sections, Properties of Curves. Part II. MIXED MATHEMATICS—comprising Mechanics in general, Statics, Dynamics, Hydrostatics, Hydrodynamics, Pneumatics, Mechanical Agents, Strength of Materials. With an Appendix of copious Logarithmic and other Tables. By OLINTHUS GREGORY, LL.D., F.R.A.S. Enlarged by HENRY LAW, C.E. 4th Edition, carefully revised and corrected by J. R. YOUNG, formerly Professor of Mathematics, Belfast College ; Author of "A Course of Mathematics," &c. With 13 Plates. Medium 8vo, 1l. 1s. cloth.

"As a standard work on mathematics it has not been excelled."—*Artizan.*

"The engineer or architect will here find ready to his hand, rules for solving nearly every mathematical difficulty that may arise in his practice. The rules are in all casess explained by means of examples, in which every step of the process is clearly worked out."—*Builder.*

"One of the most serviceable books to the practical mechanics of the country. . . . . . In the edition just brought out, the work has again been revised by Professor Young. He has modernised the notation throughout, introduced a few paragraphs here and there, and corrected the numerous typographical errors which have escaped the eyes of the former Editor. The book is now as complete as it is possible to make it. It is an instructive book for the student, and a Text-book for him who having once mastered the subjects it treats of, needs occasionally to refresh his memory upon them."—*Building News.*

The Metric System.

A SERIES OF METRIC TABLES, in which the British Standard Measures and Weights are compared with those of the Metric System at present in use on the Continent. By C. H. DOWLING, C. E. Second Edition, revised and enlarged. 8vo, 10s. 6d. strongly bound.

"Mr. Dowling's Tables, which are well put together, come just in time as a ready reckoner for the conversion of one system into the other."—*Athenæum.*

"Their accuracy has been certified by Professor Airy, the Astronomer-Royal."—*Builder.*

"Resolution 8.—That advantage will be derived from the recent publication of Metric Tables, by C. H. Dowling, C.E."—*Report of Section F, British Association, Bath.*

Comprehensive Weight Calculator.

THE WEIGHT CALCULATOR ; being a Series of Tables upon a New and Comprehensive Plan, exhibiting at one Reference the exact Value of any Weight from 1 lb. to 15 tons, at 300 Progressive Rates, from 1 Penny to 168 Shillings per cwt., and containing 186,000 Direct Answers, which with their Combinations, consisting of a single addition (mostly to be performed at sight), will afford an aggregate of 10,266,000 Answers ; the whole being calculated and designed to ensure Correctness and promote Despatch. By HENRY HARBEN, Accountant, Sheffield, Author of 'The Discount Guide.' An entirely New Edition, carefully revised. Royal 8vo. strongly half-bound, 30s.   [*Just Published.*

Inwood's Tables, greatly enlarged and improved.

TABLES FOR THE PURCHASING of ESTATES, Freehold, Copyhold, or Leasehold; Annuities, Advowsons, &c., and for the Renewing of Leases held under Cathedral Churches, Colleges, or other corporate bodies; for Terms of Years certain, and for Lives ; also for Valuing Reversionary Estates, Deferred Annuities, Next Presentations, &c., together with Smart's Five Tables of Compound Interest, and an Extension of the same to Lower and Intermediate Rates. By WILLIAM INWOOD, Architect. The 20th edition, with considerable additions, and new and valuable Tables of Logarithms for the more Difficult Computations of the Interest of Money, Discount, Annuities, &c., by M. FÉDOR THOMAN, of the Société Crédit Mobilier of Paris. 12mo, 8s. cloth.

** *This edition (the 20th) differs in many important particulars from former ones. The changes consist, first, in a more convenient and systematic arrangement of the original Tables, and in the removal of certain numerical errors which a very careful revision of the whole has enabled the present editor to discover; and secondly, in the extension of practical utility conferred on the work by the introduction of Tables now inserted for the first time. This new and important matter is all so much actually added to* INWOOD'S TABLES ; *nothing has been abstracted from the original collection: so that those who have been long in the habit of consulting* INWOOD *for any special professional purpose will, as heretofore, find the information sought still in its pages.*

"Those interested in the purchase and sale of estates, and in the adjustment of compensation cases, as well as in transactions in annuities, life insurances, &c., will find the present edition of eminent service."—*Engineering.*

Geometry for the Architect, Engineer, &c.

PRACTICAL GEOMETRY, for the Architect, Engineer, and Mechanic ; giving Rules for the Delineation and Application of various Geometrical Lines, Figures and Curves. By E. W. TARN, M.A., Architect, Author of "The Science of Building," &c. With 164 Illustrations. Demy 8vo. 12s. 6d.

"No book with the same objects in view has ever been published in which the clearness of the rules laid down and the illustrative diagrams have been so satisfactory."—*Scotsman.*

Compound Interest and Annuities.

THEORY of COMPOUND INTEREST and ANNUITIES; with Tables of Logarithms for the more Difficult Computations of Interest, Discount, Annuities, &c., in all their Applications and Uses for Mercantile and State Purposes. With an elaborate Introduction. By FÉDOR THOMAN, of the Société Crédit Mobilier, Paris. 12mo, cloth, 5s.

"A very powerful work, and the Author has a very remarkable command of his subject."—*Professor A. de Morgan.*

"We recommend it to the notice of actuaries and accountants."—*Athenæum.*

SCIENCE AND ART.

The Military Sciences.

AIDE-MÉMOIRE to the MILITARY SCIENCES. Framed from Contributions of Officers and others connected with the different Services. Originally edited by a Committee of the Corps of Royal Engineers. Second Edition, most carefully revised by an Officer of the Corps, with many additions ; containing nearly 350 Engravings and many hundred Woodcuts. 3 vols. royal 8vo, extra cloth boards, and lettered, price 4*l.* 10*s.*

"A compendious encyclopædia of military knowledge."—*Edinburgh Review.*
"The most comprehensive work of reference to the military and collateral sciences."
—*Volunteer Service Gazette.*

Field Fortification.

A TREATISE on FIELD FORTIFICATION, the ATTACK of FORTRESSES, MILITARY, MINING, and RECONNOITRING. By Colonel I. S. MACAULAY, late Professor of Fortification in the R. M. A., Woolwich. Sixth Edition, crown 8vo, cloth, with separate Atlas of 12 Plates, price 12*s.* complete.

Field Fortification.

HANDBOOK OF FIELD FORTIFICATION, intended for the Guidance of Officers preparing for Promotion, and especially adapted to the requirements of Beginners. By Major W. W. KNOLLYS, F.R.G.S., 93rd Sutherland Highlanders, &c. With 163 Woodcuts. Crown 8vo, 3*s.* 6*d.* cloth.

Storms.

STORMS : their Nature, Classification, and Laws, with the Means of Predicting them by their Embodiments, the Clouds. By WILLIAM BLASIUS. With Coloured Plates and numerous Wood Engravings. Crown 8vo, 12*s.* 6*d.* cloth boards.

Light-Houses.

EUROPEAN LIGHT-HOUSE SYSTEMS ; being a Report of a Tour of Inspection made in 1873. By Major GEORGE H. ELLIOT, Corps of Engineers, U.S.A. Illustrated by 51 Engravings and 31 Woodcuts in the Text. 8vo, 21*s.* cloth.

Dye-Wares and Colours.

THE MANUAL of COLOURS and DYE-WARES : their Properties, Applications, Valuation, Impurities, and Sophistications. For the Use of Dyers, Printers, Dry Salters, Brokers, &c. By J. W. SLATER. Post 8vo, cloth, price 7*s.* 6*d.*

"A complete encyclopædia of the *materia tinctoria.* The information given respecting each article is full and precise, and the methods of determining the value of articles such as these, so liable to sophistication, are given with clearness, and are practical as well as valuable."—*Chemist and Druggist.*

Electricity.

A MANUAL of ELECTRICITY; including Galvanism, Magnetism, Diamagnetism, Electro-Dynamics, Magno-Electricity, and the Electric Telegraph. By HENRY M. NOAD, Ph.D., F.C.S., Lecturer on Chemistry at St. George's Hospital. Fourth Edition, entirely rewritten. Illustrated by 500 Woodcuts. 8vo, 1l. 4s. cloth.

"The commendations already bestowed in the pages of the *Lancet* on the former editions of this work are more than ever merited by the present. The accounts given of electricity and galvanism are not only complete in a scientific sense, but, which is a rarer thing, are popular and interesting."—*Lancet.*

Text-Book of Electricity.

THE STUDENT'S TEXT-BOOK OF ELECTRICITY. By HENRY M. NOAD, Ph.D., Lecturer on Chemistry at St. George's Hospital. New Edition revised and enlarged, with additions on Telegraphy, by G. E. PREECE, Esq. Upwards of 400 Illustrations.
[*In Preparation.*

Rudimentary Magnetism.

RUDIMENTARY MAGNETISM: being a concise exposition of the general principles of Magnetical Science, and the purposes to which it has been applied. By Sir W. SNOW HARRIS, F.R.S. New and enlarged Edition, with considerable additions by Dr. NOAD, Ph.D. With 165 Woodcuts. 12mo, cloth, 4s. 6d.

"There is a good index, and this volume of 412 pages may be considered the best possible manual on the subject of magnetism."—*Mechanics' Magazine.*

"As concise and lucid an exposition of the phenomena of magnetism as we believe it is possible to write."—*English Mechanic.*

"Not only will the scientific student find this volume an invaluable book of reference, but the general reader will find in it as much to interest as to inform his mind. Though a strictly scientific work, its subject is handled in a simple and readable style."—*Illustrated Review.*

Chemical Analysis.

THE COMMERCIAL HANDBOOK of CHEMICAL ANALYSIS; or Practical Instructions for the determination of the Intrinsic or Commercial Value of Substances used in Manufactures, in Trades, and in the Arts. By A. NORMANDY, Author of "Practical Introduction to Rose's Chemistry," and Editor of Rose's "Treatise of Chemical Analysis." *New Edition.* Enlarged, and to a great extent re-written, by Henry M. Noad, Ph. D., F.R.S. With numerous Illustrations. Crown 8vo, 12s. 6d. cloth.
[*Just ready.*

"We recommend this book to the careful perusal of every one; it may be truly affirmed to be of universal interest, and we strongly recommend it to our readers as a guide, alike indispensable to the housewife as to the pharmaceutical practitioner."—*Medical Times.*

"The very best work on the subject the English press has yet produced."—*Mechanics' Magazine.*

Mollusca.

A MANUAL OF THE MOLUSCA; being a Treatise on Recent and Fossil Shells. By Dr. S. P. WOODWARD, A.L.S. With Appendix by RALPH TATE, A.L.S. F.G.S. With numerous Plates and 300 Woodcuts. Third Edition. Crown 8vo, 7s. 6d. cloth gilt.

Clocks, Watches, and Bells.

RUDIMENTARY TREATISE on CLOCKS, WATCHES, and BELLS. By Sir EDMUND BECKETT, Bart. (late E. B. Denison), LL.D., Q.C., F.R.A.S., Author of "Astronomy without Mathematics," &c. Sixth edition, thoroughly revised and enlarged, with numerous Illustrations. Limp cloth (No. 67, Weale's Series), 4s. 6d.; cloth boards, 5s. 6d.

"As a popular, and, at the same time, practical treatise on clocks and bells, it is unapproached."—*English Mechanic.*

"The best work on the subject probably extant . . . So far as we know it has no competitor worthy of the name. The treatise on bells is undoubtedly the best in the language. It shows that the author has contributed very much to their modern improvement, if indeed he has not revived this art, which was decaying here . . . To call it a rudimentary treatise is a misnomer, at least as respects clocks and bells. It is something more. It is the most important work of its kind in English."—*Engineering.*

"The only modern treatise on clock-making."—*Horological Journal.*

"Without having any special interest in the subject, and even without possessing any general aptitude for mechanical studies, a reader must be very unintelligent who cannot find matter to engage his attention in this work. The little book now appears revised and enlarged, being one of the most praiseworthy volumes in Weale's admirable scientific and educational series."—*Daily Telegraph.*

"We do not know whether to wonder most at the extraordinary cheapness of this admirable treatise on clocks, by the most able authority on such a subject, or the thorough completeness of his work even to the minutest details. The chapter on bells is singular and amusing, and will be a real treat even to the uninitiated general reader. The illustrations, notes, and indices, make the work completely perfect of its kind."—*Standard.*

"There is probably no book in the English language on a technical subject so easy to read, and to read through, as the treatise on clocks, watches, and bells, written by the eminent Parliamentary Counsel, Mr. E. B. Denison—now Sir Edmund Beckett, Bart."—*Architect.*

Science and Scripture.

SCIENCE ELUCIDATIVE OF SCRIPTURE, AND NOT ANTAGONISTIC TO IT; being a Series of Essays on—1. Alleged Discrepancies; 2. The Theory of the Geologists and Figure of the Earth; 3. The Mosaic Cosmogony; 4. Miracles in general—Views of Hume and Powell; 5. The Miracle of Joshua—Views of Dr. Colenso: The Supernaturally Impossible; 6. The Age of the Fixed Stars—their Distances and Masses. By Professor J. R. YOUNG, Author of "A Course of Elementary Mathematics," &c. &c. Fcap. 8vo, price 5s. cloth lettered.

"Professor Young's examination of the early verses of Genesis, in connection with modern scientific hypotheses, is excellent."—*English Churchman.*

"Distinguished by the true spirit of scientific inquiry, by great knowledge, by keen logical ability, and by a style peculiarly clear, easy, and energetic."—*Nonconformist.*

"No one can rise from its perusal without being impressed with a sense of the singular weakness of modern scepticism."—*Baptist Magazine.*

"A valuable contribution to controversial theological literature."—*City Press.*

Practical Philosophy.

A SYNOPSIS of PRACTICAL PHILOSOPHY. By the Rev. JOHN CARR, M.A., late Fellow of Trin. Coll., Cambridge. Second Edition. 18mo, 5s. cloth.

Dr. Lardner's Museum of Science and Art.

THE MUSEUM OF SCIENCE AND ART. Edited by
DIONYSIUS LARDNER, D.C.L., formerly Professor of Natural Phi-
losophy and Astronomy in University College, London. CONTENTS:
The Planets; are they inhabited Worlds?—Weather Prognostics—
Popular Fallacies in Questions of Physical Science—Latitudes and
Longitudes—Lunar Influences—Meteoric Stones and Shooting
Stars — Railway Accidents — Light—Common Things:—Air—
Locomotion in the United States—Cometary Influences—Common
Things: Water—The Potter's Art—Common Things: Fire—
Locomotion and Transport, their Influence and Progress—The
Moon—Common Things: The Earth—The Electric Telegraph—
Terrestrial Heat—The Sun—Earthquakes and Volcanoes—Baro-
meter, Safety Lamp, and Whitworth's Micrometric Apparatus—
Steam—The Steam Engine—The Eye—The Atmosphere—Time
—Common Things: Pumps—Common Things: Spectacles, the
Kaleidoscope—Clocks and Watches—Microscopic Drawing and
Engraving—Locomotive—Thermometer—New Planets: Lever-
rier and Adams's Planet—Magnitude and Minuteness—Common
Things: The Almanack—Optical Images—How to observe the
Heavens—Common Things: the Looking-glass—Stellar Universe
—The Tides — Colour — Common Things: Man — Magnifying
Glasses—Instinct and Intelligence—The Solar Microscope—The
Camera Lucida—The Magic Lantern—The Camera Obscura—
The Microscope—The White Ants: their Manners and Habits—
The Surface of the Earth, or First Notions of Geography—Science
and Poetry—The Bee — Steam Navigation — Electro-Motive
Power—Thunder, Lightning, and the Aurora Borealis—The
Printing Press—The Crust of the Earth—Comets—The Stereo-
scope—The Pre-Adamite Earth—Eclipses—Sound. With up-
wards of 1200 Engravings on Wood. In 6 Double Volumes,
handsomely bound in cloth, gilt, price £1 1s.

"The 'Museum of Science and Art' is the most valuable contribution that has
ever been made to the Scientific Instruction of every class of society."—*Sir David
Brewster in the North British Review.*

"Whether we consider the liberality and beauty of the illustrations, the charm of
the writing, or the durable interest of the matter, we must express our belief that
there is hardly to be found among the new books, one that would be welcomed by
people of so many ages and classes as a valuable present."—*Examiner.*

*⁎⁎⁎ Separate books formed from the above, suitable for Workmen's
Libraries, Science Classes, &c.*

COMMON THINGS EXPLAINED. With 233 Illustrations, 5s. cloth.

THE ELECTRIC TELEGRAPH POPULARIZED. 100 Illustrations, 1s. 6d. cloth.

THE MICROSCOPE. With 147 Illustrations, 2s. cloth.

POPULAR GEOLOGY. With 201 Illustrations, 2s. 6d. cloth.

POPULAR PHYSICS. With 85 Illustrations. 2s. 6d. cloth.

POPULAR ASTRONOMY. With 182 Illustrations, 4s. 6d. cloth.

STEAM AND ITS USES. With 89 Illustrations, 2s. cloth.

THE BEE AND WHITE ANTS. With 135 Illustrations, cloth, 2s.

DR. LARDNER'S SCIENTIFIC HANDBOOKS.

Astronomy.

THE HANDBOOK OF ASTRONOMY. By DIONYSIUS LARDNER, D.C.L., formerly Professor of Natural Philosophy and Astronomy in University College, London. Fourth Edition. Revised and Edited by EDWIN DUNKIN, F.R.A.S., Superintendent of the Altazimuth Department, Royal Observatory, Greenwich. With 38 plates and upwards of 100 Woodcuts. In one thick vol., Crown 8vo, price 9s. 6d. cloth.

"We can cordially recommend it to all those who desire to possess a complete manual of the science and practice of astronomy."—*Astronomical Reporter.*

Optics.

THE HANDBOOK OF OPTICS. New Edition. Edited by T. OLVER HARDING, B.A. Lond., of University College, London. With 298 Illustrations. Small 8vo, cloth, 448 pages, price 5s.

Electricity.

THE HANDBOOK of ELECTRICITY, MAGNETISM, and ACOUSTICS. New Edition. Edited by GEO. CAREY FOSTER, B.A., F.C.S. With 400 Illustrations. Small 8vo, cloth, price 5s.

"The book could not have been entrusted to any one better calculated to preserve the terse and lucid style of Lardner, while correcting his errors and bringing up his work to the present state of scientific knowledge."—*Popular Science Review.*

Mechanics.

THE HANDBOOK OF MECHANICS. Revised and enlarged by B. LOEWY, F.R.A.S.   [*Reprinting.*

Hydrostatics.

THE HANDBOOK of HYDROSTATICS and PNEUMATICS. New Edition, Revised and Enlarged by BENJAMIN LOEWY, F.R.A.S. With numerous Illustrations. 5s.   [*Just published.*

Heat.

THE HANDBOOK OF HEAT. New Edition, Re-written and Enlarged. By BENJAMIN LOEWY, F.R.A.S.   [*Nearly Ready.*

Animal Physics.

THE HANDBOOK OF ANIMAL PHYSICS. With 520 Illustrations. New edition, small 8vo, cloth, 7s. 6d. 732 pages.

Electric Telegraph.

THE ELECTRIC TELEGRAPH. New Edition. Revised and Re-written by E. B. BRIGHT, F.R.A.S. 140 Illustrations. Small 8vo, 2s. 6d. cloth.

"One of the most readable books extant on the Electric Telegraph."—*Eng. Mechanic.*

NATURAL PHILOSOPHY FOR SCHOOLS. By DR. LARDNER. 328 Illustrations. Fifth Edition. 1 vol. 3s. 6d. cloth.

"A very convenient class-book for junior students in private schools. It is intended to convey, in clear and precise terms, general notions of all the principal divisions of Physical Science."—*British Quarterly Review.*

ANIMAL PHYSIOLOGY FOR SCHOOLS. By DR. LARDNER. With 190 Illustrations. Second Edition. 1 vol. 3s. 6d. cloth.

"Clearly written, well arranged, and excellently illustrated."—*Gardeners' Chronicle.*

Geology and Genesis Harmonised.

THE TWIN RECORDS of CREATION; or, Geology and Genesis, their Perfect Harmony and Wonderful Concord. By GEORGE W. VICTOR LE VAUX. With numerous Illustrations. Fcap. 8vo, price 5s. cloth.

"We can recommend Mr. Le Vaux as an able and interesting guide to a popular appreciation of geological science."—*Spectator.*

"The author combines an unbounded admiration of science with an unbounded admiration of the Written Record."—*London Review.*

"No real difficulty is shirked, and no sophistry is left unexposed."—*The Rock.*

Geology, Physical.

PHYSICAL GEOLOGY. (Partly based on Major-General Portlock's Rudiments of Geology.) By RALPH TATE, A.L.S., F.G.S. Numerous Woodcuts. 12mo, 2s.

Geology, Historical.

HISTORICAL GEOLOGY. (Partly based on Major-General Portlock's Rudiments of Geology.) By RALPH TATE, A.L.S., F.G.S. Numerous Woodcuts. 12mo, 2s. 6d.

** Or PHYSICAL *and* HISTORICAL GEOLOGY, *bound in One Volume, price 5s.*

Wood-Carving.

INSTRUCTIONS in WOOD-CARVING, for Amateurs; with Hints on Design. By A LADY. In emblematic wrapper, handsomely printed, with Ten large Plates, price 2s. 6d.

"The handicraft of the wood-carver, so well as a book can impart it, may be learnt from 'A Lady's' publication."—*Athenæum.*

"A real *practical guide.* It is very complete."—*Literary Churchman.*

"The directions given are plain and easily understood, and it forms a very good introduction to the practical part of the carver's art."—*English Mechanic.*

Popular Work on Painting.

PAINTING POPULARLY EXPLAINED; with Historical Sketches of the Progress of the Art. By THOMAS JOHN GULLICK, Painter, and JOHN TIMBS, F.S.A. Second Edition, revised and enlarged. With Frontispiece and Vignette. In small 8vo, 6s. cloth.

** *This Work has been adopted as a Prize-book in the Schools of Art at South Kensington.*

"A work that may be advantageously consulted. Much may be learned, even by those who fancy they do not require to be taught, from the careful perusal of this unpretending but comprehensive treatise."—*Art Journal.*

"A valuable book, which supplies a want. It contains a large amount of original matter, agreeably conveyed, and will be found of value, as well by the young artist seeking information as by the general reader. We give a cordial welcome to the book, and augur for it an increasing reputation."—*Builder.*

Grammar of Colouring.

A GRAMMAR OF COLOURING, applied to Decorative Painting and the Arts. By GEORGE FIELD. New edition, enlarged and adapted to the use of the Ornamental Painter and Designer, by ELLIS A. DAVIDSON. With new Coloured Diagrams and numerous Engravings on Wood. 12mo, 3s. cloth boards.

"One of the most useful of student's books, and probably the best known of the few we have on the subject."—*Architect.*

"The book is a most useful *résumé* of the properties of pigments."—*Builder.*

"This treatise forms a most valuable *vade mecum* for the ornamental painter and designer.—*Scotsman.*

Delamotte's Works on Illumination & Alphabets.

A PRIMER OF THE ART OF ILLUMINATION; for the use of Beginners: with a Rudimentary Treatise on the Art, Practical Directions for its Exercise, and numerous Examples taken from Illuminated MSS., printed in Gold and Colours. By F. DELAMOTTE. Small 4to, price 9s. Elegantly bound, cloth antique.

"A handy book, beautifully illustrated; the text of which is well written, and calculated to be useful. . . . The examples of ancient MSS. recommended to the student, which, with much good sense, the author chooses from collections accessible to all, are selected with judgment and knowledge, as well as taste."—*Athenæum.*

ORNAMENTAL ALPHABETS, ANCIENT and MEDIÆVAL; from the Eighth Century, with Numerals; including Gothic, Church-Text, large and small, German, Italian, Arabesque, Initials for Illumination, Monograms, Crosses, &c. &c., for the use of Architectural and Engineering Draughtsmen, Missal Painters, Masons, Decorative Painters, Lithographers, Engravers, Carvers, &c. &c. &c. Collected and engraved by F. DELAMOTTE, and printed in Colours. Royal 8vo, oblong, price 4s. cloth.

"A well-known engraver and draughtsman has enrolled in this useful book the result of many years' study and research. For those who insert enamelled sentences round gilded chalices, who blazon shop legends over shop-doors, who letter church walls with pithy sentences from the Decalogue, this book will be useful."—*Athenæum.*

EXAMPLES OF MODERN ALPHABETS, PLAIN and ORNAMENTAL; including German, Old English, Saxon, Italic, Perspective, Greek, Hebrew, Court Hand, Engrossing, Tuscan, Riband, Gothic, Rustic, and Arabesque; with several Original Designs, and an Analysis of the Roman and Old English Alphabets, large and small, and Numerals, for the use of Draughtsmen, Surveyors, Masons, Decorative Painters, Lithographers, Engravers, Carvers, &c. Collected and engraved by F. DELAMOTTE, and printed in Colours. Royal 8vo, oblong, price 4s. cloth.

"To artists of all classes, but more especially to architects and engravers, this very handsome book will be invaluable. There is comprised in it every possible shape into which the letters of the alphabet and numerals can be formed, and the talent which has been expended in the conception of the various plain and ornamental letters is wonderful."—*Standard.*

MEDIÆVAL ALPHABETS AND INITIALS FOR ILLUMINATORS. By F. DELAMOTTE, Illuminator, Designer, and Engraver on Wood. Containing 21 Plates, and Illuminated Title, printed in Gold and Colours. With an Introduction by J. WILLIS BROOKS. Small 4to, 6s. cloth gilt.

"A volume in which the letters of the alphabet come forth glorified in gilding and all the colours of the prism interwoven and intertwined and intermingled, sometimes with a sort of rainbow arabesque. A poem emblazoned in these characters would be only comparable to one of those delicious love letters symbolized in a bunch of flowers well selected and cleverly arranged."—*Sun.*

THE EMBROIDERER'S BOOK OF DESIGN; containing Initials, Emblems, Cyphers, Monograms, Ornamental Borders, Ecclesiastical Devices, Mediæval and Modern Alphabets, and National Emblems. Collected and engraved by F. DELAMOTTE, and printed in Colours. Oblong royal 8vo, 2s. 6d. in ornamental boards.

AGRICULTURE, &c.

Youatt and Burn's Complete Grazier.

THE COMPLETE GRAZIER, and FARMER'S and CATTLE-BREEDER'S ASSISTANT. A Compendium of Husbandry. By WILLIAM YOUATT, ESQ., V.S. 11th Edition, enlarged by ROBERT SCOTT BURN, Author of "The Lessons of My Farm," &c. One large 8vo volume, 784 pp. with 215 Illustrations. 1l. 1s. half-bd.

"The standard and text-book, with the farmer and grazier."—*Farmer's Magazine.*

"A valuable repertory of intelligence for all who make agriculture a pursuit, and especially for those who aim at keeping pace with the improvements of the age."—*Bell's Weekly Messenger.*

"A treatise which will remain a standard work on the subject as long as British agriculture endures."—*Mark Lane Express.*

"One of the best books of reference that can be contained in the agriculturist's library. The word 'complete' expresses its character; since every detail of the subject finds a place, treated upon, and explained, in a clear, comprehensive, and practical manner."—*Magnet.*

Spooner on Sheep.

SHEEP; THE HISTORY, STRUCTURE, ECONOMY, AND DISEASES OF. By W. C. SPOONER, M.R.V.C., &c. Third Edition, considerably enlarged; with numerous fine engravings, including some specimens of New and Improved Breeds. Fcp. 8vo. 366 pp., price 6s. cloth.

"The book is decidedly the best of the kind in our language."—*Scotsman.*

"A reliable text-book."—*Stamford Mercury.*

"Mr. Spooner has conferred upon the agricultural class a lasting benefit by embodying in this work the improvements made in sheep stock by such men as Humphreys, Rawlence, Howard, and others."—*Hampshire Advertiser.*

"The work should be in possession of every flock-master."—*Banbury Guardian.*

"We can confidently recommend the work as useful and reliable, and of much practical utility to the class for whom it is intended."—*Salisbury and Winchester Journal.*

"Mr. Spooner has conferred a boon on agriculturists generally, and the farmer's library will be incomplete which does not include so admirable a guide to a very important branch of the business."—*Dorset County Chronicle.*

Scott Burn's System of Modern Farming.

OUTLINES OF MODERN FARMING. By R. SCOTT BURN. Soils, Manures, and Crops—Farming and Farming Economy, Historical and Practical—Cattle, Sheep, and Horses—Management of the Dairy, Pigs, and Poultry, with Notes on the Diseases of Stock—Utilisation of Town-Sewage, Irrigation, and Reclamation of Waste Land. New Edition. In 1 vol. 1250 pp., half-bound, profusely Illustrated, price 12s.

"There is sufficient stated within the limits of this treatise to prevent a farmer from going far wrong in any of his operations. . . . The author has had great personal experience, and his opinions are entitled to every respect."—*Observer.*

Horton's Underwood and Woodland Tables.

TABLES FOR PLANTING AND VALUING UNDERWOOD AND WOODLAND; also Lineal, Superficial, Cubical, Wages, Marketing, and Decimal Tables. Together with Tables for Converting Land-measure from one denomination to another, and Instructions for Measuring Round Timber. By RICHARD HORTON. 12mo. 2s. strongly bound in leather.

Ewart's Land Improvers' Pocket-Book.

THE LAND IMPROVERS' POCKET-BOOK OF FOR-
MULÆ, TABLES, and MEMORANDA, required in any Com-
putation relating to the Permanent Improvement of Landed Property. By JOHN EWART, Land Surveyor and Agricultural Engineer.
Royal 32mo, oblong, leather, gilt edges, with elastic band, 4s.

"A compendium long required by land surveyors, agricultural engineers, &c."—
Sussex Daily News.
"It is admirably calculated to serve the purpose for which it was intended."—
Scotsman.
"A compendious and handy little volume."—*Spectator.*

Hudson's Tables for Land Valuers.

THE LAND VALUER'S BEST ASSISTANT: being Tables,
on a very much improved Plan, for Calculating the Value of
Estates. To which are added, Tables for reducing Scotch, Irish,
and Provincial Customary Acres to Statute Measure; also, Tables
of Square Measure, and of the various Dimensions of an Acre in
Perches and Yards, by which the Contents of any Plot of Ground
may be ascertained without the expense of a regular Survey; &c.
By R. HUDSON, C.E.   New Edition, royal 32mo. oblong, leather,
gilt edges, with elastic band, 4s.

"Of incalculable value to the country gentleman and professional man."—*Farmer's
Journal.*

Complete Agricultural Surveyors' Pocket-Book.

THE LAND VALUER'S AND LAND IMPROVER'S COM-
PLETE POCKET-BOOK; consisting of the above two works
bound together, leather, gilt edges, with strap, 7s. 6d.

☞ *The above forms an unequalled and most compendious Pocket
Vade-mecum for the Land Agent and Agricultural Engineer.*

"We consider Hudson's book to be the best ready-reckoner on matters relating to
the valuation of land and crops we have ever seen, and its combination with Mr.
Ewart's work greatly enhances the value and usefulness of the latter-mentioned . .
It is most useful as a manual for reference to those for whom it is intended."—
North of England Farmer.

House Property.

HANDBOOK OF HOUSE PROPERTY: a Popular and Prac-
tical Guide to the Purchase, Mortgage, Tenancy, and Compulsory
Sale of Houses and Land; including the Law of Dilapidations and
Fixtures; with Explanations and Examples of all kinds of Valua-
tions, and useful Information and Advice on Building. By EDWARD
LANCE TARBUCK, Architect and Surveyor. 12mo, 5s. cloth boards.

"We are glad to be able to recommend it."—*Builder.*
"The advice is thoroughly practical."—*Law Journal.*

Scott Burn's Introduction to Farming.

THE LESSONS of MY FARM: a Book for Amateur Agriculturists, being an Introduction to Farm Practice, in the Culture of
Crops, the Feeding of Cattle, Management of the Dairy, Poultry,
and Pigs, and in the Keeping of Farm-work Records. By ROBERT
SCOTT BURN.   With numerous Illustrations.   Fcp. 6s. cloth.

"A most complete introduction to the whole round of farming practice."—*John
Bull.*

"*A Complete Epitome of the Laws of this Country.*"

EVERY MAN'S OWN LAWYER; a Handy-Book of the Principles of Law and Equity. By A BARRISTER. 12th Edition, carefully revised, including a Summary of The Building Societies Act, The Infants' Relief Act, The Married Women's Property Act, The Real Property Limitation Act, The Betting Act, The Hosiery Manufacture Act, a Summary of the Supreme Court of Judicature Act, &c., &c. With Notes and References to the Authorities. 12mo, price 6s. 8d. (saved at every consultation), strongly bound.

COMPRISING THE LAWS OF

BANKRUPTCY—BILLS OF EXCHANGE—CONTRACTS AND AGREEMENTS—COPYRIGHT—DOWER AND DIVORCE—ELECTIONS AND REGISTRATION—INSURANCE—LIBEL AND SLANDER—MORTGAGES—SETTLEMENTS—STOCK EXCHANGE PRACTICE—TRADE MARKS AND PATENTS—TRESPASS, NUISANCES, ETC.—TRANSFER OF LAND, ETC.—WARRANTY—WILLS AND AGREEMENTS, ETC. Also Law for Landlord and Tenant—Master and Servant—Workmen and Apprentices—Heirs, Devisees, and Legatees—Husband and Wife—Executors and Trustees—Guardian and Ward—Married Women and Infants—Partners and Agents—Lender and Borrower—Debtor and Creditor—Purchaser and Vendor—Companies and Associations—Friendly Societies—Clergymen, Churchwardens—Medical Practitioners, &c.—Bankers—Farmers—Contractors—Stock and Share Brokers—Sportsmen and Gamekeepers—Farriers and Horse-Dealers—Auctioneers, House-Agents—Innkeepers, &c.—Pawnbrokers—Surveyors—Railways and Carriers, &c. &c.

"*No Englishman ought to be without this book.*"—*Engineer.*

"It is a complete code of English Law, written in plain language which all can understand ... should be in the hands of every business man, and all who wish to abolish lawyers' bills."—*Weekly Times.*

"A useful and concise epitome of the law."—*Law Magazine.*

"What it professes to be—a complete epitome of the laws of this country, thoroughly intelligible to non-professional readers."—*Bell's Life.*

Auctioneer's Assistant.

THE APPRAISER, AUCTIONEER, BROKER, HOUSE AND ESTATE AGENT, AND VALUER'S POCKET ASSISTANT, for the Valuation for Purchase, Sale, or Renewal of Leases, Annuities, and Reversions, and of property generally; with Prices for Inventories, &c. By JOHN WHEELER, Valuer, &c. Third Edition, enlarged, by C. NORRIS. Royal 32mo, cloth, 5s.

"A neat and concise book of reference, containing an admirable and clearly-arranged list of prices for inventories, and a very practical guide to determine the value of furniture, &c."—*Standard.*

Pawnbrokers' Legal Guide.

THE PAWNBROKERS', FACTORS', and MERCHANTS' GUIDE to the LAW of LOANS and PLEDGES. With the Statutes and a Digest of Cases on Rights and Liabilities, Civil and Criminal, as to Loans and Pledges of Goods, Debentures, Mercantile, and other Securities. By H. C. FOLKARD, Esq., of Lincoln's Inn, Barrister-at-Law, Author of the "Law of Slander and Libel," &c. 12mo, cloth boards, price 7s.

The Laws of Mines and Mining Companies.

A PRACTICAL TREATISE on the LAW RELATING to MINES and MINING COMPANIES. By WHITTON ARUNDELL, Attorney-at-Law. Crown 8vo. 4s. cloth.

Bradbury, Agnew, & Co., Printers, Whitefriars, London.